Work in the New Economy

The Information Age Series

Series Editor Manuel Castells

There is a growing interest in the general audience, as well as in universities around the world, on the relationships between information technology and economic, social, geographic and political change. Indeed, these new relationships are transforming our social, economic, and cultural landscape. Social sciences are called upon to understand this emerging society. Yet, to be up to the task social sciences must renew themselves, in their analytical tools and in their research topics, while preserving their scholarly quality.

The Information Age series is the "Nasdaq" of the social sciences – the series that introduces the topics, the findings and many of the authors that are redefining the field. The books cover a variety of disciplines: geography, sociology, anthropology, economics, political science, history, philosophy, information sciences, communication. They are grounded on original, rigorous research and present what we really know about the Information Age.

Together, the books in *The Information Age* series aim at marking a turn in the academic literature on information technology and society.

Published

Work in the New Economy: Flexible Labor Markets in Silicon Valley
Chris Benner

Bridging the Digital Divide
Lisa J. Servon

Forthcoming

The Internet in Everyday Life
Barry Wellman and Caroline Haythornthwaite

The Geography of the Internet
Matthew A. Zook

Work in the New Economy

Flexible Labor Markets in Silicon Valley

Chris Benner

Blackwell Publishing

© 2002 by Chris Benner

350 Main Street, Malden, MA 02148-5018, USA
108 Cowley Road, Oxford OX4 1JF, UK
550 Swanston Street, Carlton South, Melbourne, Victoria 3053, Australia
Kurfürstendamm 57, 10707 Berlin, Germany

First published 2002 by Blackwell Publishers Ltd, a Blackwell Publishing
company

Library of Congress Cataloging-in-Publication Data

Benner, Chris.
Work in the new economy: flexible labor markets in Silicon Valley /
Chris Benner.
    p. cm.
Includes bibliographical references and index.
ISBN 0-631-23249-4 (alk. paper) – ISBN 0-631-23250-8 (alk. paper)
1. Labor market—California—Santa Clara Valley (Santa Clara County)
2. Manpower policy—California—Santa Clara Valley (Santa Clara County)
3. Job security—California—Santa Clara Valley (Santa Clara County)
4. Employment agencies—California—Santa Clara Valley (Santa Clara County)
5. High technology industries—Employees—Supply and demand—California—
Santa Clara Valley (Santa Clara County)   I. Title.
HD5725.C2 B46 2002
331.12'51004'0979473—dc21

A catalogue record for this title is available from the British Library.

Set in 10.5 on 12.5 pt Palatino
by Ace Filmsetting Ltd, Frome, Somerset
Printed and bound in the United Kingdom
by MPG Books Ltd, Bodmin, Cornwall

For further information on
Blackwell Publishing, visit our website:
www.blackwellpublishing.com

Contents

Figures

Tables

Series Editor's Preface

The decisive structural transformation in economy and society is the one affecting work and employment. This is where technology and wealth creation intersect with people's lives. A number of studies have argued that what characterizes work in the Information Age is the shift to flexible labor. This is to be understood as the ability of labor to adapt to constant changes in the work process, as well as the flexible arrangements in the contractual relationships between management and labor. Furthermore, the individualization of working conditions, and the networking of tasks performance within and between firms are often seen as indispensable factors in enhancing productivity and competitiveness in the new economy.

Silicon Valley offers a privileged vantage point to observe this transformation. It is arguably the most economically and technologically dynamic area in the world, and the seed-bed of the information technology revolution. Fifty years of relentless innovation have seen wave after wave of entrepreneurs taking up each one of the cutting edge technological breakthroughs, and transforming them into new industries: semiconductors in the 1950s, integrated circuits in the 1960s, microprocessors in the 1970s, powerful personal computers in the 1980s, Internet in the 1990s, software development throughout the whole process, and, in this early 21st century, genetic engineering, bioelectronics, and nanotechnology. Each time, and in each technological wave, Silicon Valley has been, and continues to be, at the heart of the process of entrepreneurial innovation.

Among the factors that explain this extraordinary capacity of Silicon Valley at reinventing itself, is the flexibility of its labor market, and the adaptability of its labor force to the changing requirements of the work process. Thus, what happens in Silicon Valley's labor market is often proposed as a necessary policy for regions around the world, engaging in the new economy to improve their prosperity and/or restructure their productive base.

Yet, as it is often the case, simplistic images belie the actual experience, so that when they are transformed into policies and strategies they tend to generate undesirable consequences. While Silicon Valley's model of development, including its flexible labor market, is undoubtedly a dynamic model, spurring growth and innovation, it also generates considerable environmental stress, declining quality of life in the region, an extremely individualistic culture, increased inequality, and a low level of social cohesion, as has been documented in the studies conducted by the Center for Technology and Society at Santa Clara University, in the heart of Silicon Valley. A substantial proportion of Silicon Valley's labor force receives little pay, has no job security, and scant chances of professional promotion. This is particularly the case for minorities. The very same flexibility that supports innovation and adaptation to a changing global market, translates into risk, insecurity, low wages, and deteriorating labor conditions for a significant proportion of the labor force. Is this the necessary price to be paid for progress? Not necessarily so. There is no one simple formula; flexibility comes in different formats, and its social outcomes depend on the institutional environment, as well as on companies' policies. Furthermore, while a flexible labor market favors adaptability, it also may undermine productivity. The reason is that, as Nonaka has argued, there are two components in the stock of knowledge invested in the company: explicit knowledge and tacit knowledge. Tacit knowledge is acquired through experience, through knowledge of the specificity of the work process in the company, and it is accumulated in the worker's mind. The willingness and ability of the worker to reinvest this tacit knowledge in the company, making it formal, communicable knowledge, is essential for the company to go up the learning curve. However, why should the worker invest in the company, rather than in his own professional portfolio, if the partnership with the company is occasional, unstable, and unpredictable? So there is, to some extent, a structural contradiction between the conditions for flexibility and the conditions of productivity in the new economy. Firms try to favor stability, leading to productivity, by developing strategies to keep its core labor force, while allowing flexibility for the larger, replaceable labor force – or, in my conceptual framework, differentiating employment policy for self-programmable labor and for generic labor. The trouble with this strategy, besides being discriminatory, is that workers respond in kind, so that self-programmable workers, with bargaining power, are the ones who tend to be job-hopping in search of opportunities, while generic workers, in less demand, are the ones hanging on to their current jobs.

Once we accept the complex dynamics of work flexibility, it becomes essential to go beyond images and generalities, to enter the realm of academic research. And this is what this book does. It presents a pioneer research on the hows and whys of the flexible labor market in Silicon Valley, and on the outcomes of this flexibility for workers, for companies, and for society at large. It focuses particularly on one of the most important, and often forgotten, components of this flexibility, the labor intermediaries – that is, the companies and mechanisms through which flexibility of labor is managed, such as temporary work agencies, hiring halls, and subcontracting firms. What emerges from this fine-grain analysis is a highly variegated picture that allows us to understand what labor flexibility really means, and in which ways it is related to the economic, technological, and social conditions in Silicon Valley, and beyond.

I will not anticipate on the conclusions of this research, because the book is clearly written and speaks by itself, but I want to emphasize its rigor, its eclectic approach to scholarly research, using diverse methodologies, benefiting from the author's deep immersion, for many years, in fieldwork in one of the most emblematic areas of the Information Age. Particularly interesting is the author's personal knowledge of the social actors involved in Silicon Valley, his intellectual independence *vis a vis* all interests present in this controversial topic, and his ability to relate his findings to the broader debates on the kind of society emerging from the knowledge economy. Thus, his research results are clearly useful for the world at large. Not because the world will be like Silicon Valley, but because Silicon Valley's reality does not fit the advertising image of the ideologues of the new economy. If you really want to know what working in Silicon Valley is, read this book. It will challenge your convictions, since it does not indulge in the myths of an ever-growing economy of opportunity, neither does it accept the simplistic notions of capitalism as usual. It will force you to rethink your perspectives, on the grounds of what actually happens in the new labor markets of the knowledge-driven economy. In other words, you will learn, and you will have at your disposal material and analysis, against which to contrast your own information, ideas, and concerns.

Professor Benner invites us on a guided tour of work and employment in the Information Age, because it stems from observing Silicon Valley as it is. Hopefully, this exemplary effort will stimulate further research in different contexts, so that we can start updating our understanding of labor markets and of regional economies within the parameters of our time.

Manuel Castells,
April 2002

Acknowledgments

This book is a study of labor markets in Silicon Valley, the region at the core of innovation in global information technology industries. My concern, however, is not simply with this extraordinary region. Instead, my hope is to contribute to a broader set of debates on the changing nature of work in the information economy. Like studying work in the textile industry in England in the early 1800s in order to understand the first industrial revolution, or studying work in the auto industry in Detroit in the early 1900s in order to understand the second industrial revolution, studying work in Silicon Valley in the 1990s provides insights into ways the information revolution is transforming work globally. While Silicon Valley is extreme in its concentration of information technology industries, the increasing integration of information technology throughout the globe, and indeed the increasing importance of information itself in all economic activity, makes an understanding of Silicon Valley valuable for a wide range of industries and regions around the world.

My choice of analyzing regional labor markets is driven by two factors. First is the somewhat paradoxical recognition, now shared by many analysts, that with increasing globalization of the economy and the increasing importance of information and knowledge in driving competitive success, regionalization plays a fundamental role in the coordination of advanced economic activity. Knowledge and information sharing is at the core of this, since the trust and common conceptual frameworks that develop through repeated social and economic interaction facilitate economic coordination, the sharing of tacit knowledge and the development of innovation that is so central to competitive success in the information economy.[1] Clearly this interaction doesn't take place solely as a

---

1 I return to this theme at various points in the book, but would refer readers to Storper (1997) for a sophisticated and insightful treatment of this issue.

result of spatial proximity, but spatial proximity makes a huge difference, and thus understanding regional labor markets is critical for understanding transformations of work and employment more broadly.

The second reason for a focus on regional labor markets is more of a political one: the region is an increasingly important scale for public policy intervention and labor and community organizing. Action at a global level, such as trying to shape World Bank policies, the World Trade Organization, or corporate human resource practices in developing countries, is important, but is far removed from most people's day-to-day lived experience. All too often these movements are led by middle-class white intellectuals and do little to directly connect with the conditions of poor and working class people in the US. Action at a truly local level on the other hand, such as in a single city, workplace, or neighborhood, often fails to address the interdependent nature of our metropolitan regions and leaves poor communities isolated in segregated ghettos. More promising strategies that promote regional coordination among cities and help link labor/community organizing strategies to opportunities at a regional scale have been emerging in the past decade.[2] I hope that this book can help provide new insights into the dynamics of regional labor markets in a way that can contribute to this growing movement for improved regional governance and community-based regionalism.

In the process of producing this book I have incurred a substantial debt to many people. Learning is indeed a collective process and I have benefited tremendously from the help of many people. First and foremost is Manuel Castells, who has been an inspiration, a mentor, a stimulating colleague and a friend. Through continually encouraging me in my intellectual pursuits and constantly pushing me to ask big questions, he has done more for my intellectual development than I can say. Richard Walker and AnnaLee Saxenian have also both been key sources of inspiration and have given me valuable feedback on the entire manuscript. Amy Glasmeier and Melissa Wright also gave me substantial feedback on the manuscript, which was greatly appreciated.

I owe a special thanks to my colleagues who have been part of a comparative study of labor market intermediaries in Silicon Valley and Milwaukee and whose ideas and insights have deeply influenced mine: Manuel Pastor, Laura Leete, Laura Dresser, Eric Parker, Annette Bernhardt, Susan Christopherson, Eileen Appelbaum, Ed Yelin, Michael

2   Pastor (2000), PolicyLink (2000b).

Reich, Katherine McFate, Mara Manus, and the staff of Working Partnership USA. There are many other fine scholars whose insights have helped shaped this book. I would particularly like to thank: Patrick Bond, Martin Carnoy, Charles Darrah, Peter Evans, Gillian Hart, Michael Johns, Jean Lave, Alan Pred, Harley Shaiken, Ari Sitas, David Szanton, Michael Teitz, Michael Watts, Eddie Webster, and David Wield. I had the good fortune to be able to share ideas and mutual support with an outstanding cohort of graduate students during my time at the University of California, Berkeley. I am particularly grateful to the following: Yuko Aoyama, Karen Chapple, Tony Chen, Nancy Erbstein, Jill Esbenshade, Gary Fields, Florence Gardner, Blanca Gordo, Julie Guthman, Peter Hall, Jonathan London, James McCarthy, Isaac Mankita, Sean O'Riain, and Matthew Zook.

Linking intellectual pursuits with applied efforts to implement social change has been the core of my engagement in the world for many years. In regard to this project, I have been extremely fortunate to have the opportunity to work with many fine visionary leaders and organizers at the South Bay AFL-CIO Central Labor Council and their affiliated research institute Working Partnerships USA. The Chief Executive Officer Amy Dean is truly an inspiring leader and I have learned a tremendous amount being able to work with her. I have benefited greatly from my relationships with many other people there, including: Bob Brownstein, Phaedra Ellis-Lamkins, Bart Fisher, Poncho Guevara, Lisa Hoyos, Anabel Ibanez, John Leopold, Christine Macias, Steve Preminger, Erica Rios, Toby Rogers, Cristina Uribe, and Sarah Zimmerman. I also want to thank the Economic Policy Institute and particularly Larry Mishel, Jared Bernstein, and David Webster. EPI copublished, along with Working Partnerships USA, two previous studies of labor market dynamics in Silicon Valley and California,[3] and I have drawn on some of that material for this book.

While writing the bulk of this book, I had the good fortune to be located at the Institute of Industrial Relations at the University of California, Berkeley. I would like to thank all the personnel at the Institute, and particularly the chairs of the Center for Labor Research and Education, Kirsten Spalding and Carol Zabin, for making it such a productive and supportive place. In the final stages of preparing the manuscript I also had the good fortune of being selected as a resident fellow at The Mesa Refuge, a writing retreat in Pt. Reyes, California managed

3   Benner (1996a), Benner, Brownstein and Dean (1999).

by the Common Counsel Foundation. This is a truly inspirational place for writing and my deepest appreciation goes to Peter Barnes for making such an opportunity available. In the process of conducting research for this book, I have been the beneficiary of financial support (sometimes directly, sometimes indirectly through Working Partnerships) from the following, whose assistance is acknowledged and greatly appreciated: University of California, Ford Foundation, Rockefeller Foundation, Russell Sage Foundation, Tides Foundation, Solidago Foundation, McKay Foundation, French-American Charitable Trust, New World Foundation, and the Unitarian Universalist Veatch Program.

Finally, thank you to Wendy for helping to make it all happen, and to Tioga for helping make the future real.

While all of the people and organizations mentioned above deserve a great deal of credit for any strengths and insights that appear here, I of course remain responsible for any and all shortcomings.

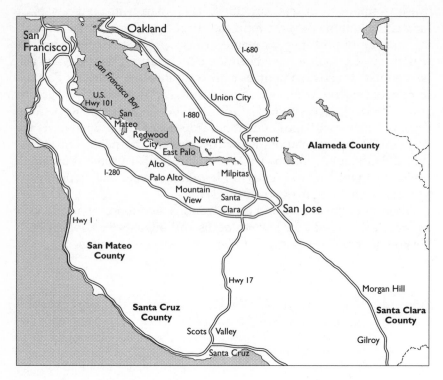

Map of Silicon Valley and environs

Introduction

Play the space between the notes just like you play the notes and never play the same thing twice.

Miles Davis

The end of the twentieth century ushered in a period of remarkable economic change in the United States. The dramatic development and diffusion of the World Wide Web, accelerating processes of globalization, a record period of sustained economic growth, an impressive stock market boom followed by an unprecedented crash in technology stocks, and a wave of new companies, industries, and business models – all provided indications of deep transformations in our economy and society. At the core of these transformations are three interrelated processes. First, the spatial boundaries of economic activity are changing, associated with the increasing globalization of the economy. Second, forms of economic organization are shifting, with a decline in vertically integrated firms and growth in complex network production systems. Third, forms of competition are being modified with the increasing importance of innovation to long-term economic success. All three processes are integrally linked with, and indeed are only made possible by, the dramatic developments in information technologies of the past three decades. The fundamental task of information technologies is to process information, and since all social and economic relations are predicated on the need to communicate, information technologies have a singular utility to almost the entire realm of human activity and permeate all economic activity. Thus, it is not at all an exaggeration to say that we are in the midst of an information revolution as significant for changing economic and social structures in the twenty-first century as the first and second industrial revolutions were for the nineteenth and twentieth centuries.

As in previous economic transformations, work is central to understanding the social implications of these changes. The technological and managerial transformation of work and employment, along with the related transformation of labor markets, is the central means by which most people experience and are affected by broader economic changes. This is not to deny that people's experiences as consumers and their political, cultural, and social interaction are not also dramatically affected by these economic changes – they clearly are. Nonetheless, paid employment (including self-employment) is the primary means of survival for the vast majority of the population and remains a primary arena of social interaction and human experience. Understanding the dramatic changes in work, employment, and the structure of labor markets is thus critical to the understanding of the broader implications of these dramatic economic changes for people at all levels of society.

The importance of understanding these changes in work is underscored by the insecurity workers feel in the face of the heightened instability of the information economy. This instability is driven in part by the rapid pace of change in information technologies themselves, with new developments potentially disrupting existing processes of economic interaction and creating entirely new economic opportunities, with all the attendant booms, speculative manias, subsequent contractions, and creative destruction to be expected. Globalization, networked production relations, and the increased importance of innovation all further reinforce the unstable tendencies of the information economy, as intense competition and constantly shifting markets and production relations undermine economic stability at a disconcerting pace. Firms and industries may come and go, but the vast majority of people depend on regular and predictable work as their main, if not sole, source of economic survival. Thus, the instability of work is more than simply an interesting economic phenomenon, it strikes at the core of human security. This makes the task of understanding the nature of this transformation of work even more urgent – an essential step in improving levels of economic security for large sectors of the workforce.

The purpose of this book is to help contribute to that understanding of the transformation of work in the information age. It is a study of labor markets in Silicon Valley, a region known globally as a center of innovation and diffusion in information technology industries. Silicon Valley is an important context for examining trends in work for two fundamental reasons. First, its very origin as an industrial region lies in information technology industries which have developed primarily in the last half-century. The relative newness of Silicon Valley's industrial structure and the dominance of these industries in the regional economy make especially visible patterns of work that are associated with the rise of information technology. Second, Silicon Valley is a global center of innovation and production in information technology industries. New products and process innovations are adopted in the region rapidly, allowing these industries to develop innovative management and human resource practices, which then often diffuse on to world markets and into other industries.

Understanding these changes in work, however, is a complex, difficult, and multifaceted endeavor. It requires challenging old assumptions about the nature of work and employment while developing and strengthening new analytical tools and concepts that are appropriate for current patterns. Is a job a "social artifact" more appropriate for an industrial era of factories and stable routine work than an information age of shifting work tasks and on-line networked relationships (Bridges 1994)? Who should be considered the real "employer" in complex subcontract and temporary employment relationships in which the company signing employees' paychecks has no control over working conditions (Gonos 1997)? What is "work" and what is "leisure" in a context in which technology is binding the world of work and the world of home in ways that redefine what it means to be in each and in which human nature itself is becoming commoditized (Carnoy 2000; English-Lueck 2002; Hochschild 1983)? These are questions that have no easy answer, but clearly require us to think about work and employment in new, different, and creative ways. In addressing these questions in the context of Silicon Valley's labor markets, this book is divided into three parts, analyzing three interrelated issues: labor market flexibility; labor market intermediaries; and careers in the information economy.

Flexibility

Part I examines labor market flexibility. Clearly labor market flexibility itself is not new, and in fact, as Sabel and Zeitlin (1997) point out, "the experience of fragility and mutability which seems so novel and disorienting today has been, in fact, the definite experience of the economic actors in many sectors, countries and epochs in the history of industrial capitalism."[1] Flexibility, however, is a highly contested and value-laden concept. The very term "labor market flexibility" holds different meanings for those analyzing it, and has taken on a variety of different meanings over the years: "Production flexibility, technical flexibility, organisational flexibility, labour process flexibility, time, wage, financial, marketing flexibility – all these issues are presumed to have a connection."[2] This lack of clarity has prompted the observation that "rarely in international discourse has [a term] gone so directly from obscurity to meaninglessness without any intervening period of coherence."[3]

Yet certain aspects of labor flexibility are critical to the competitive success of Silicon Valley and thus understanding the nature of this labor flexibility is essential for understanding work and employment patterns in the region. Much of the recent literature on labor market flexibility makes a distinction between internal (functional) flexibility and external (numerical) flexibility, using the firm as the basic unit of analysis. This approach, however, results in a core-periphery perspective that misses important aspects of how labor markets are changing. What I try to argue instead is that much of the confusion and conflict around the issue of labor market flexibility arises from the failure to make a distinction between flexible work and flexible employment. "Work" refers to the actual activities workers perform, the skills, information, and knowledge required to perform those activities, and the social interaction involved in the process of performing that work. "Employment," on the other hand, refers to the contractual relationship between employer and employee, including compensation systems and management practices. Clearly both work and employment have been changing in important ways, but the forces leading to those changes, along with their implications for both workers and employers in the regional labor market, are significantly different. Rapid changes in work – in the quantity of work, in the skills, information and knowledge required to perform that work, and the social interactions involved in that work – are largely rooted in the dynamics of competition in information technology industries, in which continual innovation is central for competitive success. This importance of innovation is related to the increasing importance of information and knowledge in the economy,

---

[1] Sabel and Zeitlin (1997: 3).
[2] Pollert (1998).
[3] US Secretary of Labor Robert B. Reich, remarks, ILO High Level Meeting on the World Summit for Social Development, Geneva, June 10, 1994, as cited in Brodsky (1994).

and the rapid change inherent in producing information and knowl-edge as commodities. These dynamics are particularly evident in infor-mation technology industries but also have applicability in a wide range of other industries as well – wherever information (both in analytical and aesthetic form) is an important part of the value of the commodity or service being produced. In essence, flexible work is an essential com-ponent of competitive success in the information economy.

In contrast, rapid changes in employment – including high levels of turnover, shorter periods of employment, and widespread contingent employment contracts – are only partly shaped by the importance of flexible work. The nature of the employment relationship is also largely shaped by a legal, institutional, and organizational environment that is deeply rooted in an older industrial economy. This older model was built largely by policies implemented in the New Deal era and in the years following World War II, an unusual period of relatively clear and long-term relationships between employer and employee. Many labor market institutions that developed during that period are poorly adapted to the changing nature of work in the information economy. This helps allow many individual firms to pursue flexible employment relations for a variety of reasons, such as simply cutting costs or shift-ing risk, that in many ways undermine the long-term competitive suc-cess of the region.

Chapter 1 elaborates on this theoretical framework for analyzing flexibility in work and employment. Chapter 2 provides empirical evi-dence of the rise of flexible work and employment patterns in Silicon Valley in the 1990s. It documents the rise of various forms of nonstand-ard employment, while also exploring the ways that work patterns and employment relationships in "standard" employment have changed dramatically as well, becoming more tenuous and temporary. It dis-cusses the links between these flexible labor markets and the character of competition in the region's high-tech industries, tracing changes in the major industries in the Valley, including Internet/software, hard-ware, semiconductors, and the defense industry.

Intermediaries

Part II examines the increasingly important role of labor market inter-mediaries in shaping the structure and dynamics of work and employ-ment in Silicon Valley. The term "labor market intermediary" covers a wide range of organizations that mediate work practices and broker employment relationships between workers and employers. These organizations build relationships on both sides of the labor market, bringing employers and workers in contact and affecting the nature and content of that relationship. Labor market intermediaries are not entirely new, nor are they unique to Silicon Valley. Temporary help firms, employment agencies, recruiters, labor contractors and the like have played an important role in a number of industry sectors and portions of the labor force for a long time. The rapid changes and unpredictability of Silicon Valley labor markets, however, is leading both workers and employers to place a greater reliance on a wide range of different types of intermediaries to help them navigate through this increasingly complex and shifting labor market. The activities of these intermediaries, in turn, shape the behavior of both workers and employers and the complex dynamics of their mutually dependent, and also at times antagonistic, relationship. Flexibility in regional labor markets contributes to the growth of intermediaries, which in turn help facilitate labor market flexibility – in essence labor market intermediaries are a fundamental feature of labor markets in the information economy.

Chapter 3 provides a conceptual framework for analyzing these intermediaries. It begins by providing a general description of the services they provide to both workers and employers related to shaping both work practices and employment relationships. Intermediaries play a critical role in job brokering, helping employers recruit workers and workers search for job opportunities, frequently shaping the character of that employment relationship. They also play a critical role in shaping changes in work, facilitating rapid adjustments in the quantity of particular work demands in the labor market and qualitatively shaping the nature of that work. On a theoretical level, this chapter argues that intermediaries perform four essential functions in the labor market for both workers and employers: reducing transaction costs, shaping compensation levels, mediating risk, and building networks.

The next three chapters analyse three broad types of intermediaries in the Silicon Valley labor market. Chapter 4 focuses on private sector intermediaries – those that ultimately have to make a profit in order to survive, including temporary help agencies, contractor brokers, online job boards, and professional employer organizations. These intermediaries are oriented toward the demand side of the labor market, responding primarily to employers' recruiting, hiring, and human resource management needs. Chapter 5 examines the rise in membership-based intermediaries, including both professional associations and union initiatives. These organizations respond primarily to the needs of workers and help workers build and maintain their employability in the broader labor market while also providing them with the networks and connections with employers to navigate the complex labor market. Chapter 6 examines the efforts of public sector institutions to increasingly play an intermediary role in the labor market. Some of these public sector initiatives are modest compared to intermediaries in the private and membership-based sphere, and are hindered by being based in institutions and programs that were built to address a more stable and predictable labor market. Nonetheless, some public intermediary initiatives, particularly those linked with adult education institutions, have grown rapidly and play a critical role in certain occupations and skill sets.

Careers

Part III then turns to an examination of the implications of this flexibility and intermediation for the careers of workers in the region. Certain aspects of the flexibility of Silicon Valley labor markets have been a critical component of the region's economic success. Flexibility in work practices, for instance, helps ensure rapid adjustment to changing technologies and market opportunities while also providing valuable learning opportunities for large sectors of the workforce. The high levels of volatility, however, make workers vulnerable to labor market shocks. Many workers with the right skills and good social networks thrive in this environment, building successful multifirm careers. Other workers, however, are threatened by skill obsolescence, periods of unemployment, and stagnating wages, with few career opportunities. This vulnerability is frequently exacerbated by flexible employment practices that weaken the tie between worker and employer, requiring workers to absorb many of the risks of economic uncertainty. These contradictory tendencies are also reflected in the activities of intermediaries, which can both contribute to and undermine career opportunities for workers in the region.

Chapter 7 provides an empirical examination of the implications of the structure of Silicon Valley's labor markets for the livelihoods of workers in the region. It acknowledges the critical importance of these new labor arrangements for economic development and innovative growth in the region, and suggests that for many workers in the regional labor market these flexible labor relations provide dynamic opportunities for learning and highly remunerative careers. The chapter emphasizes, however, the significant underside to this flexibility, documenting growing inequality and insecurity in the regional labor market in the 1990s and showing the potentially disruptive consequences for workers. It also explores the contradictory role of intermediaries in shaping these labor market outcomes. It argues that some intermediaries play a critical role in improving workforce development systems, improving firms' employment practices, building multifirm career ladders, and ensuring skills enhancement and learning across firms. On the other hand, the use of some intermediaries also puts workers at greater economic risk, and in some cases undermines skill enhancement through an underinvestment in training and learning opportunities on the part of firms.

Finally, chapter 8 explores the implications of this flexibility and the activities of intermediaries for efforts to improve labor market outcomes for workers. It begins by suggesting the need for a series of conceptual changes in the focus of labor market policy: focusing on industry and occupational clusters, rather than firms; learning, rather than training; communities and social networks, rather than individuals; and careers, rather than jobs. The chapter goes on to argue that the increasing importance of labor market intermediaries creates opportunities for public policy intervention. Traditional labor market policy focuses on either the demand or supply sides of the labor market – either regulating employers in their labor practices or trying to assist workers, primarily through investment in skills development. Intermediaries, however, can play a critical role in shaping labor market outcomes for both workers and employers. Public policy directed at intermediaries can provide support for the more beneficial aspects of their operations while restricting or hindering their more pernicious activities.

The final section explores the policy implications of the distinction between flexible work and employment. In contrast to some analysts, who characterize flexibility as the growing "individualization" of work, I argue that what we are witnessing instead is the growing individualization of employment, alongside an increasing socialization of work. This disconnection between the nature of work and the nature of employment contributes significantly to the insecurity that many workers face in the information economy. Overall the information economy is highly dynamic and capable of producing high levels of economic growth and opportunity, yet many workers are excluded from the benefits of the information economy by their individualized employment relationships. The challenge is to develop compensation systems that recognize the increasing socialization of work in the information economy while also helping to minimize insecurity by cushioning the effects of the inevitable ups and downs of the information economy.

Research Data

A brief note on data and research methods is important here. The evidence presented in this book is based on both quantitative and qualitative research methods. The quantitative analysis was essential for understanding broad trends in employment and wage patterns in Silicon Valley, and is presented in chapters 2 and 7. It is based on a variety of publicly collected labor market data available for analysis at a regional level, which are identified where appropriate in the text and tables.[4] The qualitative analysis of the activities and implications of labor

[4] This includes:
- US Census Public Use Microdata Sample (PUMS): the PUMS data set used was selected to cover the broader Silicon Valley, not simply Santa Clara County. The specific area chosen includes all of Santa Clara County (PUMAs 3401–3411) along with the neighboring cities of Fremont, Newark, and Union City in Alameda County (PUMAs 2103–2104) and the cities of Burlingame, Hillsborough, Milbrae, San Bruno, Foster City, San Mateo, Belmont, Redwood City, San Carlos, Atherton, East Palo Alto, Menlo Park, Woodside, Portola Valley, and North Fair Oaks in southern San Mateo County (PUMAs 2203–2206).
- California Department of Finance Demographic Projections: these are available from the Demographic Research Unit, at http://www.dof.ca.gov/html/Demograp/druhpar.htm. They are the most reliable inter-census demographic estimates. Data reported in this dissertation are for Santa Clara County only.
- California Employment Development Department Labor Force Data: the CA Labor Market Information Division is the primary source of labor market information for the state, county and some city-level data. Specific data include current and historical industry employment, hours and earnings, size of firm, historical and currently labor force, employment, and unemployment data. This data is available to the public at: http://www.calmis.cahwnet.gov.
- Current Population Survey–Outgoing Rotation Group: the sample used is a subset of the national sample including all households living in Santa Clara County, and is the primary source of national data on employment, unemployment, unionization, household income, and employee earnings. I use the same sample as that used by the Economic Policy Institute in their regular publication *The State of Working America* (Mishel et al. 2001). The Census Bureau does not recommend using this data source for local level analysis, given the small sample size in many local areas. It is the only source of data available, however, to calculate hourly earnings distribution at a local level, and Santa Clara County is large enough to make the sample size reasonable. The total sample size ranges from 908 households in 1979 to a low of 447 in 1985, and rising to 626 in 1998. In

market intermediaries, presented in chapters 4, 5, and 6, is based on a variety of sources, including: interviews with 75 owners, managers, program officers, and clients of labor market intermediaries; one focus group with 12 program officers from various workforce development and training institutes; participant observation in the creation of the Working Partnerships USA temporary worker employment project; and a review of a wide range of written material on the various intermediaries, including program documents, Web-based descriptive material, and secondary descriptions of the organizations. The intermediaries examined were chosen to reflect the range of organizations involved in intermediary activity.

---

order to test the representativeness of the sample for Santa Clara County, the Economic Policy Institute compared the gender and age characteristics for our sample in 1989 with the County population as reported in the 1990 census, and found no significant statistical difference.
- US Census of Manufacturers: from the US Department of Commerce and Bureau of the Census.

Part I

Flexibility and the Transformation of Work and Employment

1

Understanding Flexibility

People need to look at themselves as self-employed, as vendors who come to this company to sell their skills. In AT&T, we have to promote the concept of the whole work force being contingent [i.e., on short-term contract, no promises] though most of our contingent workers are inside our walls. "Jobs" are being replaced by "projects" and "fields of work", giving rise to a society that is increasingly "jobless but not workless".

AT&T Vice President for Human Resources James Meadows quoted in the *New York Times*, February 13,1996

[T]he job is not going to be part of tomorrow's economic reality. There still is and will always be enormous amounts of work to do, but it is not going to be contained in the familiar envelopes we call jobs . . . As a way of organizing work, [the job] is a social artifact that has outlived its usefulness.

William Bridges (Author)

Early in 1993, *Time* Magazine ran a provocative cover story called "The Temping of America" (Morrow 1993). The lead story started with the dramatic statement that Manpower Inc., a temporary help agency, had become the largest private employer in America (Castro 1993). *Time's* attention to temporary employment was indicative of a widespread interest in temporary and other forms of "contingent employment" in the 1990s (Barker and Christensen 1998). This interest was greater than seemed justified, given the small percentage of people actually employed in temporary help firms (still less than 3 percent of the labor force). Yet, in the context of corporate restructuring and economic change, the rise in temporary help agencies can be seen as simply the leading edge of a broader restructuring of labor markets in America.

In attempting to understand the nature of this restructuring, the notion of flexibility has become ubiquitous. Though efforts to promote flexible use of labor have existed for many centuries,[1] the concept gained new salience with the publication of Piore and Sabel's (1984) *The Second Industrial Divide*. Their argument, in essence, was that the economic crisis of the 1970s was resulting in *flexible specialization* replacing *mass production* as the dominant mode of economic organization. Since then, the issue of flexibility has occupied a central position in debates on economic organization, regional development, new forms of economic competition, and capital accumulation, as well as the restructuring of labor markets.[2] The debates have been particularly heated in relation to flexibility in the labor market, given the high stakes involved. Flexibility can be defined as the ability to change or react to change with little penalty in time, effort, cost, or performance. Yet change always entails some cost, and the benefits of flexibility to one actor in the economy may, and often do, come at the expense or loss of others. While at least some forms of flexibility seem to be increasingly important for firms to remain competitive in today's rapidly changing marketplace, all too often corporations' drive for flexibility is simply a desire for decreased deregulation and the ability to hire and fire employees at will (Pollert 1988). Many workers, their advocates, and policy analysts understandably challenge the drive for flexibility, showing clear evidence that it results in insecurity, declining wages, and deteriorating working conditions for a large portion of the workforce (Standing 1999).

In addition to the unequal outcomes of labor flexibility, part of the problem also lies in the diversity of types of labor flexibility and the lack of clarity around the term itself. Labor flexibility can be associated with short-term, cyclical, and temporary economic circumstances, as well as deeper structural changes, and is influenced by political forces and changing regulatory regimes along with economic changes. To understand the diversity of processes of labor market restructuring clearly requires a sophisticated appreciation for differing historical and

---

1   Indeed Harrison (1994) reminds us that neoclassical economists see the market itself as the best means of promoting flexibility in the form of rapid economic adjustment.
2   Williams, Cutler, Williams, and Haslam (1998) provide a detailed critique of Piore and Sabel's analysis. Gertler (1992) and Hirst and Zeitlin (1991) provide useful reviews of the overall debate in the 1980s and early 1990s,while Sabel and Zeitlin (1997) provides an interesting portrayal of the evolution of the debate in the 1990s.

geographic trajectories and a sensitivity to the dangers in simplifying complex social phenomenon under a term as "loaded" as flexibility. As Peck (1996:150) argues, "[t]o bundle all forms of contemporary labor market restructuring together under the generic and increasingly elastic term 'flexibility' is manifestly inadequate." Nonetheless, rapid change and unpredictability *is* a key characteristic of information technology industries, and the ability of Silicon Valley firms to innovate rapidly has been critical for the region's economic success. Rapidly changing work, new forms of networking and mobility, and contingent employment are among the most prominent features of the region's labor market. Thus, understanding the nature of this labor flexibility is critical for understanding the transformation of work and employment in the region.

This chapter attempts to provide a coherent framework for understanding flexibility in Silicon Valley's labor markets. At the core of this framework is the distinction between flexible work and flexible employment, where "work" refers to the actual tasks performed by workers in the process of economic activity, while "employment" refers to the contractual relationship (both explicit and implicit) that shapes labor control and compensation. Making this distinction between flexible *work* and flexible *employment* is particularly useful in identifying those aspects of labor flexibility that are driven by broad trends in the development of the information economy, versus those that are primarily driven by firms' human resource and management practices. Before developing this framework, however, I first turn to a brief summary of the processes of broad economic and labor market restructuring in the US since the 1970s and the role of information technology in shaping that restructuring.

Labor Markets in the Information Economy

In the past thirty years, the US economy has been dramatically restructured through a variety of processes that are related to the development of information technology. These changes have all contributed to growing volatility in labor markets. The most prominent of these changes include:

- *Changing boundaries of the economy*: Though a world economy has existed since at least the sixteenth century (Wallerstein 1979), in recent years there has been a rapid acceleration in processes of globalization, with increasing globally integrated production chains, international trade, investment, and capital flows. This increasing globalization is made possible by the infrastructure created with the rapid development and diffusion of information technology (Castells 1996; Korzeniewicz and Gereffi 1994; Sassen 1996). Though it may seem contradictory, the economy is also typified by increasing localization. This phenomenon results partly from long-term sectoral shifts in the economy, in which the share of the workforce in industries that serve only a local area (for example, retail sales, social and health services, education and so on) have increased (Persky and Wiewel 1994). Economic localization is also rooted in the increasing importance, for the competitiveness of globally integrated industries, of "relational assets" often rooted in the social interactions, sharing of tacit knowledge and development of conventions, informal rules and common cultures that are built in region-specific clusters of firms (Storper 1997). Both globalization and localization are increasing labor market volatility. Increased global competition, the frenetic pace and harsh demands of global financial markets, and the mobility of production processes greatly increases the pace of industrial shifts and economic change. Increasing localization results in more people employed in the many (though not all) locally serving industries that have long had unstable employment patterns, such as retail sales and personal services.

• *Changing industrial organization*: Information technology has also enabled new forms of management and control, both within the firm and between firm boundaries, in office and service industries as well as manufacturing (Garson 1988; Leidner 1993). Information technology creates the ability to "informate" production processes, making highly visible aspects of production and labor processes that had been previously hidden (Zuboff 1988). The digitization of information makes possible the simultaneous, precise coordination of economic activity in multiple economic locations and across firm boundaries. This enabled corporations in the 1980s and 1990s to flatten management hierarchies, eliminating multiple layers of middle management (Osterman 1996), and to increasingly subcontract or out-source major components of their operations, both locally and around the globe (Harrison 1994). In addition, firms have restructured internal operations into distinct "profit centers" that blur firm boundaries by bringing market dynamics inside the firm (Davidow and Malone 1992). The result is the increased importance of constantly shifting networks, rather than individual firms, in the structure of economic organization, which increases changes in labor markets as well (Powell 1990).

- *Changing forms of competition*: In the stable, mass-production markets that dominated the economy prior to 1970s, firms competed primarily by improving their productivity, decreasing their costs or trying to expand their market share within existing markets. With the development of an information economy, the ability of firms to effectively adapt to changing market conditions, identifying and capitalizing on new opportunities and successfully responding to new challenges, has become increasingly important, for not just competitive advantage but indeed economic survival for many firms. Researchers from a variety of fields have extensively documented the critical importance of this innovation in building and sustaining economic competitiveness.[3] This constant drive for developing new products and new production processes also contributes to the increased pace of change in labor market dynamics.

The importance of information technology and the increasing role of information in shaping new forms of competition deserves some further elaboration. Information in various forms is a growing portion of the commodities and services produced in the US economy. The Department of Commerce recently estimated that IT-producing industries themselves, including computer and communications hardware, software and related services, accounted for a full 35 percent of the nation's growth in GDP in the mid 1990s (Mayer, Price, et al 1999). Digital, microelectronics is becoming an increasingly important component of many consumer durables, ranging from wireless phone and personal data assistants to automobiles, refrigerators, kitchen appliances, and so on. If you add to this all of the sectors whose primary product is information (including media, television and movie production, research, education, and information services essential for coordinating activity in the rest of the economy), well over half of the US workforce and GDP are primarily involved in the production or processing of information and information technologies (Carnevale and Rose 1998; Hepworth 1989; Machlup 1952; Porat 1977; Williams 1988). In addition, an increasing portion of the value-added in many goods and services is information in the form of the aesthetic content of the product or service.

---

3   E.g. Braczyk, Cooke, and Heidenreich (1998) Cooke and Morgan (1998) Edquist (1997) Lundvall (1992) Nonaka and Takeuchi (1995) Simmie 1997.

The clothing and shoe industry and many components of the children's toy industry are classic examples, but there are many others (Lash and Urry 1994). With this increasing aestheticization of production goods as well, the design process comprises a larger component of the value of goods, while the material costs and labor process involved in production are less important in their contribution to value-added.

In industries that are heavily dependent on information and knowledge, there is a significant difference between high fixed costs and low marginal costs. In other words, the cost of producing the first copy of an information good, such as a software program or a movie, may be very high, involving all the research, development, and initial production processes. Most of these costs are "sunk costs" – costs that are not recoverable if production is halted:

> If you invest in a new office building and you decide you don't need it, you can recover part of your costs by selling the building. But if your film flops, there isn't much of a resale market for its script. And if your CD is a dud, it ends up in a pile of remainders at $4.95 or six for $25. Sunk costs generally have to be paid up front, before commencing production. (Shapiro and Varian 1998: 21)

Once the commodity is developed, however, the costs of reproducing additional copies is negligible, with no real natural limits to the production of additional copies:

> if you can produce one copy you can produce a million copies, or 10 million copies, at roughly the same unit costs. It is this combination of low incremental costs and large scale of operation that leads to the 92 percent gross profit margins enjoyed by Microsoft (Shapiro and Varian 1998: 21).

Firms with significant sunk costs of product development obviously need to recover those initial costs, but once these costs have been recovered, the potential for substantial profits in information industries is extremely high. The ability to sell 10 million additional copies of a product that costs next to nothing to make is obviously an attractive prospect!

A problem emerges, however, if a second firm enters into direct competition with the initial producer. For both companies the marginal costs of producing an additional unit are minimal, and thus there is tremendous pressure for each company to reduce the sales price of their product to expand their market share. Once the sunk costs have been spent and production commenced, there is no natural floor to the sale price except the minimal cost of producing and distributing another version, frequently resulting in a downward spiral in prices and lower profits. If this prevents a firm from recovering their sunk costs of product development, then they lose money.

Firms in information-intensive industries, therefore, typically try to pursue pricing mechanisms that minimize direct competition. The most obvious way of doing this is to continually develop new products, getting them to market faster than competitors so that they can charge high prices during the early stages of production, when producers can receive essentially monopoly prices for their products. The semiconductor industry provides a classic example of this dynamic. With each new round of semiconductors that Intel or AMD develops, the initial market price starts high. Once there are competing semiconductors on the market with similar levels of speed and performance capabilities there is a strong tendency for prices to drop significantly, producing very narrow profit margins and providing further stimulus to develop new products or face going out of business (Angel 1994). The result of this pattern of competition is highly fluctuating production runs with strong pressures to ramp-up and ramp-down production as rapidly as possible.

Another pricing mechanism to avoid direct competition occurs in pure information industries where firms frequently give away the product for free in the hopes of establishing a large "locked-in" customer base, thus enabling firms to charge for follow-up services or upgrades. Netscape provides a classic example of this: they initially gave away their Internet browser for free, rapidly establishing a massive customer base and making revenues through upgrades and value-added services, primarily to corporate customers. Similar patterns exist in many information industries, including Internet publishing, film, television, and customized software markets. Low marginal costs of production can result in tremendously rapid growth in the customer base, with high financial returns if firms are able to establish themselves as the front-runners in their particular niche – a classic winner-take-all market (Frank and Cook 1995). The flip side of this, however, is that firms are highly vulnerable to the development of competing products that may draw customers rapidly away to a competing (free) service or product. Again, markets tend to be highly unstable as a consequence of the nature of competition in products and services that are highly dependent on control of knowledge and information for their competitive success.

Thus, through changing boundaries of economic activity, changing forms of economic organization, and changing forms of competition, the increasing importance of information technology – and of information and knowledge more generally – has contributed to a dramatic restructuring of the US economy. As a result of these changes, US labor markets in the 1990s were significantly different from those that dominated the period from 1948 to 1973. During this earlier period of the "golden age" of US capitalism, the single most defining feature of labor markets was the importance of long-term stable employment relationships in vertically integrated large firms operating in mass production industries. This long-term employment relationship was characteristic of both unionized and nonunionized firms (Osterman 1999). Well-developed internal labor markets meant that most promotions occurred within the corporation. For both blue-collar and white-collar positions, the majority of employees were hired into entry-level positions and built long-term careers in the firm. There were relatively high degrees of job security as employers generally saw it in their interest to maintain long-term ties with their workforce (Doeringer and Piore 1971; Hall 1982; Osterman 1984). Since many skills were firm specific, public training systems were designed to get people access to entry-level positions with the expectation that firms would invest in training their own workforce (Becker 1964; Borjas 1988; Grubb 1996; Mincer 1994).

Clearly stability didn't characterize employment for everyone. Many people, particularly women and minorities, were stuck in secondary labor markets in jobs with lower wages, greater levels of insecurity, and poorer career opportunities (Averitt 1968). Furthermore, many blue-collar workers in core firms were still subject to periodic layoffs, as firms needed to adjust their labor force in response to economic cycles (Feldstein 1975; Perry 1972). Nonetheless, these jobs in secondary labor markets actually served to reinforce in many ways the importance of "good jobs" in the primary labor market (Gordon, Edwards, and Reich 1982). Moreover, the model of the standard employment relationship served as the basis for government regulation of labor markets, including the labor relations system and most antidiscrimination legislation. Most of this legislation is based on the assumption that there is a clear, long-term relationship between employer and employee in which the employer has control over and responsibility for conditions of work and employment (Friedman 1994; Gould 1993b).

This system of long-term stable employment began to break down in the early 1970s. By the 1990s it was clear that long-term stable attachments between firm and workers was no longer the dominant force in the structure of US labor markets. Routine production jobs had declined, employment of all types had become more volatile, and temporary, contract, and other forms of contingent employment had increased. In essence, labor markets are increasingly characterized by greater instability and weaker ties between workers and employers – greater flexibility. But how should we understand the character of these new labor market arrangements that are emerging?

Flexible Work and Flexible Employment

The most common way of analyzing flexibility in the labor market and in production systems is to start with firms as the unit of analysis. In this framework, firms can pursue both internal flexibility and external flexibility or, as it is sometimes put, "functional flexibility" and "numerical flexibility". Internal or functional flexibility involves a series of labor practices that increase the ability of workers inside the firm to adjust to changing demands. It includes aspects such as polyvalent skills, broad job categories, redeployability, teamwork, and so on. External flexibility or numerical flexibility is a series of practices that allows firms to take advantage of external relations, either to access specialized skills and expertise or to adjust to fluctuating labor demands. It includes practices such as high levels of employee turnover, the use of temporary and part-time employees, increased levels of subcontracting or use of home-workers. In addition, flexibility in both arenas may relate to trying to link wage rates and other forms of compensation more directly to output, through variable compensation schemes (piece-rate, incentive schemes, and so on), or simply on an individualized basis. The following quote is characteristic of what has emerged as the dominant way of understanding labor market flexibility.

> Labour flexibility refers in general to a logic of tailoring labour inputs in production to shifting levels and qualities of outputs. There are three major domains of labour relations in which producers may attempt to introduce flexibility. First, they may seek to make wage rates downwardly adjustable and strike wage bargains on an individualised (hence politically defused) worker-by-worker basis, rather than with occupational groups as a whole. Second, they may seek the advantages of *internal* (intra-firm) flexibility through strategies that enhance the redeployability of the workforce across the shop-floor. Third, they may seek *external* flexibility through strategies that promote quantitative adjustments of their labour intake (Storper and Scott 1990: 575 emphasis in original).

There were good reasons to use the firm as the primary unit of analysis during much of the post World War II era when vertical hierarchies dominated production in most major industries. Even today, a focus on firms provides important insights. The pressures on employers and their response shape much of the dynamics and structure of labor markets. Firms pay wages, determine hiring and firing decisions, and provide the bulk of training and career development opportunities. Public policy is most frequently centered around how to influence the behavior of firms and the consequences of particular policies for the ability of employers to compete (Osterman 1999).

Nonetheless, changes in the world economy since the 1970s have cast doubt on ideas that use the modern corporation as the central organizing principle in the economy. Within a broad neoclassical framework, an increasing interest in transactions costs has opened up the examination of the firm as a governance structure and the relationship between firms and markets as means of economic coordination (Williamson 1975; Williamson 1985). Network theory moves beyond this market-hierarchy spectrum, arguing that networks provide an entirely different form of economic governance and coordination (Powell 1990). The firm itself is increasingly seen as a "socio-spatial construction embedded in broader discourses and practices" (Taylor 1999; Yeung 2000). Relations of trust, "untraded interdependencies," milieux of innovation, learning communities, firm culture – these are all analytical categories that have developed in recent years that recognize the fluid boundaries of firms while identifying sources of competitiveness that lie outside of firm activities (Castells and Hall 1994; Schoenberger 1997; Simmie 1997; Storper 1997).

While this perspective of looking beyond the firm as the fundamental unit of analysis has been widely accepted in the analysis of the organization of production, it is less integrated into studies of work and the labor market. There is an urgent need to incorporate insights from the literature on industrial organization more centrally into studies of work and employment. It seems clear that the very nature of worker activities on the job increasingly cuts across firm boundaries, requiring workers to communicate more regularly with customers, suppliers, colleagues in other firms, and so on. Skills required on the job are arguably less firm specific and instead require greater knowledge of trends in the sector or among customers. Thus, a framework that assumes strong firm boundaries in the nature of work activities frequently misses these aspects of work. Similarly, employment relations stretch across firm boundaries and across multiple firms over time. Single work sites and production processes may include workers employed by multiple firms, such as when temporary, contract, and "permanent" workers all are employed side by side. Entire supply chains have now become the object of management's attention (Chopra and Meindl 2001). Workers themselves are moving more frequently from firm to firm. The skills and experiences that workers develop are built across multiple organizational contexts. To understand these trends requires a greater attention to workers' career paths and an understanding of the relationships that get built across these multiple employment contexts over time. A framework of labor market flexibility that doesn't account for these trajectories, with the ability to trace networks across firm boundaries, also is limited in its explanatory power.

Finally, the attention to the boundaries of firms leads to a core–periphery perspective, in which firms are seen to reduce the size of their core workforce while accessing "non-core" employment through the use of various external flexibility mechanisms. This approach, however, does not address the issue that much of the employment that is external to a firm may in fact be quite central or core to an industrial complex. There is a significant portion of contingent workers, for example, who have high wages, significant career mobility, and a clear preference for contingent employment arrangements (Kunda, Barley, and Evans 1999; Pink 1998). In Silicon Valley, many of these roving information technology specialists are central to the functioning of the industrial agglomeration as a whole and may provide crucial services to a string of individual firms at particular points in time, but could not be considered core to any single firm. On the other side of the coin, many workers are full-time, permanent "core" employees of certain firms whose activities could be described as "peripheral" to an industrial complex. This includes such activities as building services, commercial security services, cafeteria services, landscaping services, and so on.

Thus, an approach to labor market flexibility that is confined to examining internal versus external flexibility limits our understanding of many of the dimensions of flexibility. Rather than developing a framework that focuses on internal versus external flexibility, a more useful way of analyzing labor market flexibility is to make a distinction between flexibility in work and flexibility in employment relations, recognizing that both categories cut across firm boundaries (see table 1.1).

The term "work" refers to the actual nature of the activities people do while engaged in the process of production. It includes the physical and mental processes required, the tools and technology used, and the relations with other people – customers, co-workers, colleagues from other

Table 1.1   Aspects of flexible labor markets

Work _The actual nature of the activities people do while engaged in the process of production_	Employment _The informal and formal contractual relationship between worker and employer_
Aspects of flexible work <ul><li>Rapid changes in quantity of work required</li><li>Rapid changes in skills, knowledge, information required for work</li><li>Reflexivity in work tasks</li></ul>	Aspects of flexible employment <ul><li>Rise in external employment relations (temporary, sub-contracted labor)</li><li>Weakening of direct employment contract</li><li>Mediated management practices</li></ul>

firms, suppliers, and so on – that they engage in during the process of performing those activities. "Flexible" work – rapid change in the arena of work with little penalty in time, effort, or performance – directly influences the demand for labor in the way often described as numerical flexibility – fluctuating demand in the quantity of work needed in any particular enterprise. Flexible work also refers to changes workers experience on the job, the changing value of their skills and experience in the marketplace, the changing social relationships and patterns of communication required to be effective in performing their work, and so on.

Work is distinct from employment. "Employment" refers to the nature of the relationship with the employer, the processes employers use in directing, motivating, and monitoring workers' activities, and the nature of compensation provided for the activities performed. Temporary employment, part-time employment, self-employment, independent contractors, and various compensation schemes that link compensation to performance (such as stock options, performance evaluations, etc.) are all issues related to flexible employment, but may or may not be directly linked with flexible work. For example, temporary employees at an electronic manufacturing services firm doing routine assembly work may be performing routine work (at least for a period of time) while being engaged in flexible employment.

Flexible Work

Work in all its dimensions has become more volatile and more unpredictable. This change in work has three basic components: rapid changes in the quantity of work required; rapid changes in skill requirements;[4] and reflexivity in work tasks. The development of information technology is a critical factor driving all of these changes, making them a fundamental feature of labor markets in an information economy. To be sure, there are other factors shaping flexible work as well, including choices firms make in their employment relationships and their use of technology. Nonetheless the volatility and rapid change inherent in information technology and information processing industries suggests that the demand for flexibility in work is rooted in broad changes that are difficult to influence or shape through policy initiatives or institutional reform. Thus, flexibility in work practices is likely to continue or even increase for the foreseeable future.

Quantitative Change in Work

The debate on quantitative changes in work is frequently framed in terms of whether technology is creating jobs by improving productivity and stimulating overall demand, or whether it is eliminating jobs by replacing workers with machines and automated production processes. Doomsayers like Rifkin (1995) and Aronowitz and Difazio (1994), for instance, argue that technology is automating work in a wide range of occupations and resulting in widespread unemployment and underemployment. Such prophecies of widespread job destruction linked with technological development, however, are more ideology than fact. Technological development is a critical component of improved productivity and wealth generation. The distributional impacts of technological change are shaped primarily by institutional structures and power relations, not the technology itself. Careful empirical studies repeatedly find in practice that while technology may contribute to displacing labor at a micro scale and on a firm-by-firm basis, it also contributes significantly to overall job creation at a macro

---

4   I use the term "skill" in a comprehensive way to refer to the explicit and tacit skills, information, and knowledge workers require to perform their work activities. While the term "skill" initially developed in the context of physical abilities, it has long since been expanded to include a wide variety of communication and office-based abilities as well. It should also be emphasized that "skill" can not be understood in discrete, quantifiable, objective criteria, but must be understood in the contested nature of the social relations and power struggles that shape individuals' capacities to perform work. I include "information" and "knowledge" under the term "skill" simply as a way of avoiding unnecessary repetition in the text.

level.[5] Even on a micro scale, the net impact depends much more on the way technology is introduced and the actors involved in shaping its adoption, rather than on the nature of the technology itself (Bessant 1989; Kaplinsky 1987).

My concern here, however, is not with the creation or destruction of work overall but the way the increased importance of innovation in the economy contributes to a *more rapid destruction and creation of work*. This phenomenon is clearly visible in statistics on the simultaneous creation and destruction of jobs that is hidden within standard cross-sectional figures on net employment growth. For example, between September and December 1999, there was a total of 1.0 million net new jobs added in the US economy, representing a growth of 0.9 percent. This net growth was the result of a combination of factors: New establishments created 1.8 million jobs, while dying establishments eliminated 1.7 million others; expanding establishments created 7.2 million jobs, while contracting ones lost 6.3 million. By this measure, the combination of new jobs created and jobs lost in this single quarter was equal to a full 15 percent of all jobs in the economy (Pivetz, Searson, and Spletzer 2001). According to US Census data, in the single year between 1995 and 1996, the combination of new jobs created and jobs lost equaled nearly 30 percent of the total number of jobs in the economy. While consistent long-term data on this "churn-rate' are not available, the heightened competition and rapid pace of economic change in the last thirty years makes clear that the rate of both job creation and destruction has increased, at least compared with the stable, mass-production economy of the postwar era.

Rapid skill changes

Debates on the relationship between technological change and skill typically focus on the question of the overall skill structure of the labor market. Many analysts, following the path established by Braverman's (1975) classic analysis, argue that capitalist imperatives of control, combined with the separation of conception and execution inherent in hierarchical management structures, leads to a progressive degradation and deskilling of work.[6] Others identify a broad skill upgrading over time,

---

5 Castells (1996: 251–64) provides a useful review of the evidence.
6 Technological change is a key part of this analysis, as technological development displaces labor from high productivity industries into labor-intensive industries leading to the concentration of most workers in low-skilled and low-

the result of a variety of factors, including sectoral shifts in the economy and a range of new management techniques which recognize the increased value of workers' tacit knowledge and thus limit the usefulness of Taylorist management techniques that drive the deskilling process.[8] Still others discuss the ways that the capacities that get recognized as "skilled" are heavily contested, and have to be understood in the context of the social networks and power relations, both in the workplace and in broader society, that shape the nature of the skills and capacities exercised in individuals' work tasks.[8]

This entire debate on deskilling versus skill upgrading, however, misses one of the critical issues: *the pace of change in skill requirements*. Technological change produces both deskilling and skill upgrading tendencies, while changing the terrain in which social struggles over the value of skills are played out. It appears that this pace of change has increased over time. The term "skill" should be understood in this context to include the information and knowledge workers need to be effective in their work, including the organization context and social relations that shape individuals' capacities to perform work. The importance of innovation described in the previous section suggests that a much greater portion of the workforce is required to learn new information and integrate new knowledge into their work practices, adapting to new organizational contexts and developing new relationships in order to keep up with changes in competition and industry structure. Skills that people may have learned in the past can quickly become obsolete. This is clearly true among professional occupations. Much of what is required for engineers and programmers in the market today, for example, wasn't even taught in degree programs five to ten years ago.

wage, labor-intensive industries. It is important to note that Braverman's analysis is not limited to manufacturing production workers, and in fact has been extended in many ways. Noble (1977, 1984), along with Shaiken (1985), has documented the ways that scientific research and technological innovation in the workplace are largely the result of capitalist imperatives of control and profits. Processes of degradation and deskilling of work have been documented in occupations ranging from fast food workers and airline reservation agents (Garson 1992), to computer programmers and longshoremen (Zimbalist 1979) to office workers and managers (Greenbaum 1995).

7   See Attewell (1987) Smith (1994) Burawoy (1985) and Sturdy et al. (1992) for responses to Braverman in the labor process debate. Silvestri (1997) provides evidence of skill upgrading in the US labor market, while Castells and Aoyama (1994) provide evidence for the G-7 countries.

8   Gee, Hull; and Lankshear (1996), Hull (1997); Wenger (1998).

In this environment of continuous improvement, learning and innovation, firms have learned that the information and knowledge that is helpful in this regard is not limited to upper management and professional levels in the enterprise. In fact front-line workers have a great deal of information and knowledge that is essential for ensuring continuous improvement. Furthermore, there is a great deal of this knowledge that is tacit, rather than implicit, thus making it extremely difficult for management to "appropriate" this knowledge. Workers at all levels of enterprises have information and knowledge that can be essential for successful competition. As markets shift and competitive conditions change, workers at all levels are required to change the information, knowledge, and skills needed to perform their work.

Reflexivity in work tasks

In addition to the unstable markets, unstable demand for work, and rapidly changing skill requirements, work is becoming more volatile due to the increasing reflexivity of work tasks. This reflexivity requires workers at all levels to examine their own work activities in an effort to improve their work process. The trend is evident in the widespread proliferation of continuous improvement programs in work settings across industries (Appelbaum and Batt 1994). Firms in which workers are actively engaged in continuous improvement programs demonstrate greater ability to remain competitive in the market (Appelbaum et al. 2000). Again, these high-performance workplaces work best when workers are actively engaged in examining their own work practices rather than being driven by management directives, and when they can see the results of their work.

This reflexivity is important at a macro level as well, not just in the workplace (Lash and Urry 1994). The increasing importance of meeting rapidly shifting consumer demands in a range of aesthetic products and information commodities and services means that a growing portion of profitability is based on knowledge and accurate interpretation of shifting consumer tastes and cultural preferences at a macro level. while these interpretive tasks may be specialized among a group of design and marketing occupations, in fact the "social life" of information in this context requires reflexivity in a large portion of the workforce (Brown and Duguid 2000). Thus, reflexivity at both a micro and macro level are increasingly important components of competitive success in the new economy, resulting in constantly shifting work relationships and activities.

In sum, numerical flexibility and volatility, rapidly changing skill requirements, and reflexivity are all aspects of greater flexibility in work activities. These various types of flexible work practices are largely driven by factors that operate at a fundamental level in the economy – widespread diffusion of information technology, the need for constant innovation to remain competitive, the nature of competition in information-rich commodities and markets, and so on. These work practices cut across firm boundaries and are distinct from employment. This is not to suggest that they are entirely independent of employment relations – clearly the nature of the employment contract does influence the nature of work activities. What I am arguing, however, is that it is possible analytically to separate work from employment and recognize that there are a wide range of forces shaping the drive for increasing work flexibility that operate at a broader level than the contractual relationship between workers and their employers. The forces that shape work activities themselves are more diffuse, more fundamental, and less malleable than the forces that shape the employment relation, to which I now turn.

Flexibility in Employment Relations

Changes in employment relations are more direct and more visible than many of the changes in the nature of work. Employment relations are more directly shaped by institutional factors, including the legal and regulatory framework, the organizational structure and dynamics of firms and their management practices. The implications of the employment relationship have a much more visible, immediate and direct impact on the livelihoods of workers, since it fundamentally shapes compensation.

There is a significant mismatch between the conception of employment embodied in the regulatory system and employment relations as currently practiced by many firms. The legislative framework shaping the employment relationship (e.g. the National Labor Relations Act, the Taft-Hartley Act, the Title VII Civil Rights Act, the Age Discrimination in Employment Act, and so on) assumes a clear, long-term relationship between employers and employees (Friedman 1994; Gould 1993a; Gould 1993b). Similarly, much of current labor legislation and regulation is geared toward clarifying and strengthening that direct, long-term employment relationship in a variety of situations, assuming the continuation of a standard employment contract. The employment relationship, however, is increasingly characterized by temporary ties between worker and employer, and a relationship mediated by a set of external institutions, such as temporary agencies, subcontracting arrangements, or more informal mediated management practices.

Nonstandard Employment and Network Production

There is a voluminous literature on changing employment relations, and particularly the growth in various forms of "nonstandard employment".[9] This term generally refers to all employment that is not characterized by what have become the three fundamental components of standard employment in the post World War II era: full-time employment; a single employer who controls the conditions of employment; and employment for an indefinite period of time (i.e. not on a temporary status). Employment relations that fall outside this standard employment relation include temporary, part-time, contract employment, and self-employment.

The total of nonstandard employment has grown significantly in the United States since the 1970s.[10] This is most visible in the growth of temporary employment. Nationally, between 1982 and 2000, employment in help supply services grew by 736 percent compared to a growth in total nonfarm employment of 47 percent in the same period, thus growing from 0.5 percent of the workforce to 2.6 percent of the workforce.[11] This figure, however, underestimates the total number of people who are affected by temporary employment during the year. Researchers estimate that anywhere from 1.5 to 5 times as many people are employed in a temporary agency as at any single point during the year (Erickcek and Houseman 1997; Segal and Sullivan 1997). Furthermore, there has been a steady shift away from using temporary labor simply to fill temporary surges in labor requirements, toward outsourcing agreements with temporary agencies that permanently fill entire tiers of companies' labor forces.

9   Carre, Ferber, Golden, and Herzenberg (2000) provide a recent collection and summary of the literature.
10   Belous (1989); Bronstein (1991); Callaghan and Hartmann (1991); duRivage (1992); Messmer (1994); New Ways to Work (1991); Parker (1994); Pfeffer and Baron (1994); SEIU (1993); Sparke (1994); Tilly (1996).
11   According to data from the Current Employment Statistics, Bureau of Labor Statistics. Note that employment statistics from the CES include only employees on payroll, and thus exclude the roughly 7 percent of the workforce who are self-employed.

Part-time work and self-employment have also increased in the US, though somewhat less dramatically than temporary employment. Between 1972 and 1993, part-time employment grew from 15.8 percent to 17.8 percent of the total US workforce (Tilly 1996). This suggests that one out of every six US jobs (that is, about 22 million), is a part-time job. This yearly average, however, understates the dimension of the part-time work experience, since a much larger portion of the workforce is employed part-time at some point during the year. In 1985, for example, the number of people who worked part-time for a portion of the year was double that of the annual average number of part-time workers (Christopherson 1990).

Self-employment has also risen as a proportion of the total workforce. This is particularly true in nonagricultural industries since 1970, reversing a long-term decline. Between 1970 and 1994, self-employment rose from 6.9 percent of the nonagricultural workforce to 7.5 percent (Bregger 1996). If people who are incorporated but remain the sole employee of their own firm are included as self-employed, the total rises to 10.5 percent of the workforce, up from 9.8 percent in 1979 (Manser and Picot 1999).

Another aspect of the demise in full-time stable employment is the rise in various types of informal employment. For many years economists believed that the informal economy would disappear with the development of the modern industrial economy. In the last twenty years, it has been increasingly recognized that not only is this not the case in the developing world, but that informal employment is increasing in industrialized economies as well. Furthermore, it is clear that informal employment is not limited to survival strategies for the economically marginalized, but instead includes both low- and high-skilled workers and is intimately tied with changes in the organization of production in the formal economy.[12]

So, overall, there is a clear trend in the US toward changes in the employment relationship, with a decline in the "standard employment relationship" and the rise of various forms of nonstandard employment.[13] Furthermore, this trend appears to cut across all skill levels,

---

12   Benton (1989); Capechhi (1989); LaGuerre (1993); Lozano (1989); Sassen (1989); Stepick (1989); Zlolniski (1994).
13   This trend is not limited to the United States. Carnoy and Castells (1997) present evidence that between 30 and 45 percent of all workers in G-7 countries have some form of "flexible" work – either self-employed, part time, or temporary – and this percentage has been rapidly increasing in recent years.

and increasingly defies characterization as a "peripheral" workforce, as has been common in the literature. Certainly a large portion of people in nonstandard employment and a majority of those in temporary or involuntary part-time employment could be classified as a "peripheral workforce". Nonetheless, a large and growing number are in highly skilled occupations, performing work that is crucial for the value-added activities of firm and industry sectors, and finding such work preferable to standard employment. Thus, it is inaccurate to portray the rise of nonstandard employment as simply the rise of a peripheral workforce. The trend represents broader restructuring of employment relations.

The Changing "Standard" Employment Contract

Tenuous employment relations are not limited to firms' increased use of nonstandard employment. The "standard" employment relationship is shifting in fundamental ways as well. The nature of the contract between employer and employee has changed, such that workers can no longer expect to retain long-term stable employment with their employer, even when the firm is doing well. This trend is reflected in the quote from James Meadows, vice-president of AT&T, at the beginning of this chapter, in which he argues that all workers have to consider themselves as being on short-term contract with no long-term promises.

There has been a growing literature in the 1990s examining changes in job instability, measured by turnover rates and lengths of tenure. There has been some disagreement over the empirical findings because of data inconsistencies and the fact that trends vary by demographic group.[14] The clearest analysis for distinguishing changes in employment relationships from demographic shifts is found by examining

---

[14] For instance, using data from the CPS, Swinnerton and Wial (1995) find evidence of a secular decline in job stability, whereas Diebold, Neumark, and Polsky (1994) and Farber (1996) do not. This difference is in part due to changes in the wording of the CPS tenure questions after 1981, how researchers treat those who are self-employed, and how researchers treat other non-respondents. The interpretation is also difficult since there is evidence of increased tenure levels for women. The primary factor driving this, however, is the increased participation of women in the labor force and particularly more women pursuing long-term careers and taking less time off for child rearing, rather than changes in the nature of the employment relationship itself. For a good review of the evidence on job stability, see Neumark (2000 and Bernhardt and Marcotte (2000).

Table 1.2 Median years of tenure with current employer, by age and sex, 1983–2000

	1983	1987	1991	1996	1998	2000
Men						
(age in years)						
20–24	1.5	1.3	1.4	1.2	1.2	1.2
25–34	3.2	3.1	3.1	3.0	2.8	2.7
35–44	7.3	7.0	6.5	6.1	5.5	5.4
45–54	12.8	11.8	11.2	10.1	9.4	9.5
55–64	15.3	14.5	13.4	10.5	11.2	10.2
Women						
(age in years)						
20–24	1.5	1.3	1.3	1.2	1.1	1.0
25–34	2.8	2.6	2.7	2.7	2.5	2.5
35–44	4.1	4.4	4.5	4.8	4.5	4.3
45–54	6.3	6.8	6.7	7.0	7.2	7.3
55–64	9.8	9.7	9.9	10.0	9.6	9.9

Source: BLS Employee Tenure CPS Supplement: http://www.bls.gov/news.release/ tenure.toc.htm
Note: Data for 1996 and later are not strictly comparable with data for 1991 and earlier years because population controls from the 1990 census, adjusted for the estimated undercount, are used beginning in 1996. Figures for the 1983–91 period are based on population controls from the 1980 census. Also, beginning in 1996, the figures incorporate the effects of the redesign of the Current Population Survey introduced in January 1994. Data exclude the incorporated and unincorporated self-employed.

changes in tenure for men, where it is increasingly clear that, at all age levels and all education levels, job tenure has been declining. The median tenure for men aged 45 to 54, for instance, has declined to 9.5 years in 2000, down from 11.2 at the beginning of the decade and 12.8 in 1983. For men aged 54 to 64, the median tenure in 2000 was 10.2 years, down from 13.4 years in 1991 and 15.3 years in 1983 (see table 1.2).

The differences when comparing longitudinal cohorts can be quite significant. Studying the first 16 years of work experience for two different cohorts from the National Longitudinal Survey, for instance, Bernhardt et al. (1999) find that the recent cohort (who entered the labor market in 1979) were 34 percent more likely to experience job changes than a cohort who entered the labor market in 1966. Even in traditionally stable industries, the odds of a job separation for the recent cohort were 30 percent higher. By their early 30s, the recent cohort was 21 percent less likely to hold tenures of seven years or longer compared to the original cohort.[15]

Perhaps more important than increased turnover, however, is the changing implicit contract on the job (Rousseau 1995) . The rules, procedures, expectations, and norms regarding the employment relationship within firms are changing:

> People mourn its passing: The longtime covenant between employee and employer. We remember fondly the days when IBM could offer lifetime employment. And even if we didn't work for the likes of IBM, most of us understood that respectable companies would offer at least a measure of job security in exchange for adequate performance and some exhibition of loyalty. No longer. While a few prominent companies argue that the old covenant still exists, most people – and most companies – now hardened by downsizings, delayerings, right-sizings, layoffs, and restructurings, have concluded that the old covenant is null. (Waterman, Waterman, and Collard 1994: 88)

Employers no longer provide even implicit job security. The employment relationship has become a more open-ended negotiation based in large part on market power (Cappelli 1999). As Cappelli et al. (1997) argue, this has primarily been implemented on employers' terms, placing greater demands on workers while offering them less in terms of pay, benefits, or security. On the other hand, in some cases it does create significant challenges for employers as well. This is particularly true in tight labor markets, where the level of turnover and mobility may be significantly higher than employers desire, as highly sought-after workers move from firm to firm in search of better employment opportunities.

Mediated Employment Relations

The other significant development in the nature of the employment relation is the increasing mediation of that relationship by forces or institutions external to the firm. Sometimes this has been referred to as "market-mediated employment relations" (Abraham 1990; Cappelli 1999) in which pressures from outside the firm boundaries are used as a management tool:

---

15   See also Bernhardt, Morris, Handcock, and Scott (2001a).

We found that traditional methods of managing employees and developing skilled workers inside companies are breaking down. What we see in their place is a new employment relationship where pressures from product and labor markets are brought inside the organization and used to mediate the relationship between workers and management. Employees now bear many more of the risks of doing business through reduced job security and contingent pay. Jobs demand more of workers but seem to offer them less. Employees are pressed to manage their own career development in work settings that may be reducing the incentives for employers to provide training, especially for entry-level jobs. At the same time, sharp declines in employee commitment have forced employers to rethink how to manage employees in ways that do not rely on traditional commitments to the organization. (Cappelli et al. 1997: 4)

These types of mediated management relationships have particularly been documented in service industries that involve high levels of customer interaction. In those cases, the management relationship can only be understood in the context of the triangular relationship between employer, workers, and customers (Fuller and Smith 1996; Leidner 1993; Macdonald and Sirianni 1996). Firms employ this strategy in order to de-emphasize bureaucratic control methods and instead use customer feedback as a way of ensuring high-quality work. Fuller and Smith (1996) find evidence of this in a wide range of industries, including automobile sales, supermarket, hospital, child care, banking, hotel, restaurant, insurance, and liquor. Similar dynamics are observable in many information technology industries where close relationships between customers and suppliers are often critical in ensuring quality control and rapid delivery of product. This is reflected in the following quote describing Electronic Manufacturing Services (EMS) firm Solectron's shop-floor management system.

At the operational level, every customer and product has a focused team of people who essentially own that customer's product and own that service to that customer through the manufacturing process. If they feel that they need to do something, they have all the empowerment and all the authority for that particular customer. The managers manage between the customer-focus teams and different teams themselves, to make sure everything fits. There is no person at the operation saying, "You will do this. You will do that.". (Suzik 1999: 57)

Again, the employment relationship is fundamentally mediated by a set of relationships that cross firm boundaries. Workers are immediately subject to changing customer demands and desires, and must adjust their work accordingly. Compensation systems are then frequently linked with workers' ability to respond to these customers' desires.

On the whole, the rise in nonstandard employment relationships and the various ways of restructuring the standard employment contract reflect ways that firms are trying to achieve greater flexibility in their relationships with workers. It is important to keep in mind, however, the distinction between employment and work in this regard. Ultimately what is important for the competitiveness of the firm and for the broader economy is the work itself. Flexibility in work activities seems to be increasingly important in ensuring long-term competitiveness. Firms introduce flexible employment relations in many cases in an effort to promote flexible work. Firms also promote flexible employment practices, however, for a variety of other reasons, such as cutting costs, shifting economic risk, improving control mechanisms, and the like. Such practices may have negative impacts on working conditions and compensation for employees, while doing little to promote long-term competitiveness of the economy. Furthermore, since the institutional framework shaping employment relations is based on the firm, it limits the ability of workers to develop career mobility across multiple firms.

Flexibility, therefore, clearly has both beneficial and detrimental aspects. To the extent that it contributes to improved economic performance, this may have beneficial aspects for both firms and workers. To the extent that it shifts risk from firms to workers and makes workers more vulnerable, it may harm workers. To the extent to which it undermines long-term investments in human resource development, it may harm both employers and workers. To distinguish the various implications of labor market flexibility requires specifying in more detail the mechanisms that promote flexibility and examining the implications of those mechanisms for the innovativeness and flexibility of firms as well as for the welfare of workers (Zabin and Ringer 1997). Part III returns to this theme, but for the moment I will turn to the empirical analysis of labor market flexibility in Silicon Valley.

2

Silicon Valley: Changing Industry Structure and Employment Practices

We estimate that close to 70 percent of Intel's profits in 1997 will come from products that were not on the market as of January 1st of this year.

Gordon E. Moore
Chairman of the Board, Intel
May, 1997

It is not the strongest of the species that survive, nor the most intelligent, but the ones most responsive to change.

Charles Darwin

Silicon Valley is an important context for examining new trends in flexible labor and regional development. Though certain trends may be more exaggerated in Silicon Valley than elsewhere, it is nonetheless a trendsetter, both for the United States and for the world. As mentioned in the Introduction, this is true for two fundamental reasons. First, its origins as an industrial region lie in information technology industries, which have developed primarily in the last half-century. As recently as 1950 the region's economy was still dominated by agriculture and food processing industries in a largely rural setting. This agriculture-based economy has now almost entirely disappeared, and the structure of the region's labor markets are primarily shaped by work and employment trends in information technology (IT) industries. The relative newness of Silicon Valley's industrial structure, at least compared to older industrial regions, makes especially visible patterns of work and employment that are associated with the rise of information technology. Second,

Silicon Valley is a global center of innovation and production in these information technology industries, which are linked together in complex networks of production, customer, and supplier relations. Product and process innovations are adopted in the region rapidly, allowing firms to develop innovative management and human resource practices. These practices then often diffuse on to world markets and into other industries. Again, this is not to suggest that trends in work and employment that develop in Silicon Valley are inevitably replicated in other regions or other industries. Indeed, the region has a unique history and the concentration of IT industries in the region is unrivaled, making for particular labor markets that may seem more exceptional than typical of the rest of the United States. Nonetheless, many important trends in labor market practices develop sooner and are rooted more deeply in Silicon Valley's economic structure. These practices often then diffuse in varying degrees to other regions and other industries as firms in other regions and industries make use of new technological developments in their own restructuring efforts.

Flexible labor is deeply rooted in Silicon Valley labor markets, which are characterized by rapidly changing skill requirements and volatile employment conditions. New forms of flexible labor – networking, mobility, and nonstandard employment – are prominent features of industrial organization in the region. The Silicon Valley region has twice the national percentage of the workforce employed in temporary agencies, with up to 40 percent of the region's workforce involved in nonstandard employment relationships. Rapid turnover has become the norm, even for people classified as having "permanent" employment (Carnoy, Castells, and Benner 1997; Gregory 1984; Saxenian 1996). Even for people in more stable, "permanent" employment, changing skill requirements creates constant change, a need for ongoing learning, and high levels of uncertainty. Very few people in the region's information technology industries are insulated from the high levels of volatility and rapid change that characterize work and employment in the region. Furthermore, many people outside the high-tech sector, in locally serving industries, are also heavily affected as the rapid fluctuations in the core sectors of the region's economy ripple through regional labor markets.

The volatility in the region's labor markets is fundamentally tied to the nature of competition in the region's high-tech industries. Competitive success for firms and industries in information technology industries depends on constant innovation in both developing new products and services and in improving production processes. As Angel (1994:4) describes, "[i]n an era of intensified global competition, it is the ability to anticipate and create new market opportunities, to develop new products ahead of competitors and to reconfigure production processes rapidly in response to changing production requirements that offers the best prospect for long-term profitability of firms and industries." This drive for constant innovation leads to a continual cycle of creative destruction, with new products, firms, and even entire industries replacing existing products, firms, and industries, while surviving firms are forced to restructure their operations and products. The rate of these volatile changes has accelerated since the early 1990s as the rapid development of the World Wide Web and related telecommunications and networking technologies have created opportunities in entirely new industries, dramatically altered competitive conditions in a wide range of existing industries, and made possible entirely new organizational forms. Volatile employment conditions, however, are not limited to the recent decade, but in fact have characterized Silicon Valley's IT industries since their earliest days. Indeed, flexible employment practices, with open labor markets and widespread circulation of skilled personnel among multiple firms, has been a key component in the long-term competitive success of firms and industries in the region. These employment conditions are rooted fundamentally in a set of competitive conditions characteristic of information technology industries.

This chapter begins by providing evidence of the pervasiveness of flexible work and employment in Silicon Valley. It argues that rapidly changing work and employment conditions are the dominant experience for the majority of all workers in the region's labor markets. The second half of the chapter connects these flexible labor markets to the character of competition in the region's leading information technology firms and industries.

Flexible Work and Employment Practices

There are three growing trends that characterize Silicon Valley's labor markets in recent years. The first is a rapid growth in various forms of nonstandard employment, including temporary, independent contracting and outsourcing employment. Second is the high level of turnover and mobility, including for employees classified as having full-time, "permanent" employment. Third, rapidly changing technology and market conditions are leading to high levels of skill obsolescence along with these flexible employment practices.

Nonstandard employment

Estimates of the size of the growing workforce employed in nonstandard arrangements are at best approximations, since government statistics on nonstandard work are limited and the many different types of
nonstandard employment often overlap statistical categories. There
are also multiple interpretations of what constitutes nonstandard employment.[1] The broadest definition of nonstandard employment, however, includes: temporary help services; part-time labor;
self-employment or independent contracting; and subcontracted business services. The following presents what is currently known about
the extent of temporary, part-time, and contracted work in Silicon Valley in comparison to trends at a national level. While the exact numbers may be debatable, the trends clearly show a rising level of
nonstandard employment. It is also clear that Silicon Valley shows a
particularly high concentration of nonstandard employment compared
to the country as a whole.

Temporary Employment

Temporary employment is the most obvious and visible type of nonstandard employment. In Santa Clara County, the number of people
employed in temporary help firms has grown dramatically. Between
1984 and 1998, employment in temporary agencies grew from a yearly
average of 12,340 to 33,850, growing from 1.6 percent of the workforce
to 3.5 percent of the workforce (see table 2.1).

In this 14 year-period, employment in temporary agencies grew by
174 percent while total employment grew by 26 percent. *Between 1990
and 1994 employment in temporary agencies grew by 30 percent while overall
employment actually declined by 2 percent!*

Self-employed Workers

It is difficult to obtain regular information on self-employment at a
county level, since statistics are not regularly kept at a local level. According to the US Census, however, in 1990 a total of 52,000 people, or
approximately 6.5 percent of the workforce of Santa Clara County, were
self-employed. This was up from 5.9 percent in the 1980 census. Joint

---

1   Discussed in Carnoy, Castells, and Benner (1997).

Table 2.1   Temporary employment and total employment in Santa Clara
County, 1984–98

Year	Temporary employment	Total employment	Temporary as % of total
1984	12,340	764,400	1.6
1985	12,450	770,900	1.6
1986	14,310	761,500	1.9
1987	16,920	779,700	2.2
1988	18,150	808,900	2.2
1989	17,020	814,100	2.1
1990	16,580	819,500	2.0
1991	14,720	810,900	1.8
1992	15,510	797,200	1.9
1993	17,370	802,000	2.2
1994	21,820	805,000	2.7
1995	28,160	836,400	3.4
1996	30,660	885,000	3.5
1997	33,230	931,700	3.6
1998	33,850	961,500	3.5

Source: California Economic Development Department, Labor Market Information Division.
Note: Figures are yearly averages. 1998 only includes the first three-quarters.

Venture Silicon Valley estimates that over 7 percent of the workforce were fully self-employed in 1995. This figure, however, does not take into account people who identify themselves as self-employed but who are legally employees of their own incorporated business. There is no accurate estimate of this in Silicon Valley, but one indicator is the number of single-employee business operations in Silicon Valley communities. In the four largest cities in Silicon Valley, the number of single-employee business licenses increased 44 percent between 1989 and 1996, from 19,600 to 28,400. Another indicator is the percentage of people who report at least some self-employed income on their tax returns, a total of 15 percent of all tax returns in Santa Clara and San Mateo counties in 1999 (JV:SVN 2000).

Part-time Employment

Obtaining estimates of part-time employment in Silicon Valley is impossible, since no statistics are regularly kept at a county level. Part-time employment in the State of California, however, has followed

Table 2.2 California part-time employment as percentage of all employment, 1983–98

Year	Total part-time	Involuntary part-time	Voluntary part-time
1983	18.4	5.6	12.8
1984	17.8	5.1	12.7
1985	17.7	4.8	12.8
1986	17.0	4.6	12.3
1987	17.5	4.5	13.0
1988	17.4	4.6	12.8
1989	15.9	2.7	13.2
1990	14.9	2.5	12.4
1991	15.6	3.1	12.5
1992	15.7	3.8	11.9
1993	16.3	4.2	12.1
1994*	19.9	4.1	15.8
1995	19.3	3.7	15.6
1996	18.7	3.3	15.4
1997	18.8	3.0	15.8
1998	18.8	2.7	16.1

Source: California Employment Development Department.
* Figures for 1994 and after are not directly comparable with previous figures due to a change in survey methodology.

national patterns of growth and decline quite closely. In essence, part-time employment, particularly involuntary part-time employment, grew rapidly in the 1970s and early 1980s, but then stabilized. In 1998, in California, 18.7 percent of the workforce was employed in regular part-time work, up from 14.9 percent in 1990 but down from a high of 19.9 percent in 1994 (see table 2.2).

Contracting Out

The current trend toward increased outsourcing of both manufacturing and services represents the most significant change in the structure of employment. In many cases, contracted employees perform jobs that were previously held by workers directly employed by these same employers. For many corporations, a variety of functions including much of the manufacturing activity can be farmed out to networks of relatively small outside contractors. Employers are also increasingly using contract employees in highly skilled positions. Computer programmers, engineers, and a range of other highly skilled professionals in the Valley work as independent contractors, often working through a variety of consulting companies and business service firms. These workers move between workplaces, filling particular positions and working on particular projects on demand (Kunda, Barley, and Evans 1999).

In the 1980s, outsourcing of lower-level building services and landscaping operations was common. In the 1990s, there was a rapid expansion in the outsourcing of a more diverse array of functions, including everything from payroll and human resource administration to manufacturing. The Electronic Manufacturing Services (EMS) industry, for example, is one of the most rapidly growing segments of the high-tech sector, as original equipment "manufacturers" like Hewlett-Packard, Cisco Systems, and Sun increasingly outsource their manufacturing functions to EMS companies like Solectron, Flextronics, and Sanmina. For a typical PC company, the costs of components, software, and services purchased from outside increased from less than 60 percent in the mid 1980s to more than 80 percent of total production costs in 1997 (Ernst 1997).

While reliable data on the number of jobs in outsourced employment does not exist, one "proxy" number that has been used in various studies is employment in "business services" (Belous 1989; Clinton 1997). Under this label is a diverse range of companies that provide a large number of subcontracting services, including advertising, computer and data processing services, consumer credit reporting and collection, protective services, building services, and personnel services. In Santa Clara County, employment in business services has risen from 48,500 in 1984 (6.3 percent of civilian employment) to 132,100 in 1998 (13.7 percent) (see table 2.3). The use of "business services" as a proxy for subcontracted work, however, is at best only a rough estimate, especially in Silicon Valley. Due to the deficiencies of our Standard Industrial Classification system, it includes most of the software industry. It also definitely double-counts some people in nonstandard employment, since the category also includes people employed in temporary agencies (a subcategory of business services). On the other hand, it does not include any people employed in subcontracted manufacturing activities, who constitute a large number of the people in the electronics industry in Silicon Valley. In the absence of more detailed statistics, it can be used as a rough proxy.

Table 2.3 Employment in business services, Santa Clara County, 1984–98

Year	Total employment	Business services	
		No.	Percent
1984	764,400	48,500	6.3
1985	770,900	49,800	6.5
1986	761,500	50,200	6.6
1987	779,700	53,200	6.8
1988	808,900	56,700	7.0
1989	814,100	56,400	6.9
1990	819,500	58,000	7.1
1991	810,900	59,000	7.3
1992	797,200	65,500	8.2
1993	802,000	74,200	9.3
1994	805,000	81,900	10.2
1995	836,400	96,200	11.5
1996	885,000	109,500	12.4
1997	931,700	120,600	12.9
1998	961,500	130,300	13.6

Source: California Employment Development Department.

Total Nonstandard Employment

Richard Belous (1989) was the first person to try to make a comprehensive estimate of the nonstandard workforce in the US and its growth in the 1980s. Including temporary workers, part-time workers, business services, and the self-employed, Belous estimated that by 1988 between 25 and 30 percent of the US workforce were nonstandard workers. Belous used two different estimates, the upper estimate included all people in the categories identified and the lower estimate tried to eliminate some potential double counting.[2] In either case, the nonstandard workforce was growing from 50 to 100 percent faster than employment in the economy as a whole, and between one-third to one-half of all new jobs created in the 1980s were for nonstandard workers.

Using Belous's methodology, between 277,992 and 421,832 people in

2 Belous's lower estimate doesn't count business services at all, since it assumes that all business services workers are already counted in one of the other groups, and it counts only 60 percent of the temporary workers, since survey data suggests that 40 percent of temporary workers are part-timers.

Table 2.4   Growth of the nonstandard workforce in Santa Clara County, 1984–98

	Workers		Percent change	No. increase
	1984	1998		
Temporary workers	12,340	33,850	174	21,510
Part-time workers	136,200	180,762	33	44,562
Business services	48,500	130,300	169	81,800
Self-employed	45,700	76,920	68	31,220
Upper estimate of size of nonstandard workforce	242,700	421,832	74	179,132
Lower estimate of size of nonstandard workforce	189,300	277,992	47	88,692
Total civilian employment	761,200	961,500	26	200,300

Sources: Figures for temporary workers and business services come from the California Employment Development Department. Figures for self-employment are projections based on US Census data. Figures for part-time employment are from the Bureau of Labor Statistics and assume Santa Clara County has the same percentage of part-time workers as the nation.

Santa Clara County had some form of nonstandard employment in 1998, which accounts for between 29 percent and 44 percent of the Santa Clara County labor force (see table 2.4). The nonstandard workforce is growing roughly two to three times as fast as the overall labor force, and *between 44 percent and 89 percent of all net job growth in the county between 1984 and 1998 was accounted for in the growth of nonstandard employment.*

Labor Turnover, Mobility, and Skill Obsolescence

An additional sign of the rapid changes in work and employment conditions in Silicon Valley's volatile labor market is evident in the high levels of turnover and rapid pace of skills obsolescence in high-tech occupations. Some of this turnover is driven by highly skilled professionals who voluntarily change employment in search of better employment opportunities. In the words of a human resource manager in an electronics firm: "The job market for engineers is extremely volatile . . . People are moving from job to job, and can gain tremendous offerings from new places. The majority of our engineers have been with the company for two years or less. It was somewhat lower three years ago, but still high"(HR manager in an electronics manufacturer, 1996).

Younger workers in particular are less tied to a single firm, and often move in search of new work challenges and earnings opportunities, often in smaller start-up firms. As one human resource manager in a major software firm describes: "[We have] an increase in attrition . . . People are getting a lot of offers from start-up companies . . . [and] a lot of technically inclined individuals are really ready to roll the dice. We have a fairly young workforce, most of our fellow companies out here do. Lots of people are saying you got to take a shot at this kind of thing once in a life . . ." (HR Manager at a major software company, 1996).

Much of the turnover, however, is also driven by layoffs and corporate restructuring. Layoffs in high-tech industries are frequently not related to cyclical downturns but are more related to structural changes in the industry or in a company's operations. Many companies simultaneously layoff part of their workforce while hiring for other positions. While there is no data source on this at a regional level, national figures suggest information technology industries are particular prone to this. In their tracking of announced layoffs starting in 1993, for example, outplacement firm Challenger Gray & Christmas found that the computer and telecommunications industries are leaders in job loss at a time when the industries have shown significant net job growth. From 1993 to 1998, companies in more than thirty industries announced a combined total of 3.1 million layoffs, with seven industries accounting for more than half of that total. The computer industry ranked third, while telecommunications ranked fourth, outpaced only by aerospace/ defense (subject to declining federal government defense expenditures) and the retail industry, a widely acknowledged unstable employment sector.

These layoffs occurred in the midst of the longest economic expansion in US history, and are thus linked primarily to restructuring within firms and within industries, rather than recession. In Silicon Valley, for example, in 1998, a year in which total employment in Santa Clara County grew by over 3 percent, many Silicon Valley firms were in the midst of laying off significant portions of their workforce due to restructuring. Prominent Silicon Valley firms that announced layoffs included the following: Seagate (10,000, 10 percent of their global workforce); Applied Materials (4,200, 30 percent); Intel (3,000, 5 percent); National Semiconductor (1,400, 10 percent); Silicon Graphics (1,000, 10 percent); Silicon Valley Group (900, 26 percent); Lam Research (700 people, 15 percent); Netscape (400, 12.5 percent); Komag (480, 10 percent);

Cypress Semiconductor (100, less than 5 percent); S3 (100, 15 percent); Spectrian (200, 25 percent); Read-rite (250, 10 percent); Adaptec (250, 7 percent); and VLSI (10 percent). These layoffs were in part due to a downturn in demand as a result of the Asian financial crisis, but they also reflect responses to technological changes in various industries as firms try to restructure to meet new competitive conditions.

Available data on turnover at a state-wide level also provide evidence of high levels of mobility and turnover in high-tech industries. California's economy in the 1990s has come to be increasingly dominated by information technology industries, and though not as concentrated as Silicon Valley, the state faces similar trends (Benner, Brownstein, and Dean 1999; Levy and Arnold 1999). A recent University of California, San Francisco survey found that almost half of California's workers have been with their current employer for two years or less. Median job tenure in the state is only three years. The UCSF study found that only 21 percent of employed adults had been with their current employer ten years or more in 1998.[3] This compares with a national figure of 35.4 percent of employed workers with more than ten years on their current job (Mishel, Bernstein, and Schmitt 2001).

In a similar vein, in a comparison of all 50 states, Atkinson et al. (1999) find that California had the second highest "churn rate" of all states, second only to Nevada. The churn rate is a measure of the extent of both firms failing and new firms starting as a percent of all companies in each state. As Atkinson et al. (1999) argue, steady growth in employment masks the constant churning of job creation and destruction, as less innovative and less efficient companies downsize or go out of business and more innovative and efficient companies grow and take their place. They argue that such turbulence increases the economic risk faced by workers, companies and regions, but is also a major driver of economic innovation and growth.

Changing skill demands

The turbulence in employees' work lives, however, is not limited to changing jobs or employers. The rapid pace of technological change and rapidly changing market conditions requires workers to continually learn on the job, to stay on top of new technology and to develop

---

3   California Work and Health Survey: http://medicine.ucsf.edu/programs/cwhs/

new skills. Without new knowledge, companies rapidly fall behind. Without continual learning, employees become less valuable to their employers, becoming "obsolete" with successive waves of technological innovation. In the words of Michael Curran, director of the NOVA Private Industry Council, an award-winning training center and workforce development resource in the Valley, "The nature of industry in the Valley is constantly changing, and employers just can't tell you what skills they're going to need two years from now . . . In the past, the skills that employees had lasted longer, maybe 8-10 years. Now a current skill set might be valuable for only 18 months" (interview, June, 1999).

This trend toward skills obsolescence in the high-tech industry is evident in analysis of comprehensive national data conducted by University of California Professor Clair Brown and her colleagues. They compared the earnings growth based on experience (the experience premium) for engineers and managers in high-tech industries versus in the economy as a whole. As figure 2.1 shows, earnings growth based on experience has stagnated for high-tech engineers and managers while growing substantially for engineers and managers in the economy as a whole. In the entire economy, a professional with 20 years of experience in 1985 earned 48 percent more than a professional with no experience, and by 1995 this had increased to 73 percent. In high-tech industries, an engineer or professional with 20 years of experience earned 55 percent more than a new-hire in 1985 but only 59 percent more in 1995. Wages actually start to decline for engineers and managers with more than 24 years experience.

In addition to the increasing pace of change in skill requirements, it is important to note that the nature of many of the skills required in the region's industries are nonfirm specific. Skills are more general, related to technological changes that rapidly diffuse throughout many companies and industries. To remain productively employed, many workers have to consistently upgrade their skills and knowledge, maintaining close communication with many other individuals and firms in the broader industry. Since a larger portion of their skills are not firm specific, they are able to move from firm to firm more easily, contributing to the lack of long-term attachment between firms and many individuals in the region.

From the analysis in this section, it should be clear that both the nature of work and employment relations in Silicon Valley change rapidly and in unpredictable ways. The percentage of the workforce in nonstandard employment is significantly higher than the national

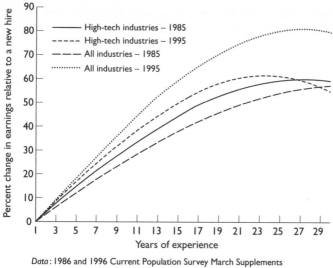

Data: 1986 and 1996 Current Population Survey March Supplements
Source: Courtesy of Clair Brown et al., University of California, Berkeley

Figure 2.1   Manager and professional experience premiums, 1985 and 1995

average, accounting for as much as 44 percent of total employment in the Valley and 89 percent of recent job growth. Even for people in permanent employment, however, their relationship with employers is shaped by short periods of time and rapidly changing skill demands. The rapid changes in work demands and the tenuous employment relationships are driven largely by the dynamics of competition in information technology industries. With rapidly changing product markets, short product life-cycles, and intense competition, firms in the various information technology sectors in Silicon Valley have placed a high premium on the flexible use of labor. The following section traces these economic dynamics in the regional economy as a whole and in the various industry subsectors.

Economic Change and Flexibility

The rapid turnover and volatility in employment in Silicon Valley is integrally connected to the nature of competition in the region's high-technology industries. In these industries, markets and technology change extremely rapidly and in unpredictable ways. Those firms that succeed are those that are able to innovate by developing both new products and improved production processes to shorten the time-to-market. The pace of change pushes firms to pursue high levels of flexibility in their labor practices. While the specific technological changes and market conditions are unique within the various subsectors that make up the regional high-tech complex, there is a common experience of rapid change and volatility.

Silicon Valley's economy is dominated by the concentration of electronics and related information technology industries in the area. The semiconductor industry is the oldest and most significant sector in the region's economy and provided the basis for the early development and expansion of the region. While semiconductors still provide a major core of the region's high-tech agglomeration, in the last twenty-five years the regional economy has become significantly more diversified and complex. Computer systems and workstations, with leading companies such as Sun Microsystems and SGI (formerly Silicon Graphics), became a major component of the region's economy, particularly in the 1980s, along with disk drives, storage devices, and other peripherals. With the expansion of the Internet in the 1980s and 1990s, networking equipment companies such as Cisco, 3Com, and Bay Networks became prominent employers in the area. Software, multimedia, and Internet companies are the most rapidly growing sector of the Valley in the 1990s. Table 2.5 presents the core information technology industries in the area, the major companies in each sector, and the approximate local and global employment of the top 20 companies in each industry sector.

Table 2.6 shows total employment in the major driving industry clusters, along with other major employment sectors in Silicon Valley from 1992 to 1998.[4] The leading industry clusters identified here, all linked with the region's high-tech industrial complex, accounted for 41 percent of total employment in the Valley in 1998 (see figure 2.2). Software is the most rapidly growing industry in the region, adding more than 45,000 jobs in six years, an increase of 171 percent from 1992 to 1998.

---

4   The approach to analyzing employment in regional industry clusters represents a significant improvement over our currently outdated and misleading Standard Industrial Classification System. Nonetheless, it still requires using available data on employment by SIC code and recombining it into clusters of related firms that more accurately reflect economic dynamics in the regional economy. The appendix to this chapter explains more about the industry cluster analysis of the regional economy and provides the SIC codes that make up the clusters identified in this section.

Table 2.5 Silicon Valley information technology sectors

Industry segment	Major companies	Largest 20 firms 1997 employment	
		Local	Global
Computer systems	Hewlett-Packard, Apple, Sun, SGI, Tandem	~35,000	180,000
Semiconductor manufacturers	Intel, National Semi., AMD, LSI, VLSI	~31,000	140,000
Semiconductor manufacturing equipment	Applied Materials, LAM, KLA/ Tencor, SVG, Varian,	~19,000	38,000
Disk drives/storage	Seagate/Conner, Maxtor, Quantum, Western Digital	~17,000	133,000
Network equipment	Cisco, 3Com, Bay Networks	~13,000	35,000
Contract manufacturing/ PCBs	Solectron, SCI, Flextronics, Sanmina	~13,000	35,000
Software developers/ Internet	Oracle, Cadence, Adobe, Yahoo, Excite, Lycos	38,000	
Biotechnology/ Biopharmaceutical	Alza Corp, SRI International, Scios, Molecular Dynamics	~4,000	

Source: For employment: *San Jose Business Journal* and company reports. Adapted from Luethje (1998).

Significant employment growth has also occurred in various types of business services, including outsourcing and innovation services. Employment in outsourcing services – a category including primarily temporary help agencies, building services, mailing, reproduction, and security services – grew by 68 percent between 1992 to 1998, reflecting the rapid trends toward outsourcing lower-skilled, non core corporate functions. Employment in innovation services – a category that includes wholesale distribution of computers and components, along with engineering and research/testing services – grew by 52 percent in this period, reflecting the outsourcing trend for more highly skilled functions. Employment in the core computers/communication sector has been nearly flat over this time-period, while growth in printed circuit board fabrication and other electronic manufacturing services grew by 55 percent, reflecting the restructuring in the computer systems industry. Meanwhile, employment in defense and aerospace firms declined by 40 percent in this time-period, continuing a decline that began in the late 1980s.

Table 2.6 Employment by industry sector, Silicon Valley, 1992–98

	Employment*		Change, 1992–98	
	1992	1998	Number	Percent
"Driving cluster industries"				
Software	26,715	72,320	45,605	171
Business services – outsourcing	50,298	84,561	34,263	68
Innovation related services	56,705	86,243	29,538	52
Semiconductors	56,681	77,698	21,017	37
Computers/Communication contract mfg.	22,858	35,364	12,506	55
Business services – professional	31,003	38,336	7,333	24
Computers/Communication – orig. equip. mfg	72,080	76,754	4,674	6
Bioscience	19,990	23,787	3,797	19
Defense/Aerospace	37,707	22,796	−14,911	−40
Other manufacturing industries				
Fabricated metal products	8,870	11,628	2,758	31
Transport equipment (nondefense)	5,030	6,021	991	20
Food processing	6,462	7,053	591	9
Miscellaneous manufacturing	45,093	51,805	6,712	15
Other major employment sectors				
Construction	38,580	61,802	23,222	60
Non food retail	82,950	94,761	11,811	14
Travel, tourism, leisure	24,194	35,095	10,901	45
Eating and drinking places	53,698	64,190	10,492	20
Nonfood wholesale	31,662	37,600	5,938	19
Private sector hospitals and health services	53,408	62,927	5,441	10
Private sector social services	14,530	19,269	4,739	33
Finance, insurance, real estate	50,008	52,482	2,474	5
Private educational services	23,074	24,533	1,459	6
Food distribution – wholesale and retail	28,716	29,960	1,244	4
Personal services	8,625	8,231	−394	−5
Other	62,784	72,674	6,537	10
Federal, state, and local government	111,412	115,749	4,337	4
Total, all industries	1,023,133	1,273,639	250,506	24

Source: EDD

* Figures are average employment for fourth quarter in each year.

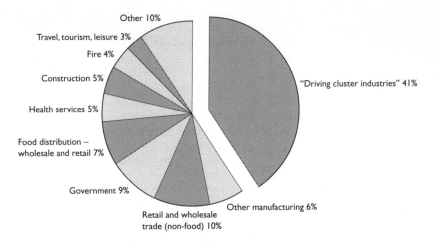

Figure 2.2 Total employment by industry cluster, Silicon Valley, 1998, fourth quarter

In sum, there has been a significant restructuring of the Silicon Valley economy in the 1990s with rapidly changing work and employment demands. This trend, however, reflects similar restructuring that has struck the Valley's economy since its origins. The following sections trace some of these changes in the region's economy, first in overall employment, and then in significant industry sectors including software, semiconductors, the computer industry, and defense/aerospace.

Overall Industry/Company Change

One clear sign of the rapid changes in employment in the Valley is the turbulence in the largest public companies in the region. These large public companies provide a significant portion of employment in the information technology sector, and are at the core of the region's high-tech agglomeration, providing a source for spin-offs which form many of the smaller start-ups in the area and important markets for many smaller supplier firms. Yet despite their importance and size, they have faced dramatic change. Of the 100 largest Silicon Valley companies in 1985, only 19 still existed and were in the top 100 in 2000 (see table 2.7). Of the 81 that no longer appeared in the top 100 list in 2000, 39 were acquired or merged into other companies, 22 were still independent

Table 2.7 Firms in the top 100 Silicon Valley firms in 1985 that still were in the top 100 in 2000

		Sales rank	
Company	Major product	1985	2000
Advanced Micro Devices	Semiconductors	6	13
Alza	Drug-delivery systems	54	45
Apple Computer	Computers	2	9
Applied Materials	Semiconductor manufacturing equipment	18	8
Coherent	Lasers	22	66
Hewlett-Packard	Computers/Instruments	1	1
Integrated Device Technologies	Semiconductors	61	47
Intel	Semiconductors	4	2
KLA Instruments/KLA-Tencor	Semiconductor manufacturing equipment	45	27
Lam Research	Semiconductor manufacturing equipment	66	31
LSI Logic	Semiconductors	21	17
Maxtor	Hard disk drives	56	19
National Semiconductor	Semiconductors	3	23
Plantronics	Communications accessories	35	85
Quantum	Hard disk drives	25	12
Silicon Valley Group	Semiconductor manufacturing equipment	63	48
Siliconix	Semiconductors	28	78
3Com	Computer networking equipment	62	16
Varian Associates	Diversified electronic products	5	57

Source: San Jose Mercury News, from company SEC filings.

public companies but were too small to make the list in 1994, 13 more entered bankruptcy proceedings, six more moved out of the area and one became private through a management buy-out (see table 2.8). Many of the companies that merged or were acquired did so because of pressing financial problems. For example, Businessland, which was rated 10th in total sales in 1985, was acquired in 1991 only after suffering huge losses from its chain of computer stores. When the new owners couldn't turn around the company, the remaining stores were shut down in 1993. Avantek, which was rated 15th in total sales in 1985, mostly manufactured microwave communications equipment for the military and was acquired by Hewlett-Packard in 1991 when it couldn't recover

Table 2.8 Silicon Valley top 100 firms in 1985 that were not in the top 100 in 2000

Firm	Rank in 1985	Industry	Event	Date
Activision	74	Computer and video games	Changed name in 1988, entered bankruptcy proceedings in 1991, emerged from bankruptcy proceedings, changed name back to Activision and moved to Los Angeles.	1988
Adac Laboratories	46	Medical imaging equipment	Acquired by Konin Klijke Philips Electronics	2000
Altos Computer System	23	Networked computer systems	Acquired by Acer Group of Taiwan	1990
Amdahl	7	Mainframe computers and services	Acquired by Fujitsu, Inc. of Japan	1997
Anderson Jacobson Inc.	51	Telecommunication equipment	Acquired by CXR Corp. of San Jose	1988
Anthem Electronics	26	Semiconductor distributor	Acquired by Arrow Electronics of Melville, NY	1994
Argosystems Inc.	44	Defense electronics	Acquired by Boeing Co. of Seattle	1987
Ask Computer Systems	40	Manufacturing control software	Acquired by Computer Associates International of Islandia, NY	1994
Avantek	15	Microwave communications equipment	Acquired by Hewlett-Packard of Palo Alto	1991
Boole & Babbage	73	Enterprise software	Acquired by BMC Software of Houston, TX	1999
BR Communications	98	Military communication equipment	Merged with TCI Internation of Sunnyvale. Combined company is now too small to make the Silicon Valley 150 list	1988
Bridge Communications	69	Computer networking equipment	Acquired by 3Com Corp of Santa Clara	1987
Britton-Lee	71	Database Software	Changed name to Sharebase Corp. in 1989, acquired by Teradata Corp. of Los Angeles in 1990. Teradata was acquired by AT&T in 1992	1989
Businessland	10	Computer stores	Acquired by JWP of Rye Brook, NY in 1991 after heavy losses. JWP shut down remaining retail operation in 1993	1991

Firm	Rank in 1985	Industry	Event	Date
California Microwave	30	Wireless, satellite communications	Acquired by Northrop Grumman	1999
Circadian	100	Medical equipment	CEO resigned in 1995, in midst of laying off a third of their workforce. Now out of business	1995
Collagen	94	Medical implants	Dropped off list in early 1990s (too small), and by 1997 spun-off its medical implants business	1997
Compression Labs	96	Video compression devices	Acquired by Vtel of Austin, TX	1997
Convergent	9	Computer workstations	Acquired by Unisys Corp of Blue Bell, PA	1997
Cooper Biomedical	36	Pharmaceutical research	Changed name to Cooper Development Co. in 1986. Now too small to make the Silicon Valley 150 list.	1988 1986
Cooper Lasersonics	37	Surgical lasers	Acquired by Heraeus Holding GmbH of Germany	1988
Corvus Systems Inc.	38	Computer networking	Entered bankruptcy proceedings in 1988; reorganized in 1990 with most assets transferred to a new privately held company called Ceron Corp.	1988
Daisy Systems Corp.	24	Electronic design automation	Entered bankruptcy proceedings in 1990 after running into financial trouble related to the acquisition of rival Cadnetix Corp. The remaining assets of Daisy were acquired by Intergraph Corp. of Huntsville, AL. later that year	1990
Dest Corp.	87	Desktop scanners for personal computers	Entered bankruptcy proceedings in April 1989, taken private in a management buy-out one month later. Reorganized as New Dest Corp., the business was acquired by Behavior Technology of Taiwan in 1994	1989

Company	No.	Products	Notes	Year
Diasonics Inc.	19	Medical equipment	Split into three public companies in 1993: Diasonics Ultrasound Inc. of Milpitas, acquired by Elbit Ltd. of Israel in 1994; Focus Surgery Inc. of Milpitas, which is too small to make the Silicon Valley 150 list; and OEC Medical Systems Inc. of Salt Lake City. Ranked 129 in Silicon Valley in 2000.	1993
Dionex	64	Chromatography systems		
Drexler Technology Corp.	91	Optical memory cards		
E-H International Inc.	99	Disk-drive controllers		
EIP Microwave Inc.	85	Microwave test equipment	No longer exists. Acquired by privately owned Phase Matrix Inc in 1999 amidst declining revenues	1999
Engineered Systems & Development Corp.	50	Disk-drive manufacturing equipment	Entered bankruptcy proceedings in 1988 and ceased operations in 1989.	1988
Equatorial Communications Co.	48	Satellite telecommunications networks	Acquired by Contel Corp. of Atlanta	1987
Exar	47	Semiconductors	Ranked 166th in Silicon Valley in 2000	
Finnigan Corp.	39	Analytical instruments	Acquired by Thermo Instrument Systems Inc. of Waltham, MA	1990
Hytek Microsystems Inc.	84	Integrated circuits	Moved to Carson City, NV	1990
Icot Corp.	76	Computer networking equipment	In 1993, 3 senior executives left in the midst of a restructuring. Merged with Amati Communications which was later bought by Texas Instruments	1993
ILC Technology	79	Lasers, light sources	Acquired by BEC Group of Rye, NY	1996
Intech Inc.	88	Circuit boards	Went private through management buy-out	1992
Margaux Controls Inc.	75	Refrigeration control systems for supermarkets	Changed name to Margaux Inc. in 1987, entered bankruptcy proceedings in March 1989, emerged from bankruptcy court protection in October 1989 and relocated its headquarters to Conyers, GA	1987

Firm	Rank in 1985	Industry	Event	Date
Masstor Systems Corp.	77	Computer disk drives	Entered bankruptcy proceedings in September 1994; too small to make the Silicon Valley 150 list	1994
Measurex	17	Industrial measurement devices	Acquired by Honeywell, Inc. of Minneapolis, MN	1997
Micro Mask Inc.	78	Semiconductor manufacturing equipment	Acquired by Hoya Corp. of Japan	1989
Monolithic Memories Inc.	16	Semiconductors	Acquired by Advanced Micro Devices Inc. of Sunnyvale	1987
Nanometrics Inc.	86	Semiconductor manufacturing equipment	Ranked 206th in Silicon Valley in 2000	
NCA Corp.	82	Manufacturing management software	Acquired by Ask Computer Systems Inc. of Mountain View	1987
Optical Specialties Inc.	97	Semiconductor manufacturing equipment	Closed doors to business in 1998, following long decline	1998
Priam Corp.	31	Computer disk drives	Entered bankruptcy proceedings in 1989, and remaining assets were sold to Orca Technology Corp. of San Jose in 1990	1989
Pyramid Technology	67	Computers	Acquired by Siemens Nixdorf Americas	1995
Quadrex Corp.	50	Nuclear engineering services	Moved its headquarters to Gainesville, Fla., in 1990, then to St. Louis in 1994, and entered bankruptcy proceedings.	1990
Radionics Inc.	80	Electronic equipment for building security systems	Acquired by Expamet International PLC of Britain	1989
Ramtek Corp.	55	Computer disk drive components	Entered bankruptcy proceedings in 1993; assets were acquired by The Cerplex Group Inc. of Tustin in 1994	1993

Company	No.	Product/Service	Notes	Year
Scientific Micro Systems Inc.	60	Computer disk drive controllers	Entered bankruptcy proceedings in March 1989, acquired by Chips and Technologies Inc. of San Jose	1989
Seagate Technology	13	Disk drives	Acquired by Veritas Software Corp. in the midst of major downsizing.	2000
Seeq Technology Inc.	58	Semiconductors for data networks	Acquired by LSI Logic in 1999	1999
Sigmaform Corp.	83	Heat-shrinkable coverings for electrical cables	Acquired by Raychem Corp. of Menlo Park	1988
Siltec Corp.	57	Semiconductor manufacturing equipment	Acquired by Mitsubishi Metals Corp. of Japan	1986
Silvar-Lisco	95	Electronic design automation software	Changed name to Silicon Valley Research Inc. in 1994; still exists but too small to make the Silicon Valley 150 list	1994
Software Publishing	62	Prepackaged software	Acquired by Allegro New Media	1996
Spectra-Physics Inc.	14	Industrial lasers	Acquired by Ciba-Geigy Ltd. of Switzerland in 1987, sold by Ciba-Geigy to Pharos AB of Sweden in 1990	1987
Stanford Telecommunications	68	Digital communications	Merged with Newbridge Networks in 1999, selling off many of its divisions in the process, and later purchased by Alcatel (France)	1999
Supertex Inc.	93	Specialty semiconductors	Ranked 191st in Silicon Valley in 2000	
Systems Industries Inc.	33	Computer disk drive equipment	Entered bankruptcy proceedings in 1993; assets were acquired by MTI Technology Corp. of Anaheim	1993
Tab Products	27	Office furniture	Ranked 154th in Silicon Valley in 2000	
Tandem Computers	8	Computers	Acquired by Compac Computers	1997
Technology for Communications International Inc.	70	Broadcasting equipment	Merged with BR Communications Inc. of International Inc.; the combined company is too small to make the Silicon Valley 150 list	1988
Telco Systems Inc.	34	Telecommunications equipment	Moved its headquarters to Norwood, MA	1986

Firm	Rank in 1985	Industry	Event	Date
TeleVideo Systems Inc.	32	Personal computer peripherals	Sales, which peaked in 1983 at $169 million, had dropped to less than $20 million by 1995, when it tried to refocus business on multi-media efforts, without significant success	1995
Triad Systems Corp.	29	Inventory control software	Moved its headquarters to Livermore	1987
Trilogy Ltd.	72	Semiconductors	Suspended most operations in 1986; changed its name to Elxsi Ltd. in 1987 and moved its headquarters to Greenwich, CN	1986
Ungermann-Bass Inc.	43	Computer networking equipment	Acquired by Tandem Computers Inc. of Cupertino in 1988	1988
Valid Logic Systems Inc.	49	Electronic design automation software	Acquired by Cadence Design Systems Inc. of San Jose in 1991	1991
VLSI Technology	41	Semiconductors	Acquired by Philips Electronics of Amsterdam	1999
Watkins-Johnson	15	Semiconductor manufacturing equipment	Sold portions of its semiconductor business to Applied Materials and to Silicon Valley Group. Maintains a wireless communications group	1999
Western Micro Tech/ Savoir Tech Group	53	Computer systems distribution	Acquired by Avnet of Phoenix	2000
Wyse Technology	42	Computer terminals	Acquired by Channel International Corp. of Taiwan in 1990	1990
Xebec Corp.	20	Disk drive controllers	Relocated its headquarters to Carson, City, NV in 1987	1987
Xicor	67	Semiconductors	Ranked 157th in Silicon Valley in 2000	
Xidex Corp.	11	Computer floppy disks	Acquired by Anacomp Inc. of Indianapolis in 1988	1988

Zentec Corp.	92	Computer terminals	Relocated its headquarters to Tallahassee, FL, in 1988	1988
Zeta Laboratories Inc.	81	Microwave communications equipment	Acquired by Whittaker Corp. of Los Angeles in 1986, then sold to Lucas Industries PLC of England in 1989	1986
Zitel Corp.	90	Data storage equipment	In 1999, lost $13 million on revenue of only $20.9. Changed name to Fortel in May 2000, with revenues too small to make top 150 list	
Zymos Corp.	89	Personal computer chip sets	Changed name to Appian Technology Inc. in 1990; Appian entered bankruptcy proceedings in 1994 and most of the company's assets were acquired by Cirrus Logic Inc. of Fremont	

from declining defense spending. Ask Computer Systems, listed 40th in 1985, was taken over by Computer Associates International in 1994 after falling far behind its competitors in the market for manufacturing control software. As the *Mercury News* acknowledges, "it's clear that working for a Silicon Valley High-Technology Company in 1985 was a risky proposition" (Langberg and Davis 1995).

Similarly, many of the largest companies in the Valley in 2000 were founded only in recent years, experiencing exponential growth to reach the upper tiers of the region's high-tech industries. More than half of the top 100 companies in the 2000 listing of Silicon Valley's largest firms were not on the list only ten years previously. This includes many companies that had only been founded in the 1990s, but soon rocketed to be among the Silicon Valley elite in terms of sales revenue, including:

- JDS Uniphase, the maker of fiber optic communications products, was only formed in 1999 with the merger of JDS Optics (founded in 1982) and Uniphase (which had its IPO in 1993). By 2000, JDS Uniphase had $2.6 billion in sales, making it the 21st largest company in the valley.
- Siebel Systems, a sales and marketing software systems company which shipped its first product in 1995 was already ranked 29th in 2000, with total sales of nearly $1.8 billion.
- E*Trade, the on-line brokerage firm, first started operating on-line in 1993 and founded www.etrade.com in 1996, the same year it went public. By 2000 it had rocketed to $1.4 billion in sales, making it the 33rd largest firm in the Valley.
- Yahoo! started in 1994 and only went public in 1996. By 2000, it had total sales of $1.1 billion, making it the 43rd largest on the list.
- Juniper Networks, the maker of Internet infrastructure systems that are now challenging Cisco Systems for dominance in the router industry, had its IPO in 1999 and with sales of $674 million in 2000 was the 62nd largest company in the valley.
- Verisign, which provides Internet security products, opened its headquarters in 1995 and first went public in 1998, and by 2000 was ranked 77th on the list, with sales of $475 million.

The region has also continued to exhibit tremendous growth in the small firm sector, a trend which accelerated in the late 1990s. One way to measure this growth is to look at the number of "gazelle" firms – those publicly traded companies that have grown at least 20 percent for four straight years, starting from at least $1 million in sales. According to

Joint Venture Silicon Valley, high numbers of gazelles reflect high levels of innovation, and, by generating accelerated increases in sales, these firms stimulate the development of other businesses and personal spending throughout the region. The number of gazelles in the Valley started to accelerate in 1996 as opportunities for growth in Internet sales and firms abounded. In 1995 there were 39 firms that met the criteria of four consecutive years of 20 percent growth. By 1998 that number had grown to 92 (JV:SVN 1999).

The level of churning that exists in large high-tech firms, however, is even greater in the small firm sector. For every successful small firm, there are many more unsuccessful failures. The rule of thumb for venture capitalists in the area is that only one out of ten investments in new start-ups will provide significant returns and a full seven out of ten are expected to lose money or fail entirely. In the culture of Silicon Valley, such failures are a common experience and are seen as an important part of the entrepreneurial spirit that contributes to the region's vibrancy. At the same time, it contributes to the high levels of rapid change in employment.

The dynamics in the regional economy that link economic dynamism with high levels of labor flexibility are even more apparent in examining specific industry sectors in the Valley. The industrial base of the Valley's economy has evolved over time as new economic sectors have emerged to replace older ones as the dominant drivers in the region. Thus, in the 1950s, defense industries dominated the region's economy. As the integrated circuit was developed, the semiconductor industry emerged in the 1960s as the leading industry. Later, companies involved in the production of computer systems and their components became more prominent. Finally, in the 1990s, software and Internet companies became leading growth sectors. With each round of industrial succession, Silicon Valley faced new rounds of employment churning. Older companies frequently faced decline or moved operations overseas. Meanwhile, companies in newer industries grew most rapidly. Even within each of the Valley's leading industries, the pattern of rapid change is evident.

Software/Internet industry

Software and the Internet has been the leading industry growth sector in Silicon Valley since the early 1990s. It has been the single largest source of employment growth, and has been a driver in changing employment practices in other sectors as well. Competition in the industry is fierce, with rapid change the norm, leading to rapid churning in firms and employment. In Kanter's words: "To respond to rapid change and cutthroat competition, software companies need constant innovation, and that means constant workplace flux . . . the future of any job is highly uncertain . . . Experience has taught people not to count on the company but on their ability to move" (Kanter 1995). Careers in the software industry in Silicon Valley have been described as "careers in the fast lane" (White 1998). Based on in-depth interviews with more than 56 people in the industry, a study sponsored by the NOVA Private Industry Council in Sunnyvale concluded that the project nature of software work allows for people to leave companies more readily, and the resultant employee turnover rate rose significantly between 1995 and 1998:

> Nowhere is the "jobshift" phenomena more evident than in software, where the concept of a job is being replaced by work-to-be-done. Jobs are dying and it is becoming a project world. This places the focus of the individual and organization on tasks and results to be accomplished, not static positions. It also demands career self-reliance as a new pattern of employee behavior. The highly-flexible and portable nature of software work makes it easier to experiment with new workplace policies such as flex-time, telecommuting, and instant collaboration over great distances. The latest advances in workplace technology are being developed by software companies, who become the first to use them. (White 1998)

Similar trends are noted strongly in the emerging interactive digital multimedia industry as well. The industry is structured similarly along project lines, and the result is that many companies do not have the resources or the desire to hire large numbers of employees and prefer to hire independent contractors to supplement their workforce. Even when hired as an employee, a worker can often expect to be hired only for the duration of a project (Regan and Associates 1997).

The high mobility of software professionals is further enforced by the small size of firms in the software industry, which averages only 27 employees. This is compared to the average size in semiconductor firms in the Valley of 151, and in computer original equipment manufacturers of 175. With employment in smaller firms, there is much less likelihood of significant internal labor markets or long-term career paths (see table 2.9).

Part of the turnover also seems to be as a result of people leaving and

Table 2.9 Average firm size and total employment growth, Silicon Valley cluster industries

Driving industry cluster	Average number of employees/firm 1998	Employment change 1992–8
Software	28	45,605
Business services – outsourcing	27	34,263
Innovation related services	17	29,538
Semiconductors	151	21,017
Computers/Communication contract manufacturing	80	12,506
Business Services – professional	8	7,333
Computers/Communication – original equipment manufacturing	175	4,674
Bioscience	71	3,797
Defense/aerospace	422	−14,911

Source: EDD.

entering the entire occupation, not just their current position. The number of openings that result from employees leaving the programming occupation exceeds the number of net, new positions. An estimated 36 percent of all graduates with majors or degrees in computer engineering have left that field and are working in other occupations (Veneri 1998). A study by George Mason University found that information technology workers overall were twice as likely to have changed careers as were those in other occupations.[5] The National Survey of College Graduates finds that while 52 percent of civil engineering graduates are still in that field 20 years after they graduate (typically in their early 40s), only 19 percent of computer science graduates are still in that field 20 years later.[6]

Rapid turnover in the industry in the region has also been driven by the highly volatile Internet industry, which grew rapidly in the mid to late 1990s and then had a spectacular crash in 2000. There are no completely accurate figures on total number of Internet firms in Silicon Valley, but one indicator is the amount of venture capital funds being invested in the region's software and Internet firms. Between 1990 and

5 This report is cited in Cappelli (2000:13).
6 Cited in Matloff (1999).

1998, total venture capital financing in Silicon Valley grew from $0.5 billion to $6.1 billion a year. Software/Internet companies accounted for 45 percent of the total in 1998 and 33 percent in 1999 (JV:SVN 2000).

The speculative bubble in Internet companies clearly came to a rapid halt in 2000, as a large number of Internet companies went bankrupt. Nationwide, between January 2000 and April 2001, at least 435 Internet companies folded, with at least half of those occurring in the first four months of 2001 (Reuters 2001). In April 2001, according to outplacement firm Challenger, Gray & Christmas, more than 17,000 people were laid off from dot.com companies, more than double the previous month. In the Bay Area, out of 37 consumer Internet firms that made the *San Francisco Chronicle's* list of 500 largest firms in 2000, only 20 remained one year later (Kopytoff 2001). Despite the bursting of the dot.com bubble, few analysts doubt that many Internet companies will continue to grow and thrive, and the Internet will provide a basis for significant growth over the long term. The rapid churning in jobs and companies reflects innovative entrepreneurial efforts to explore new markets and production possibilities, a part of the process of successful development in the industry as a whole even though many individual firms and products are bound to fail.

Computers and Components Industry

The computer systems industry has seen dramatic change in the Silicon Valley since the 1980s. At the core of this restructuring is the rise of electronic manufacturing service firms. The original equipment manufacturers (OEMs) in the computer industry have increasingly outsourced their manufacturing operations to firms such as Solectron, Flextronics, and Sanmina that specialize in manufacturing services. As technology becomes increasingly complex, financing and upgrading manufacturing facilities has proven to be a considerable burden. The electronic manufacturing services industry was made possible by the development in the 1980s of Surface Mount Technology (SMT), which involved computer-controlled machines replacing manual work in placing electrical components on printed circuit boards. The development of this technology was driven by, and in turn further enabled, manufacturers' desire to develop more sophisticated boards and computer systems. But the capital costs involved in manufacturing facilities using these sophisticated technologies is substantial. With money not tied up in inventory, OEMs that outsource can more heavily invest in other parts of their businesses, such as new product design and developments. Electronic manufacturing services firms are able to spread the costs of capital improvements and technological upgrades across multiple clients. The work of the electronic manufacturing service firms may be limited to simply inserting components on to printed circuit boards. Major electronic manufacturing services firms, however, also provide more comprehensive services in design, assembly, testing, procurements, quality assessment, and materials management.

The electronic manufacturing services sector has seen dramatic growth in the 1990s. There are estimated to be over three hundred firms providing electronic manufacturing services in Silicon Valley alone (Ewell and Ha 1999). The five largest companies in Silicon Valley (Solectron, Flextronics, Sanmina, International Manufacturing Services, and CMC Industries) grew 56 percent in combined revenues to $7.7 billion in 1998, from $5 billion in 1997. Nationally, the electronic manufacturing services industry started in the early 1980s, and has grown to over $112 billion in 2000, with a continuing 40 percent per year annual growth rate.[7] While a large portion of employment in electronic manufacturing services firms takes place in Asia, and increasingly in Guadalajara, Mexico, there has also been rapid growth in local employment in Silicon Valley. The close relationship between manufactures and OEMs that is made possible by maintaining production facilities in the Valley, rather than moving them overseas, allows for better communication and design assistance, especially in the early stages of production. During short production runs, all of the production may remain at facilities locally while in longer production runs, electronic manufacturing service firms may rapidly reassign production to lower-cost areas once design flaws are rectified and quality assurance controls perfected in the Silicon Valley facilities. Electronic manufacturing service firms place a heavy premium on ensuring exact duplication of production facilities in multiple sites, facilitating the rapid transfer of production runs to different areas, to maximize use of capital equipment and minimize production costs (Ha 1999b; Luethje 1998).

Employment in electronic manufacturing service firms is highly insecure. Employers need to be able to rapidly ramp up and ramp down production to respond to employers' needs. Time-to-market is a crucial competitive factor in the industry, leading to rapid fluctuations in employment. Such fluctuations occur not simply on a week-to-week or

---

7   http://www.mfgmkt.com/top_50release.html

day-to-day basis, but even hour to hour. Based on her in-depth, ethnographic research while working in an electronic manufacturing service firm, Chun (2001) argues that workers experience "tremendous twists and turns of flexible production as an "objective" condition of highly marginalized work in a fiercely competitive, highly volatile and constantly changing global market.":

> Just-in-time manufacturing principles keep the exact supply of materials in stock for a daily production. Yet, if the day's shipments does not send the appropriate amount of materials to run the assembly line, production is shut-down. Fully operational assembly lines depend on fully operational SMT machines and computerized quality control systems. However, if a machine breaks down, the entire line is sent home early . . . workers could not always expect to show up to the production site, work a full eight and a half hour shift, and punch out. They could not always expect to be given advance notice for canceled shifts nor could they expect to be paid for work lost when shifts were canceled for there were no guarantees that production lines would be running.

Another, more recent factor shaping volatility in the computer industry is the profit squeeze that emerged in the late 1990s as a result of plummeting prices for low-end computers. In 1999, PCs with performance capabilities superior to the highest-end models of only two years before were available in the retail market for less than $500, challenging computer makers to explore new business models. With sub-$500 PCs now on the market, many PC manufacturers moved toward bundling their hardware with various services, such as a year of free Internet access, or rebates tied to Internet service contracts. These rebates made the computer itself almost free. PC makers are thus increasingly moving beyond the manufacture and sale of computer hardware, adding a whole range of services from remote computer training to online auctions, in order to take a slice of what consumers spend (Claymon 1999).

There is also increasing speculation that the personal computer market may be nearing saturation in US markets. The model of "a PC in every household" may be replaced by both smaller custom hand held "smart devices" linked to the World Wide Web via wireless technology and simpler television set top-boxes linked to the Web. These new technologies are expanding, which, in addition to facilitating the convergence of the Internet, telecommunications and video entertainment industries, also provides the potential for storing software and data on central services and delivering them over the Web, rather than being stored on individual PCs. Such trends are in their infancy, but they represent fundamental challenges to "traditional" business models of computer companies.

There has also been a recent crisis for manufacturers of computer peripherals, particularly disk drive and other storage systems firms. Intense competition in the industry led to dramatic price cuts: worldwide hard drive sales revenues decreased 5.2 percent in 1998, despite an 11.1 percent increase in units shipped. In 1988, the average price per megabyte for a hard drive was $11.54. By 1998, that price had fallen to 4.3 cents, and was expected to drop to less than 1 cent by 2002 (Espe 1999). The result has been multiple rounds of layoffs in the industry. IBM's San Jose based Storage Systems Division, where the world's first disk drive was developed in the 1950s, announced in June 1999 that it was slashing 1,100 jobs. The bulk of job losses were in its server disk drive business, with the additional loss of assembly positions in the company's tape drive assembly operations, which were moved from San Jose to Guadalajara, Mexico. In January, 1998, Seagate cut 10,000 jobs, or 10 percent of its workforce, and a further 10 percent cut was announced in September of 1999. Quantum Corp. announced the layoff of 13 percent of their workforce in July of 1999, while Western Digital Corp. eliminated 2,500 jobs in August (Ha 1999a; Quinlan 1999). Recent improvements in drive technology include the ability to store as much as 8.6 megabytes of information on a single magnetic disk or platter, and other technology advances have also made disk drives faster and more reliable. Four companies came to market with these new 8.6 megabyte disk at the same time, however, preventing any company from reaping the normal windfall for months while competitors struggle to keep up. Since more than 75 percent of disk drives sold in 1999 went into desktop PCs, the price pressures in the computer industry has undermined profit margins in disk drive manufacturing as well (Quinlan 1999).

Thus, to summarize, the computer industry has been a significant part of Silicon Valley's economy since the 1970s and an important source of employment for large numbers of people in the regional workforce. In the last decade, however, the industry has gone through dramatic changes as the growth of outsourced manufacturing facilities and the development of new technologies has challenged traditional companies and business models. Employment in the most rapidly growing sector of the computer systems industry, in electronic manufacturing services firms, is highly volatile, despite the rapid growth in that industry. Overall the result has been an increase in levels of volatility and uncertainty for workers in the industry.

Semiconductor Industry

The semiconductor industry is the oldest and most established industry in Silicon Valley and still one of the largest employment sectors. Throughout its history it has faced cycles of rapid change and volatility as part of the industry's successful adaptation to changing technologies and market conditions. In the 1960s and 1970s, periodic restructuring was primarily related to changes in defense spending and the growth of global production networks. The industry then faced a major crisis in the 1980s as a result of intense competition from Japanese producers, from which it emerged with a significantly different organizational structure and product mix. Finally, the increasing miniaturization of components and shrinking of product life-cycles has accelerated volatility in the 1990s.

The semiconductor industry owes much of its early years to the federal government, and particularly the Department of Defense and NASA, which provided a ready market for early semiconductor producers. This dependence on federal government spending actually predated the development of solid-state technology in an era when the region's electronics firms were still primarily building vacuum tube technology. A Stanford Research Institute (SRI) report in the 1960s found that over 60 percent of industry sales of 46 electronics firms in the peninsula during the 1957–8 period were directly or indirectly made to government military procurers (Ingerman 1970). The whole Bay Area was a major center of defense spending, and the combination of the outbreak of the Korean War in 1950 and the Soviet Union's launching of Sputnik in 1957 created a ready market for electronics producers throughout the 1950s. From 1954 to 1961, nearly 80 percent of new jobs in factories in the entire Bay Area could be accounted for by defense industries in Santa Clara County (Sevilla 1992).

Much of this early growth was in technology based on vacuum electron tubes. The development of the solid state semiconductor technology, however, began in 1947 with the invention of the point contact transistor at Bell laboratories. Four years later, the Bell affiliate of Western Electric introduced the first commercially available transistor device. Shockley Transistor Corp. established the first semiconductor plant in Palo Alto in 1955, and Fairchild Semiconductor was founded two years later. With the development of the integrated circuit (IC) in the early 1960s, demand for semiconductors took off. With the Department of Defense and NASA as key customers, the initial development and expansion of IC production was made possible. Total sales of ICs jumped from less than $20 million in 1963 to $40 million in 1964, and production tripled each year throughout the late 1960s (Sevilla 1992). The result was a dramatic expansion and transformation of the region's electronics complex, away from vacuum tube technology and toward technology built on integrated circuits.

The dependence on military contracts made the region's electronics industries vulnerable to fluctuations in defense spending. With cutbacks in space and defense budgets in 1962 and 1963, the electronic industry went into recession. In the nine-county Bay Area electronics complex, employment declined from 49,000 in 1962 to 45,000 in 1964. Partly as a result, firms increasingly pursued commercial markets for their products. Between 1961 and 1965, military sales as a percentage of total business in the electronics industry in the Bay Area decreased from 70 percent to 55 percent (Sevilla 1992).

This development of a commercial market was also critical in the restructuring of the industry because it led to a shift away from heavy security restrictions and procurement regulations characteristic of the military market. Without these restrictions, firms were able to explore establishing production facilities in other countries, leading to the globalization of Silicon Valley's electronics industries, particularly of the most labor-intensive phases of production (Henderson 1989). Fairchild first set up a plant in Hong Kong in 1963. By 1974, a sample of 32 semiconductor firms in the US representing 75 percent of the country's production controlled 69 assembly plants in less developed countries, mostly in Southeast Asia (Sevilla 1992).

The development of overseas production facilities resulted in a rapid shift of the occupational character of the workforce in Silicon Valley, with a decline in production worker jobs and growth in more professional and technical positions. The advent and expansion of IC technology also created new opportunities for product customization and differentiation. During the 1970s, there was an extraordinary rate of horizontal disintegration in the industry. An explosion of new entrants into the market was made possible by development of the MOS (metal oxide on silicon) chip and new product technologies associated with large scale integration (LSI). This was also fueled by the rapidly rising demand for semiconductors that required more specialized units engaged in small batch production (Henderson and Scott 1988). The wave of new entrants increased competition in the industry.

This heightened competition resulted in significant fluctuation in employment, even within a single firm. John Keller (1981) provides data on employment changes within Fairchild Semiconductor Corporation in Mountain View, from 1974 to 1977, which show quarter-to-quarter change in overall total employment by as much as 14 percent (see table 2.10). Note that these figures are simply for total employment, and don't reflect the level of turnover of people, which would likely be somewhat greater. There was a steep recession in the 1974–5 period, and during this time the company reduced its production workforce by one-third. Yet there were also significant reductions in the first quarter of 1976, and again in 1977, with significant hiring in between.

The industry faced another period of crisis and restructuring in the 1980s. After three decades of technological and commercial domination, US semiconductor firms lost market share and technological leadership to Japanese competitors. Leading US semiconductor firms such as Intel, AMD, and National Semiconductor had focused on memory chip production, but Japanese semiconductor firms increasingly were entering this market and producing higher-quality chips at a lower price. US producers faced problems of low yields in production, poor manufacturing quality, and fluctuating capacity utilization (Angel 1994; Winslow 1995). This made them vulnerable to fast-moving competitors with higher-quality production process, and the move of Japanese manufacturers into the market for semiconductor memories was swift, particularly in the production of the latest-generation 256 DRAM memory chips. With an early lead developed in 1984, Japanese producers captured virtually the entire market and, when US producers tried entering the field in 1985, price cutting was so fierce that they suffered tremendous financial loses. By 1986, all Silicon Valley semiconductor producers had dropped out of DRAM production. This loss of the memory business spurred the worst recession in Silicon Valley history, resulting in the loss of 25,000 jobs in the space of two years (Saxenian 1994). Observers began predicting the demise of Silicon Valley (*Business Week* 1985). Saxenian (1994: 95) summarizes the trend as follows:

> By pursuing an autarkic production strategy just as competitive conditions were changing, however, Silicon Valley's leading chipmakers made themselves vulnerable both to the more efficient Japanese mass producers and the region's innovative start-ups. As a result, they lost market share in commodity memories to Japanese firms throughout the 1980s, while ceding the highly profitable semi-custom and specialty markets to a new generation of more flexible Silicon Valley-based ventures.

This crisis, however, did not result in the demise of the Silicon Valley semiconductor industry. Instead, semiconductor firms developed more innovative networked production processes, and discovered new and

Table 2.10   Hourly and salaried employment fluctuations at Fairchild
Semiconductor Corporation, Mountain View, California, 1974–77

Business Quarter	Employment			Quarterly % Change		
	Total	Hourly	Salaried	Total	Hourly	Salaried
1 1974	7,537	5,581	1,956	–	–	–
2 1974	7,360	5,613	1,747	–2	1	–11
3 1974	6,532	4,939	1,593	–11	–12	–9
4 1974	5,618	4,069	1,549	–14	–18	–3
1 1975	4,882	3,712	1,170	–13	–9	–24
2 1975	4,858	3,899	959	0	5	–18
3 1975	5,245	4,165	1,080	8	7	13
4 1975	5,779	4,215	1,564	10	1	45
1 1976	5,607	3,876	1,731	–3	–8	11
2 1976	5,768	3,997	1,771	3	3	2
3 1976	6,336	4,390	1,946	10	10	10
4 1976	6,592	4,658	1,934	4	6	–1
1 1977	6,521	4,361	2,160	–1	–6	12
2 1977	6,175	4,240	1,935	–5	–3	–10

Source: Keller 1981, 327.

more profitable markets, both in custom and specialty semiconductors and in the rapidly expanding market for microprocessors. Writing in the early 1990s, Angel (1994: 3–4) describes the transition as follows:

> It is now clear that the US semiconductor industry is currently undergoing a new round of restructuring . . . the most visible aspect of change has been the proliferation of partnership agreements among semiconductor firms . . . the traditional Schumpeterian dualism of the entrepreneur and the large firm is rapidly being replaced by new organizational forms centered on networks of small and large firms. Of equal importance have been changes in the internal manufacturing operations of many US semiconductor firms, from the restructuring of basic research activities to changes in relations with equipment manufacturers, customers, and suppliers. Processes of industrial restructuring have substantially enhanced the manufacturing performance of US firms, improving product quality, production yields, and time-to-market for new technologies. These changes constitute nothing less than a remaking of the US semiconductor industry.

The character of the semiconductor market in the 1990s is further pushing semiconductor firms to continually innovate or rapidly face declining revenue. The lifetime of any new product is now measured in months rather than years. Intel, the largest semiconductor maker in the world, provides an instructive example of the competitive pressures even the largest companies face. Intel faces stiff competition in its microprocessor business from major competitors. The time-to-market of new products can make the difference of millions of dollars in revenue as competitors seek to match or improve performance characteristics. With capital costs of new wafer fab plants rising to as much as $2–3 billion, semiconductor firms depend on the period of time before competitors enter the market for a new technology to charge higher unit prices. The mark-up rate over production costs often reaches more than 80 percent in the early stages of production runs, with prices having to be slashed once competitors enter the market. This means that being second-to-market can result in serious losses on a new microprocessor that cost millions of dollars in development costs.

An indication of the pace of change in the industry was given by Intel's 1997 Annual Report (SEC 10-K) filed with the US Securities and Exchange Commission, which reads:

> The year 1997 was one of major product transitions for Intel. The Company introduced two major new microprocessor products [Pentium processor with MMX-Technology, and Pentium II processor], effectively replacing its previous product lines in this area. *Over 90 percent of the microprocessors shipped in the fourth quarter were introduced in the first five months of 1997.* (Intel, SEC Form 10-K, 1998, p. 2; emphasis added)

By the following year, revenue from MMX-Technology Pentiums had already declined significantly, and Intel had introduced two new lines of microprocessors for the PC market, the Intel Celeron and Pentium III, which provided the majority of their revenue.

Thus, throughout its history, the semiconductor industry in Silicon Valley has faced significant challenges, and has responded through significant restructuring. The pace of change in the industry is extremely high and, as a result, employment churning and turnover in jobs and companies have characterized the semiconductor industry since the early days of its growth in the 1960s.

Defense/Aerospace Industry

The defense industry, another critical part of the Silicon Valley industrial complex, has also been highly volatile. Silicon Valley was heavily dependent on military expenditures in the early stages of its development. While the 1970s saw the influence of defense spending decline somewhat, defense spending expanded again in the 1980s under the Ronald Reagan presidency. By 1987, Joint Venture Silicon Valley estimated that the defense industry accounted for 10 percent of employment in Silicon Valley's economic base. In the early 1990s a major decline in defense spending contributed to a significant recession in the Valley. Total US Department of Defense Procurement, in inflation-adjusted dollars, reached a peak in 1987 and had declined by nearly 50 percent by 1995 (JV:SVN 1995). By the latter half of the 1990s, the significance of defense spending to the regional economy had once again declined substantially, yet the defense/aerospace industry continued to employ more than 20,000 people in 1998.

Through its history, there have been four major defense contractors in the Silicon Valley area: Lockheed Missiles & Space, FMC, United Technologies Corporation, and Westinghouse Corporation. Lockheed Missiles & Space Co (LMSC), the largest of the four, moved to Sunnyvale in 1954 to develop and produce the Polaris missile. LMSC was also responsible for manufacturing the MILSTAR communications satellite, the Poseidon and Trident fleet ballistic missile systems, and key components of the Space Shuttle, the Hubble Space Telescope, and numerous classified national security surveillance satellites (JV:SVN 1995). The second largest defense contractor in the region is FMC (now renamed United Defense). Though its headquarters were moved from San Jose to Chicago in 1972, the San Jose based defense group continued to play a key role in the development and delivery of high-tech Infantry Fighting Vehicles. In particular they produced the Bradley Fighting Vehicle and a range of derivative vehicles including the Multiple Launch Rocker System, the Electronic Fighting Vehicle System, a Command and Control Vehicle and the Bradley Fire Support Vehicle. These vehicles all used the latest vehicle electronic systems and technology to significantly enhance their effectiveness in the field, as was demonstrated with their extensive deployment during Operation Desert Storm in the Persian Gulf (Winslow 1995). United Technologies Corp. (UTC), now the Chemical Systems Division of UTC, originally located in Santa Clara County in 1960, produced the solid-fuel propulsion boosters for Titan missiles in 1962. Westinghouse Corporation began producing fleet ballistic missile launch systems and ship propulsion systems in the Valley in the 1950s. By the 1960s, these four contractors accounted for an estimated 90 percent of defense contracting activity in Silicon

Valley.

The 1980s saw a tremendous increase in defense spending during the Reagan administration, and between 1981 and 1987, total prime contracts to Santa Clara County rose 40 percent, reaching a peak of $5.35 billion dollars ($1993) in 1987. In addition to the top four, there were at least 19 other smaller prime contractors in the Valley who received contracts worth at least $10 million (in 1993 dollars), including Loral ($385 million in 1993 dollars), Varian Associates ($83.6 million), Hewlett-Packard ($48.1 million), Teledyne ($47.0 million), and Watkins-Johnson ($34.9 million) (JV:SVN 1995).

Between 1987 and 1990, however, Department of Defense contracts in Santa Clara county declined by nearly 25 percent, and by another 17 percent between 1990 and 1993. Total employment in defense-related industries in Santa Clara County declined from a peak of 39,000 in 1987 to 25,800 in 1993 (JV:SVN 1995). The decline in defense spending also contributed to a decline in other high-tech industries in the area during this period. From 1990 to 1993, a total of 16,200 jobs were lost in the high-tech industries (including computers, communication equipment, semiconductors, other electronic components, measuring, and controlling). In all sectors, employment declined by 25,000 in the 1991–2 period alone (Winslow 1995).

The decline in defense spending created particular employment problems for workers in Lockheed and other defense contractors. This workforce had been largely isolated from the open labor markets, high turnover and high levels of mobility that characterize the rest of the high-tech labor markets. Lockheed is one of the few high-tech firms in the area whose workers are represented by unions, and the loss of these well-paying jobs was devastating to many union members and their families. The decline of these secure, insulated jobs, however, contributed to the overall increase in volatility and flexibility in the labor market.

Conclusion: Flexibility and Volatility

This chapter has argued that employment in Silicon Valley is increasingly characterized by high levels of nonstandard employment, rapid change in employment opportunities, and high levels of turnover and employee mobility. It is undoubtedly an exaggeration to say, as some analysts do, that the concept of a traditional "job" has entirely disappeared, replaced by people performing tasks on a project-by-project basis under short-term contracts. Some employees still do build long-term careers with a single firm and employers compete fiercely to try to retain highly skilled personnel on more long-term relationships. Nonetheless, for a significant majority of employees in the high-tech industries in the area, employment is increasingly volatile and uncertain.

These characteristics are rooted in the structure of competition in the region's high-tech industries. Rapid technological change and intense global competition has led to the importance of innovation in the long-term competitiveness of firms in the area. This innovation leads to rapid fluctuations in product markets and production processes. As a result of these rapid changes, firms place a high premium on the flexible use of labor, which in turn is essential to the ability of firms to take advantage of new technologies and market opportunities. The implications of this labor flexibility for workers' livelihoods will be examined in part III. For now, I will turn to another implication of this flexibility – the growth of intermediaries.

APPENDIX 2.1: Industry Cluster Analysis

Table 2.6 provides employment figures for Silicon Valley based on industry clusters. Industry clusters are concentrations of complementary industries. All industry employment figures are from ES-202 data from the California Economic Development Department, Labor Market Information Division. The geographic area covered is not just Santa Clara County, but includes neighboring cities of Fremont, Union City, Newark (Alameda County), Scotts Valley (Santa Cruz County), and southern San Mateo County (cities of Menlo Park, Atherton, Redwood City, San Carlos, Belmont, San Mateo, Foster City, and East Palo Alto). The industry categories are built from the SIC codes (table A2.1).

A2.1   Silicon Valley industry cluster analysis

Driving cluster industries	SIC codes
Semiconductors	3559, 3674, 3825
Computers and communications industry – original equipment manufacturing	3571–3577, 3661, 3663, 3695
Computers and communications industry – contract manufacturing	3672, 3679, 3669
Bioscience	283, 384, 3821, 3823–24, 3827–3829, 8071
Defense/Aerospace industry	348, 372, 376, 381, 3671, 3795
Software industry	7371, 7372, 7373, 7374, 7375
Innovation/Manufacturing related services	5045, 5065, 7376–7379, 8711, 873
Business services – professional	275, 276, 279, 731, 732, 81, 8712, 8713, 872, 874
Business services – outsourcing, security and building maintenance	733, 734, 736, 738
Environmental industry – manufacturing	3564, 3589
Environmental industry – sanitary services, scrap and waste materials	495, 5093

Other manufacturing industries	SIC code
Food processing	201–209
Fabricated metal products/metal working	341–9 (except 348), 354
Non-defense transport equipment	371, 373–5, 3791–9 (except 3795)
Miscellaneous manufacturing	21–6, 271–4, 278, 281–2, 284–339, 351–3, 3551–3558, 3561–3, 3565–9, 3578–9359, 361–5, 3675–8, 3691–4, 3696–9, 3822, 3826, 385–9, 39

Other major employment sectors	SIC code
Eating and drinking places	58
Food distribution – wholesale and retail	514, 515, 541–9
Other retail	52–3, 55–7, 59
Other wholesale (not food, not computers)	501–3, 5041–44, 5046–49, 505, 5061–4, 5066, 6069, 507–9, 511–13, 516–9
Private hospitals	806
Other private sector health services	801–805, 8072, 808–809
Private educational services	82
Private social services	83
Travel, tourism, and leisure activities	45, 472, 701–704, 783–99
Personal services (e.g. barber, laundry, etc.)	720–9

Miscellaneous services	735, 738, 75–6, 781–2, 84–6, 89
Government	FE
State government	ST
Local government	LO

Part II

Flexibility and Intermediaries

3

Flexibility and Intermediation

Music is the space between the notes.

Claude Debussy

Up to this point, my primary focus has been on the changing nature of work and employment in Silicon Valley's labor markets. I made the distinction between flexible work and flexible employment, since this is essential for understanding the ways that flexibility is linked with economic trajectories in the region and the ways flexibility shapes labor market outcomes for workers. The forces pushing for flexible work are primarily rooted in competitive dynamics of the region's leading information technology industries, in which constant innovation provides the basis for profitability. The constantly shifting tasks people perform in their work, the information, skills and knowledge required to do that work, and the relationships they engage in as part of that work are a product of and in turn contribute to the innovative success of the region's high-tech industries. Flexible work is thus fundamentally linked with competitive success in the information economy. The forces pushing for flexible employment, on the other hand, are only partially driven by these competitive dynamics. The tenuous, temporary and mediated employment relations that exist between employers and employees do, in some cases and in some ways, contribute to flexible work practices and thus innovation. In other cases, however, they are driven by narrow, short-term profit motives, or by an institutional and regulatory climate that not only contributes little to innovative success but also, in the long run, potentially undermines the success of the region, through increasing inequality and underinvesting in learning.

Both flexible work and flexible employment have given rise to another striking feature of the region's labor markets – the existence of a wide range of organizations that act as intermediaries between employers and workers. The term "labor market intermediary" traditionally refers to job brokering or matching activities in which individual employers and job seekers turn to a third party that helps them find the best match of skills, attitudes, interests, and needs (National Commission for Manpower Policy 1978). In the environment of rapid change and uncertainty that characterizes labor flexibility, both employers and workers are turning to a variety of these intermediaries to help them navigate through the complex and unpredictable labor market. Workers turn to intermediaries to help find jobs and to deal with changing information and skill requirements. Employers turn to intermediaries to help find workers and to help address fluctuating work demands. Intermediaries of various types have taken advantage of these needs of both workers and employers and have actively expanded their activities, helping to further reinforce their importance in the regional labor market. In this role, intermediaries respond to critical problems that are prevalent in flexible labor markets, such as high search costs, imperfect information, and increased risk. Intermediaries are thus emerging as critical institutions shaping the dynamics of flexible labor markets and thus labor market outcomes for both workers and employers.

Temporary agencies are the most visible and well-known type of labor market intermediary, and have grown rapidly in recent years. In addition, however, a wide variety of other organizations have been increasingly acting as intermediaries in the labor market, including:

- headhunters, recruiters, and contractor brokers, who have expanded in number and in the scope of their activities;
- Internet-based intermediaries, including literally thousands of job sites, which have emerged with the rapid expansion of the World Wide Web. These sites gained instant media and popular exposure when two sites – monster.com and hotjobs.com – were among the first "dot.com" companies to advertise during the Super Bowl, the most prominent commercial advertising spot on television (Beatty 1999; Tharp 1999);
- unions, who are increasingly experimenting with a wide range of intermediary programs, including worker-run temporary agencies and multi-employer training institutions (Dresser and Rogers 1997);
- an increasing number of community organizations which are experimenting with job placement and job linkage programs particularly focused on disadvantaged workers (Molina 1998; Seavey 1998);

- a wide range of public sector and education based intermediary programs, ranging from community college contract training programs to public sector placement programs, which have also gained increasing visibility and stature in today's volatile labor markets (Kogan et al. 1997; Lynch, Palmer, and Grubb 1991).

Many of these newer initiatives go beyond the traditional narrow function of job brokering and can no longer be thought of as simply playing a passive role in linking employees and employers. They are having a much greater impact, structurally altering and in some cases improving employment training and workforce development systems, restructuring employer hiring practices, and developing new forms of representation for workers, such as through advocacy efforts or innovative changes in collective bargaining structures.[1]

What is driving this trend toward the increasing use of intermediaries in the labor market? What do these various types of intermediaries have in common, and how are they distinct from each other? To what extent are intermediaries becoming integral components of the structure and dynamics of regional labor markets? What are the implications of this rise in intermediary activity – both for economic development trajectories and for the labor market outcomes of workers?

This section addresses these questions on both a theoretical and empirical level. This chapter starts by briefly reviewing a range of classification frameworks different researchers have used in studying the activities of intermediaries, which provide some useful insights into the various roles intermediaries play. This is followed by a more theoretical discussion of four essential labor market functions of intermediaries: reducing the transaction costs that both workers and employers face in the labor market; setting the price of labor and thus shaping the power relations between workers and employers; mediating risk for both workers and employers, through diversification and displacement; and building networks, both production networks for employers and social networks for workers. The following chapters examine the activities of three broad types of intermediaries in Silicon Valley's labor markets: private sector, membership-based, and public sector agencies. Through both the theoretical and empirical presentations it seems clear

1 Recent initiatives are described in the following studies: Carre and Joshi (1997); Harrison and Weiss (1998) Kazis (1998); Melendez and Harrison (1998); Molina (1998); Osterman and Lautsch (1996); Seavey (1998); Wolf-Powers (1999).

that intermediaries have become an essential institution for the functioning of flexible labor markets.

Labor Market Intermediaries

One of the first issues that arises in trying to examine the role of intermediaries is definitional – what actually *is* a labor market intermediary? Can all of these various organizations really be included under the same category and, if so, what do they have in common? Few studies of labor markets even recognize the existence of intermediaries. Labor markets are typically analyzed in the context of the complex dynamics between workers and employers. These dynamics in turn are shaped by contradictory pressures based on the mutual interdependence and antagonistic interests of workers and employers, in the workplace and in the broader community (Peck 1996; Storper and Walker 1989). The relationship between employers and workers is clearly shaped by a range of labor market institutions. These institutions, however, are typically analyzed based on how they shape dynamics of supply and demand or shape the power struggles between workers and employers, rather than as a third actor in the labor market relationship mediating the relationship between workers and employers. To the extent that research has been done on particular intermediaries in the US, they have been analyzed in isolation, for example examining the role of temporary help agencies,[2] or job training programs.[3] The few attempts that have been made to link the study of multiple types of intermediaries have been useful in describing their activities but have spent less time on developing theories that might help explain the functions they play in labor markets and why intermediaries are needed for labor flexibility.[4]

On a broad descriptive level, intermediaries of all types provide services to employers and to workers. The services they provide relate both to employment relations and to work practices.

● Employment: The most common service intermediaries provide is connecting people to new employment opportunities and helping employers find workers. This service is often provided through a

2   Parker (1994); Rogers (2000); Smith (2001).
3   Molina (1998); Osterman and Lautsch (1996); Seavey (1998).
4   Carre and Joshi (1997); Kazis (1998).

formal placement program, such as a temporary agency or contractor broker provides, in which the intermediary takes responsibility for ensuring the best match of skills, experience and interests. The function may also be provided through more informal networking opportunities. In this context, the intermediary provides the organizational infrastructure that brings employers and workers together, but the employer and worker must still directly negotiate the conditions of employment. The role of some intermediaries may stop once a placement has been made – again leaving the employment contract in the hands of the employer and worker to negotiate. In many cases, however, intermediaries will have some ongoing involvement. Temporary agencies, contractor brokers and professional employer organizations take a strong role, acting as the legal employer. Union intermediary initiatives that include a collective bargaining relationship, as in the construction industry, also shape the employment relationship through collective bargaining agreements that set wages, benefits, and other conditions of employment. Many public sector placement agencies play a more limited role in providing follow-up and support services for disadvantaged workers once they are on the job, and intervene between the employer and worker when necessary.

- Work: Intermediaries can also play a critical role in shaping the work process, through facilitating rapid changes in work demand, shaping skills development over time, and shaping the reflexivity of work tasks. Clearly firms' use of temporary agencies and contractor brokers, for instance, allows them to rapidly ramp up or ramp down the number of workers in response to rapidly changing work demands. Some workers also use temporary agencies and brokers to find work fast. Intermediaries can play a critical role in shaping skills development. This may be done in a formal manner, through training and certification programs and responding directly to employer or worker demands. This may also proceed in more informal ways in which the intermediary provides the organizational infrastructure for building the social networks that are so essential for ongoing learning. These learning networks fundamentally shape work practices on a day-to-day level, building communication across work sites. Intermediaries also provide important information on changing work demands in the labor market, among different firms and different industries, providing signals to both workers and firms of the need to respond to these changing work demands.

These intermediary services are provided by a range of organizations that have been characterized in different ways. Richard Kazis (1998), for example, distinguishes among different intermediaries based on their strategic approach to the labor market:

1   those that accept both supply and demand in the labor market as given and try to improve the efficiency of the *job matching* process;
2   those that accept employer demand as given but work to improve the ability of supply-side *workforce development* institutions to meet employer needs;
3   those that take the supply side as given but try to *change employer demand for labor* in ways that reduce inefficiencies and inequalities in wages, benefits, job security, and advancement.

Osterman (1999: 134) develops an alternate classification system based on the extent of the intermediary's intervention in the labor market.

1   Traditional "one-on-one" intermediaries that passively accept job orders from firms and match these orders with people who have registered with the intermediary. The Employment Service is the classic example of such an intermediary.
2   Intermediaries who are more active and aggressive in their relations to both sides of the labor market. These "customized" programs recruit employers to their service, design efforts – recruitment, training, and placement – to be responsive to the needs of those employers, and also reach out and recruit a labor force to match these job requirements.
3   Intermediaries active on both sides of the labor market who also bargain with firms or deploy power in order to alter firm behavior. These intermediaries see themselves as not only providing a service but also changing the terms of trade in the labor market.

In another project aimed at comparing intermediaries in Silicon Valley and Milwaukee, Wisconsin,[6] our team of researchers developed a framework that builds on Osterman's approach, differentiating intermediaries based on the depth of the relationship that the intermediary

---

5   see http://www.willamette.edu/dept/pprc/lmi/ for a description of the project and available research papers.

Table 3.1 The relational structure of intermediaries

Relationship to workers	Relationship to employers	
	Weak	Strong
Weak	"Job-bank" databases Some welfare-to work programs	Temporary agencies Contract-based training organizations
Strong	Professional and membership organizations Community colleges	Union hiring halls Intensive community-based organizations that have employer commitments

has with each side of the labor market. This relationship can be considered either strong or weak. On the worker side, a weak relationship might consist of a visit to an employment center or job-board website, or taking a one-time course on résumé writing. By contrast, a strong relationship would involve a more intensive and longer-term interaction, such as for skills development or access to health benefits and professional networks. The same logic could be used on the employer side. A weak relationship would consist of simply listing a firm's job openings with a placement agency. A strong relationship would entail repeated use of an agency or a commitment to hire workers from the intermediary. This framework makes it possible to develop a two-by-two matrix, based on the strength of the relationship of the intermediary to workers and employers (see table 3.1).

These typologies and frameworks are useful for examining the activities of intermediaries within the labor market in descriptive terms. They leave unanswered, however, the deeper questions of the functions intermediaries play in the labor market. Why is it that employers and workers use intermediaries rather than finding each other in more decentralized, direct ways in the labor market? Before turning to this question directly, it is useful to examine the role of intermediaries in other types of markets.

Intermediation and Markets

Theories of intermediation and markets have emerged primarily in the context of research on trade,[6] financial markets,[7] and information markets.[8] These theories also struggle with the question of defining what is an intermediary. In the narrowest view of intermediation, intermediaries are pure "middlemen," bringing together buyers and sellers without changing or significantly modifying the commodity that is bought or sold (Rubinstein and Wolinsky 1987). Yet even in this narrowest sense intermediaries provide value-added services, even if they are buying and selling the same good. Intermediaries in trade, for instance, may provide a spatial function, linking buyers and sellers from different locations, or a credit function, covering temporal differences between delivery and payment. Likewise, financial intermediaries perform such functions as changing lot size, aggregating small investments into large-size credit contracts, or mediating risk through diversification and credit rationing.[9] If intermediaries did nothing to modify the good or service there would be no need for buyers and sellers to use intermediaries rather than finding each other in a decentralized market, and intermediaries would be unlikely to exist.

A much broader approach is to treat intermediaries as any organization that brings together buyers and sellers. Spulber (1999), for instance, develops an intermediation theory of the firm, in which all firms coordinating the actions of buyers and sellers are analyzed as market intermediaries: "Firms carry out transactions, operating the system of payments, inventory control, and record keeping that is essential for markets to function. In addition, firms provide a central place of exchange, thus reducing the search costs of buyers and sellers" (Spulber 1999: XIX). Using this approach, Spulber estimates that at least 25 percent of GDP is accounted for by intermediation.[10] Clearly there is a danger in this approach of casting too broad a net. If intermediaries are understood to be all market-making organizations that bring together buyers and sellers, the term becomes perhaps so broad as to lose its explanatory value. In this light, it is perhaps not surprising that the

---

6   e.g. Perry (1992).
7   e.g. Rubinstein and Wolinsky (1987).
8   Bhargava, Choudhary, and Krishnan (2000); Rose (1999); Wimmer, Townsend, and Chezum (2000).
9   See Rose (1999), especially ch 3.
10   Spulber comes up with the 25 percent figure by including all retail and wholesale trade, finance, insurance, and a significant portion of business services. He believes this is actually an underestimate, since a significant portion of activity in manufacturing, transportation, public utilities, agriculture, and so on is not actual production, but includes intermediation functions such as pricing, marketing, inventory management, and ordering from suppliers.

study of intermediaries has been frequently subsumed under the broader treatment of economic organization.

Nonetheless, using this definition of intermediaries – organizations that bring buyers and sellers together – provides useful insights that get lost in broader treatments of economic organization or that are missed by efforts that define intermediaries so narrowly that they seem insignificant. Intermediaries play a critical role in bringing buyers and sellers together in many contexts. As Coase (1937) described in his classic article on the nature of the firm, there are costs involved in any transaction, including the buying and selling of any commodity. Buyers and sellers have to find each other, prices have to be discovered, negotiations undertaken, contracts drawn up, inspections made, arrangements made to settle disputes, and so on. According to the new institutionalist school of economic theory that Coase's work inspired, these transaction costs are sometimes more efficiently handled through hierarchical control within firm boundaries or through some intermediate set of contractual relationships, rather than through the open market.[11]

At the most basic level, transactions can be described on the basis of three main factors – their frequency, the level of uncertainty involved, and the specificity of the assets and information involved in the transaction. The greater the frequency of transactions, the higher the levels of uncertainty, and the more asset specificity, the greater the tendency for the transactions to take place within hierarchical arrangements rather than through market mechanisms. Viable intermediate hybrids between markets and hierarchies develop through contractual arrangements between multiple firms. In this approach, intermediaries emerge as specialists in performing transactions – in arranging the buying and selling of a good or service. They are defined as independent, profit-maximizing economic agents mediating between two market sides in the presence of market imperfections. The source of their efficiency is a reduction in the costs of these transactions as compared to transactions without an intermediary. Thus, within the body of economic theory that has examined intermediation, intermediaries are primarily understood as critical markets actors that minimize transactions costs, allowing markets to function more efficiently and effectively.

11 Alchian and Demsetz (1972); North (1981); Williamson (1975); Williamson (1985).

Intermediation and Flexible Labor Markets

It is also possible to gain insights about the role of intermediaries in flexible labor markets from within this transactions costs framework. Given the growth in labor market flexibility, intermediaries have arisen as an efficient alternative to internal labor markets while still being more efficient than decentralized open market transactions. Both workers and employers face problems of uncertainty in evaluating job availability, job quality, and worker qualifications. With rapidly changing and unpredictable market conditions, and rapid change in technology, skills, and knowledge, the importance of firm-specific skills has declined in relative terms. With increasingly frequent job/employee search, the amount of information needed for matching workers to jobs has been ratcheted up. Employers are often in need of particular skill sets, or in need of people at a particular time. All this increases the transaction costs for both workers and employers. Intermediaries have stepped neatly into the resulting market niche. Intermediaries provide useful customized information and access to people with the right skills or experience. For both employees and workers, using intermediaries can be a way of taking advantage of the expertise and information they hold to shorten the job search process. It is costly and difficult for both employers and job seekers to learn as much as might be useful about the labor market: what (or who) is available, what going wages are, what skills are needed, and so on. Firms can recognize significant cost savings by cutting their human resource departments and not having to engage in employee search and hiring processes. Workers save the considerable costs involved in fully researching job opportunities in the labor market and finding an appropriate match for their skills. There are economies of scale to information collection that an intermediary can capture, allowing intermediaries to specialize in this information (Osterman 1999). This may involve, for instance, the specialized knowledge of particular skills required in an industry, or the information built from relationships with a large number of employers that can be centralized in one place. Employees may benefit from this information concentration and gain access to information that would be more costly and difficult to achieve through other means.

Thus, one function of intermediaries in the labor market is to reduce transactions costs for both workers and employers. There are limits, however, to the transaction costs approach. Its neoclassical assumptions about price-setting mechanisms and market efficiency, which

neglect the social embeddedness of economic activity and the nonmar-
ket social relations that shape economic interactions, have been heavily
criticized.[12] These limitations are particularly evident in the study of
labor markets, since labor cannot be treated as simply another commodity or as just another factor of production. Labor is embodied in
living, conscious human beings and human activity is an irreducible,
ubiquitous feature of human existence and social life (Storper and
Walker 1989). Therefore, understanding the role of intermediaries in
labor markets requires an understanding of the ways intermediaries
are embedded in their relationships with workers and with firms; the
ways they are socially constructed and politically mediated. Ultimately
we need a theory of labor market intermediation that isn't driven solely
by pricing and efficiency considerations but takes into account the complex patterns of both conflict and accommodation that exist between
workers and employers.

One step in helping develop that theory is to recognize the role
that intermediaries play in shaping compensation levels. In labor markets, intermediaries play a role in shaping the power of workers and
employers to negotiate pay levels. Employers frequently turn to intermediaries as a means of cutting their labor costs. This is particularly
true with the use of intermediaries who become the legal employer of
people working for clients, such as temporary agencies or some contractor brokers. These agencies then take on all the legal liabilities of
being the employer, including costs of workers compensation and legal liability in the case of employment discrimination lawsuits as well
as any costs of health insurance and other benefits they may provide.
Obviously some of these costs absorbed by the intermediary are passed
on to the clients in the form of higher fees charged for their services.
But it also comes out of lower wages for the worker, who frequently
are hindered in their negotiating strength by being in precarious employment with little information about prevailing wage levels or alternative employment opportunities. This is particularly true in the case
of lower-skilled workers, who are clearly disadvantaged by their relationship with their ultimate employer being buffered through the use
of an intermediary. Employers use intermediaries as a cost cutting
mechanism even with higher-skilled workers. In this case, they may
even pay higher levels of compensation on an hourly basis, but they
save in the long run by not entering into long-term agreements with

12   Granovetter (1985); Peck (1996); Powell (1990).

workers, thus avoiding expensive benefit packages they may provide to their more permanent workforce.

Intermediaries, however, can also be part of a strategy for workers to gain bargaining power in the labor market in an effort to improve their own salaries. On an individual level, this is evident in the case of skilled contractors who, because of their contract status, are often able to charge higher hourly rates than if they were in a permanent status performing the same work. Without the use of an intermediary, these contractors would face periods of slack employment while they searched for new opportunities – a situation that is still implicitly assumed in the pricing of temporary contracts. By using an intermediary, these highly sought-after contractors are able to minimize nonwork time and gain much higher annual income than they would working for a single employer. The key here is that by having easy access to other employment opportunities, they have greater negotiating leverage with employers than if they were dependent on a single employer for their livelihood – a power significantly strengthened by their use of intermediaries. The additional bargaining leverage provided by intermediaries is not limited to more highly skilled workers. For workers at middle and lower ends of the labor market, certain types of intermediaries can strengthen their bargaining position too. This is particularly true of membership-based intermediaries (unions or professional associations) and some community-based intermediaries. By combining the voices of many workers in the labor market, and by expressing that collective voice with multiple employers, intermediaries can increase workers' wages. This is clearly the case in industries where craft-based unions have developed collective bargaining arrangements with industry associations, but it can also have an impact through less formal means. The ability of intermediaries to strengthen the power of workers in the labor market will be addressed in some depth in chapter 5. Here my point is simply to argue that intermediaries serve both employers and workers in their contradictory efforts to shape compensation levels in the labor market – another key function of intermediaries in labor markets.

A third function intermediaries play in the labor market is managing risk. The information economy creates more risky labor markets than older, stable, production regimes, for both employers and workers.[13] Clearly workers face more dire consequences of unanticipated misfortune in the labor market – an issue which I address in more detail in

13   Mandel (1996); Reich (2000).

part III – but employers also face risk. Unexpected competition, rapidly changing markets, technological obsolescence, volatile financial markets, and so on, can threaten firms' profitability and even survival in unexpected ways. Both employers and workers use intermediaries as part of their efforts to minimize exposure to risk and the consequences of misfortune in the labor market. Intermediaries attempt to minimize their own exposure to risk through diversifying their relationships among multiple firms and groups of workers.

The use of intermediaries to manage risk is particularly strong for employers. Here, both cyclical and structural factors play a role. On the one hand, all firms experience cyclical fluctuations in demand. By using intermediaries, they can delay hiring permanent employees till later in cyclical upturns and layoff temporary employees earlier in cyclical downturns.[14] On the structural side, an increase in the volatility experienced by firms has led many businesses to attempt to reduce their own internal labor force and shift economic risk through a series of more short-term contracts with external agents. Firms also are able to shift risks to intermediaries by reducing their own human resource screening, hiring, and administration functions, reducing their exposure to unexpected downturns while still benefiting from access to workers during upturns.

Many workers are clearly made more vulnerable to labor market risk by the tenuous and temporary employment relationships associated with the rise in intermediaries. This is especially true during an economic downturn, when absolute levels of unemployment increase. Workers, however, also use intermediaries as a way of reducing their exposure to risk. Obviously, using intermediaries to help find employment can shorten a period of unemployment after being laid off. Many workers using temporary agencies will maintain ties with multiple agencies as a way of trying to maximize their employment opportunities. For workers with needed skills in the labor market, intermediaries help them take advantage of multiple employment opportunities without their being subject to the ups and downs of any single firm. These workers also can use intermediaries as a way of staying informed about

14   This phenomenon is clearly evident in the economic slowdown that began in September 2000. Between September 2000 and May 2001, as the unemployment rate rose from 4.0 percent to 4.5 percent, employment in temporary staffing firms fell by more than 20 percent, shedding some 500,000 jobs, more than the total of auto-makers, restaurants, hotels and department stores combined. Reported in the *New York Times*, May 19, 2001, p.1 and B14.

changing skills and occupational demands, helping to ensure that their own skills don't become obsolete and identifying new skills they should be developing. In essence, intermediaries, by increasing their exposure to new employment opportunities and keeping up on changing work demands, help workers increase their employability in the labor market, thus decreasing their vulnerability to unexpected shocks.

A final function of intermediaries in the labor market is their role in shaping networks for both employers and for workers. For businesses, economic success comes primarily from the ability to innovate. One of the central insights from research on economic innovation processes is the recognition that firms rarely innovate in isolation, but typically do so in the process of interacting with a wide range of other organizations. Through communicating with suppliers, customers, and competitors, and through their relationships with universities, research institutes, investment firms, government agencies, and so on, firms develop and exchange various kinds of information and knowledge that are critical to their ability to innovate.[15] This inter-organizational communication is built and maintained in large part through people's social networks. Economic competitiveness is closely linked with the information flows and diffusion of information built on strong social ties (Saxenian 1994; Saxenian 1996; Storper 1997). Firms use intermediaries as a way of building and strengthening these networks.

On the worker side, it has long been recognized that social networks provide the most common way workers find jobs (Fernandez and Weinberg 1997; Granovetter 1995; Piore 1980; Wial 1991). Social networks are also important for developing skills and learning over time, advancing and improving earnings across firms, coping with layoffs and job loss, and effectively dealing with a range of other issues that shape long-term employment outcomes.[16] In relatively stable labor markets, these social networks are built over a long period of time and become stable channels for job searches and flows of information about labor market dynamics. In the context of highly complex flexible labor markets, with rapidly changing employment opportunities and work requirements, social networks function somewhat differently and are more directly related to the activities of labor market intermediaries. At upper levels in the labor market, intermediaries play an important

15   Braczyk, Cooke, and Heidenreich (1998), Cooke and Morgan (1998); Lee, Miller, Hancock; and Rowen (2000).
16   Herzenberg et al (1998); Hull (1997); Lave and Wenger (1991); Wenger (1998); Wial (1991).

role in helping build and strengthen high-quality social networks for workers. In this role, they essentially form an organizational infrastructure for the development and maintenance of high-quality social networks that help workers in their job search processes and in keeping abreast of changing skill requirements in the labor market. Workers at the bottom end of the labor market, however, face a different challenge, since they often lack not only marketable skills but also have "poor-quality" social networks that lead to poor employment opportunities. In these cases, intermediaries sometimes help these workers "bridge" across those social boundaries, essentially providing a substitute for poor social networks.[17] Thus, as both an infrastructure for high-quality social networks and a substitute for poor-quality networks, intermediaries can play a role in shaping both "bridging" and "bonding" social networks for workers.

Conclusion: Increasing Intermediation

Reducing transaction costs, shaping compensation levels, risk displacement, and network building – these are fundamental functions intermediaries play in the labor market. With increasing importance of innovation, and the related increasing flexibility in labor markets, there are strong forces in each of these areas pushing both workers and employers to turn to intermediaries of various types. It is not the case that labor market intermediaries are new or unique to informational economies. Indeed, public sector employment agencies and for-profit temporary agencies have existed for a long time (Gonos 1997; National Commission for Manpower Policy 1978). Labor contractors are a common feature in agricultural labor markets (Wells 1996). Hiring halls are central organizations in the construction industry and have even existed among waitresses in some regions (Cobble 1991). As labor markets have become more volatile in the 1980s and 1990s, however, intermediaries have expanded into a much wider array of occupations and industries.

A more robust theory that can fully explain the role of intermediaries in the labor market remains to be developed. What has been attempted in this chapter is to help build a basis for such a theory by examining some of the functions they play in the labor market related

17 Harrison and Weiss (1998); Johnson, Bienenstock, and Farrell (1999); Pastor and Adams (1996); Pastor and Marcelli (1998).

Table 3.2   The organizational structure of intermediaries

Organization type	Examples
For-profit sector	Temporary agencies and for-profit training providers
	Contractor brokers
	Professional employer organizations
	Online job search web sites
Membership based	Union-based intiatives
	Membership-based employee associations
Public sector	Employment Training and Workforce Development System (One Stop Career Centers and PICs)
	Education-based initiatives (adult extension, community college contract training programs)
	Non-profit initiatives (publicly funded training programs)

to reducing transactions costs, mediating risk, building networks, and shaping compensation. The characteristics of flexible labor markets, with rapid change and uncertainty, help explain why these functions of intermediaries are becoming more important for both workers and employers in the process of navigating the labor market.

In turning in the next chapter to an empirical analysis of specific labor market intermediaries in Silicon Valley, it is most useful to distinguish between intermediaries by their organizational structure and origins. The financial base of an intermediary and its primary organizational base imposes a set of fundamental constraints on the activities of intermediaries. Organizational structure largely determines the types and range of different constituencies interacting with the intermediary which may shape their mandates or missions in important ways. Thus, the typology that is used here for the examination of intermediaries is based on the delineation of organizational origins of intermediaries shown in table 3.2.

4

Labor Market Intermediaries –
Private Sector

The time has long passed since the clerical/light industrial sector was
considered "the center of the universe" of the temporary help industry.
Today, virtually any skill can be, and is, provided on a temporary basis.
Interim Personnel Services Annual Report, 1994

The best way to think about our industry is as a series of pipes and shunts.
We get the resources where they need to be efficiently. I can think of no
other system that would do this.
Owner, Contractor Broker Firm, June, 1999

Private-sector intermediaries are the largest and most prominent category of labor market intermediary. Temporary agencies and other
private sector intermediaries place workers with many different skill
levels across a range of occupations, working with employers in a variety of different industries. Thus, in Silicon Valley it is not accurate to
characterize firms' use of temporary agencies as simply a cost-cutting
strategy in an effort to shrink the size of their "core" workforce and
reduce labor costs for noncore positions. Firms use intermediaries to
find and employ people for many purposes, including many "core"
functions within the region's high-tech industries. To be sure, temporary employees do include many assembly, shipping, light industrial,
and clerical positions, which combined still account for well over half
the employment in temporary agencies in the region. Temporary
employees, however, also include highly skilled technicians, engineers,
and computer professionals, who are the most rapidly growing seg-
ment in the temporary help industry and form the core of workers placed
through many of the other types of private sector intermediaries.

Furthermore, many other private sector intermediaries specialize in highly skilled occupations and thus, as a category, private sector intermediaries cut across all skill levels.

There are four major types of private sector intermediaries that will be reviewed in this chapter:[1]

- Temporary help firms – Temporary help firms are the most visible and well-known type of intermediary, and the number of firms and the number of people employed in those firms have grown dramatically in recent years. More importantly, temporary help firms have become increasingly integrated into the human resource practices of many high-tech firms, entering into long-term contracts, providing management and recruiting staff on the work-site of client firms, and providing a variety of other value-added management and administrative services for a growing sector of the workforce.
- Consultant brokerage firms – While somewhat less well known, contractor or consultant brokerage firms play a critical role in the regional labor market, particularly at middle and upper levels of the occupational structure. Contractor brokers are very similar to temporary help firms in that they recruit professional contractors for temporary positions in firms in the area. They are distinct from typical temporary help firms in that they specialize in more skilled positions, they recruit often for permanent positions as well as contract positions, and will place contractors who are incorporated or prefer to remain self-employed.[2]
- Web-based job sites – A third category of private sector intermediary,

---

1   It is possible to identify additional types of private intermediaries that play an important role in the Valley. Recruiters, for instance, play a role in finding highly skilled engineers, managers, and executives for permanent positions in the region's high-tech firms (Hunt and Scanlon 1998). Similarly, job fairs play an important role in bringing job seekers and potential employers together, particular for people trying to get into the industry for the first time (Eisenhart 1998). The purpose of this chapter, however, is not to provide a comprehensive treatment of all labor market intermediaries, but instead to demonstrate their importance in the labor market, give some indication of the diversity of their structures and activities, and outline possible future areas of research.

2   This distinction between temporary help firms and contractor brokers is clearly a fuzzy boundary, since the temporary agencies are increasingly developing expertise in placing contractors as well. The large temporary agencies also are developing complex subcontracting relations with contractor brokers in order to fill many highly skilled positions. The distinction remains useful on an analytical level, since contractor brokers have a significantly different focus than temporary help firms.

and one that has mushroomed since 1994, are Web-based job sites. The largest job sites are general purpose national sites, such as monster.com and hotjobs.com, which attempt to cover all occupational categories in regional labor markets across the country. Other sites are more specialized, such as dice.com (Data processing Independent Consultants Exchange), or Jobs for Programmers (www.prgjobs.com). Many sites are stand-alone, and only have a presence online. Other sites are linked to various industry associations and recruiting networks in which the Web-based "cyber-mediary" work is an extension of their other activities.

- Professional employer organizations – Professional employer organizations (PEOs) are firms that provide a variety of human resource administrative services to firms. They are similar to temporary help firms in that they act as the legal employer of record for employees who are doing work for a client firm. They are distinct from temporary help firms in that their employees are "permanently" working for the client firm. Typically, the PEO and the client firm have a joint-employer relationship to the employee. PEOs generally don't actively do recruiting, but they do provide a wider range of additional human resource administrative services for a more comprehensive range of employees than temporary help firms typically provide. This includes administering benefits packages, providing payroll services, ensuring compliance with employment regulations, and sharing responsibility for management of employees. While PEOs are relatively small as a category of intermediaries in Silicon Valley, they are growing very rapidly. They act as labor market intermediaries in the employment sphere by developing economies of scale in the "business of employment" for a range of small and mid-sized firms.

What distinguishes all private sector intermediaries from public-sector and membership-based intermediaries is that they are market-based organizations dependent on selling their services, and ultimately making a profit, in order to survive. This shapes their activities in ways that are profoundly different from membership-based and public sector intermediaries. Private sector intermediaries are primarily oriented toward meeting the needs of employers. While they may provide some assistance to job seekers, their revenue and thus their profits come from employers. While they clearly contribute to the profitability of their client firms, and to the flexibility of the regional economy, the implications of their activities for workers' career paths or the long-term

sustainability of the regional production complex is much more contradictory.

Private sector intermediaries rarely engage in significant skills development or training for the workers they place. Though many temporary agencies offer self-paced computer courses, they offer no
personalized attention and thus these courses are primarily useful for
people who are already at least computer literate and have significant
self-motivation. In practice, this training serves largely as a screening
device to identify workers with significant initiative rather than as a
substantial investment in worker training (Autor, Levy, and Murnane
1999). In an environment where skills and ongoing learning are so essential for workers' career paths, private temporary agencies do little
to improve labor market outcomes for workers. Furthermore, to the
extent to which they contribute to an underinvestment in training by
their client firms – because of more limited attachment to their workforce
– these private sector intermediaries may actually undermine the long-
term competitiveness of the region.

This chapter is organized into five sections. The first section discusses
the rise in employment in temporary help agencies, including discuss-
ing their increasing integration into the human resource practices of
their client firms. The second section discusses the rise in contractor
brokerage firms, highlighting their various subcontracting relationships
with the temporary help firms. The third section discusses the rise of
Internet-based job search sites. The fourth section discusses the growth
of professional employer organizations, placing them in the context of
the legal importance of being employer of record (legal employer). The
final section summarizes the overall trend toward an increase in private sector intermediaries and their importance within the regional
production complex.

Temporary Help Agencies

The most visible growth in intermediaries is in the temporary help industry. Temporary help companies are private businesses that recruit
workers to perform a variety of job tasks and then sell these workers'
labor to client firms for a set fee. The number of firms and total employment in temporary help firms exploded in the mid 1980s, in part as a
response to the economic downturn that the Valley faced during this
period. In the words of the regional president of one of the largest temporary help firms in the region:

Many Valley companies, led by AMD, which had said it would never lay people off, began laying people off. Companies re-evaluated and recognized the need to maintain flexibility to be competitive. Many companies are now keeping a 20–25 percent buffer, some lower, some higher, so they can develop new products quicker, ramp-up for production at a greater speed, etc. (Local president of a major national temporary agency, April, 1996)

The number of people employed in temporary help agencies nearly tripled between 1984 and 1998, now representing 3.5 percent of total employment in Silicon Valley. This number represents only the number of people employed in a temporary agency in any particular month. Since many people move from temporary into permanent positions, this understates the percentage of the workforce that actually use temporary agencies at different times, which is significantly higher. Based on employer interviews, Erickceck and Houseman (1997), for instance, estimate that the number of temporary jobs that client firms have during the year is typically seven to eight times the number of temporary jobs at any one time. A similar large number is suggested by the fact that Manpower, the largest temporary agency in Silicon Valley, in an average week in 1997 had 6,900 temporary employees assigned to a job, but over the course of a year placed nearly 40,000 people in temporary positions in the Valley. Both the Erickcek/Housman study and the Manpower data are likely to overstate the number of total people in temporary employment during the year, since the same person may fill multiple jobs with the same client firm or with different temporary agencies. A somewhat lower estimate is suggested from a study of employment in temporary help industries in Washington State, using data from the unemployment insurance system. In their study, Segal and Sullivan (1997) found that in 1994 approximately one and a half times as many workers got a paycheck from a temporary services firm sometime during the year as received a paycheck in the fourth quarter (3.7 percent compared to 2.4 percent), and that this ratio had increased steadily through the ten-year period of their study. Note that this ratio is for yearly employment compared to quarterly employment, not monthly employment. Given this, and given the nature of the Silicon Valley labor market, it seems reasonable to estimate that the ratio in Silicon Valley of yearly employment to monthly employment in temporary help agencies is likely to be between two and three to one. This would suggest that between 7 and 10 percent of the workforce in Silicon Valley are likely to be employed by a temporary help agency at some point during the course of a single year.

Table 4.1 Number of temporary help firms by firm size, Santa Clara County, 1987 and 1997

Employees	1987	1997
1–4	26	49
5–9	13	12
10–19	7	21
20–49	19	41
50–99	18	51
100–249	34	64
250–499	8	24
500–999	7	12
1000+	0	5
Total	132	279

Source: County Business Patterns.

Along with the growth in total employment in temporary help agencies there has been a growth in the number of firms in the Valley, which more than doubled between 1987 and 1997, rising from 132 to 279. In addition, there was a significant growth in the size of these firms. While in 1987 there were no temporary help firms in the Valley that had more than 1,000 employees in the region, by 1997 there were five such firms (see table 4.1).

When multiple offices of the same firm are included, there are well over 300 offices of temporary help agencies in broader Silicon Valley (including southern San Mateo and Alameda Counties). This includes a wide range of companies, from major multinational temporary help agencies like Manpower Temporary Services, Kelly Services and Olsten, to a range of small, individual- or family-run temp firms. Major companies operating in Silicon Valley include:[3]

- Manpower Temporary Services – formerly the largest temporary agency in the world with over 800,000 workers in the US and over 2 million globally, operates over 3,200 offices in over 50 countries, with global sales in 1998 of over $10 billion, double their sales from 1994. They have a total of 20 offices in Silicon Valley, placing close

3 National and international employment data provided in the annual reports of each company. Silicon Valley specific data from the *San Jose Business Journal Book of Lists*, 1999.

to 7,000 employees per week. They grew rapidly in the mid 1990s, with US sales increases of 17 percent in 1992, 20 percent in 1993, and 22 percent in 1994. Sales have slowed somewhat in more recent years, with a growth of 10 percent in 1996, 14 percent in 1997 and 7 percent in 1998, as they have faced more competition. Their most rapid growth sector, however, is in information technology services, which grew by 26 percent in 1998.

- Interim Personnel Services – places over 4,000 employees per week in Silicon Valley, working out of over 20 different offices. Headquartered in Fort Lauderdale, this company operated a total of 877 offices in 12 countries, as of December 31 1998. Their 1998 revenues totaled $1.9 billion, up 36 percent from 1997. They estimate globally they placed over 375,000 people in 1998.

- Adecco Personnel Services – places over 2,400 employees per week in Silicon Valley, operating out of 12 different offices. This is a multinational corporation which now claims to be the largest temporary agency in the US as well as the world, having passed Manpower when it acquired the General Services and IT staffing components of Olsten Corporation in August 1999. The company is headquartered in Switzerland, operating with 3,000 offices in 50 countries throughout the world. Their 1998 revenue was $10.8 billion, a 34 percent increase from the previous year. Their US revenues jumped more than 50 percent in 1998.

- Kelly Services – places some 2,300 employees per week, with seven different offices in Silicon Valley. They are also a major multinational corporation, with 1994 sales of $2.6 billion, up 21 percent from the previous year. They operate 1,500 offices in 19 different countries. They placed approximately 740,000 people in 1998.

The character of the workforce placed through temporary agencies has also changed significantly in the last twenty years. Temporary agencies originally focused on clerical and light-industrial work. More recently, however, there has been an expansion into technical, professional and managerial fields as well, as shown in table 4.3. Clerical and administrative support positions still form over half of all temporary help placements, but this percentage is declining. The second largest occupational category, accounting for another quarter of all placements, is production, construction, and materials handling positions. Placements in these occupations are estimated to grow 82.6 percent between 1995 and 2002. Many of the electronic manufacturing services firms in the area have expanded their use of temporary workers dramatically in the 1990s,

Table 4.2   The 25 largest temporary agencies in Silicon Valley, 1997

Name	Average number of temporary employees to jobs per week	Total number of 1997 placements in Valley	Number of recruiters in Valley	Offices in Valley
Manpower Staffing Services	6,900	39,100	145	20
Adecco Employment Services	2,800	18,750	12	12
Barrett Business Services	2,400	7,702	21	3
American Technical	1,500	4,793	9	2
Accustaff Inc.	1,350	5,525	18	4
Crossroads Staffing Services	1,200	11,250	29	6
Nelson Staffing Solutions	1,085	2,804	27	6
Advanced Technical Resources	800	2,090	22	1
Olsten Staffing Services	750	N/A	27	8
Spectrum Personnel	550	5,000	30	4
Trendtec Inc.	479	3,028	10	2
Ann Wells Personnel Services	470	2,800	7	1
Echo Design & Development Corp.	450	1,902	6	2
Josephine's Personnel Services Inc.	350	1,750	4	2
Management Solutions Inc.	225	1,225	26	1
Silicon Valley Technical Staffing	200	350	9	2
Certified Personnel	175	2,000	12	2
Balance Your Staffing Solutions	150	200	5	2
Advanced Technology Staffing	100	300	8	3
Accountants on Call	115	600	90	6
Bay Span Construction Inc.	85	200	4	3
Albin Engineering Services Inc.	70	60	4	1
Palo Alto Staffing Services	60	750	12	1
Target Personnel Services	60	187	1	1
Complimate Technical Staffing	48	572	9	1

Source: San Jose Business Journal 1999 Book of Lists.
Ranked by average number of temporary employees assigned to jobs per week in Silicon Valley. This list is compiled by the San Jose Business Journal from voluntary reporting by firms. It doesn't include some prominent temporary agencies, such as Kelly Services or Interim Staffing, and the numbers of placements should be treated with some skepticism. Nonetheless, it does give a good indication of the mix of well-known national firms and small-scale local firms within the regional complex.

and the larger ones frequently maintain 15–30 percent of their employment through temporary help firms. In addition, much of the warehouse, shipping, and receiving employment in the Valley's wholesale and distribution networks is employed through temporary agencies.

Table 4.3 Santa Clara County occupational employment projections for
temporary jobs, 1995–2002

Occupation	1995	2002	Temp jobs (%) 1995	Temp jobs (%) 2002	Change 1995–2002 #	Change 1995–2002 (%)
Managerial and administrative	480	860	1.7	1.9	380	79.2
Professional and technical	2,880	4,810	10.4	10.7	1,930	67.0
Sales	810	1,390	2.9	3.1	580	71.6
Clerical and administrative support	15,740	24,020	56.7	53.3	8,280	52.6
Service	1,160	1,770	4.2	3.9	610	52.6
Agriculture	20	40	0.1	0.1	20	100.0
Production, construction and materials handling	6,670	12,180	24.0	27.0	5,510	82.6
Total temporary jobs	27,760	45,070	100.0	100.0	17,310	62.4
Total all jobs	831,900	1,025,300			193,400	23.2
Temporary jobs as percent of total	3.3	4.4				

Source: Adapted from Baru (2001). Data from California EDD.

Despite the continued dominance of these clerical and blue-collar positions, managerial, professional and technical positions combined account for over 12 percent of temporary placements and constitute one of the fastest growing sectors of the temporary services industry. According to Staffing Industry Report, 1998, revenue for the IT sector in the US was estimated to be $18.5 billion, representing a compound annual growth rate of 24 percent since 1992. Most of the major temporary agencies are prioritizing expansion in information technology occupations and have established additional units that focus exclusively on technical placements. For instance, Manpower has created a division called Manpower Professional, which focuses on technical and professional placements. In addition, they have a Silicon Valley specific division called US Caden which specializes in information systems/ technology specialists in the Silicon Valley. Adecco has various technical divisions, including Ajilon, Computer People and ICON for information technology positions, TAD for engineering and technical placements, and TAD Telecomm for telecommunications. In August 1999, Adecco purchased the IT staffing division of Olsten to enhance and expand their technical placements.

Vendor on Premise Agreements

More important than simply the expansion of employment, and the increasing focus on information technology related occupations, is the increasing integration of temporary help firms into the human resource practices of major client firms in the area. Temporary help agencies have increasingly entered into "vendor on premise" (VOP) agreements with their clients, involving long-term contracts that include on-site offices and the provision of various management services. The experience of Olsten Corporation is typical in this regard.

> By the end of 1994, we had extended our Partnership Program services to more than 180 major corporations including some of the world's best-known companies, and the list continues to grow. In many of these relationships, we place dedicated managers on site to supervise the partnerships and, in effect, become extensions of their corporate human resources departments. The benefits to corporations are many. At Lotus Development Corporation's North American manufacturing and distribution center near Boston, we provide up to 250 people, allowing Lotus to run this major operation with only six of its own employees . . . . At the end of 1994, these Partnership Program services accounted for about 20 percent of our Staffing Services business. They have helped to give the business a solid foundation and make it less cyclical. (Olsten Staffing Services 1994)

Nationally, total revenue from VOP contracts exploded from $500 million in 1992 to some $6.5 billion in 1997, rising from only 2 percent of total temporary help revenues to an estimated 12 percent (*Staffing Industry Review* 1997).

Vendor on premise agreements range in size and scope of their activities. A single-site contract might involve only one on-site coordinator equipped with a computer terminal to take, fill, and follow-up on orders for temporary workers. Larger contracts might include several on-site staff to handle interviewing and testing of applicants as well as testing the client's candidates for full-time jobs. Other value-added services that might be part of a VOP program include doing on-site management, producing cost and quality reports, managing relations with subcontractors, monitoring targets for women- and minority-owned businesses, ensuring vendor quality control, and other administrative tasks. VOP managers often have to have an extensive background in the client's industry, be very familiar with their needs, and be able to develop management systems around the client's particular business, including setting benchmarks and evaluating and meeting those benchmarks on a consistent basis. National firms dominate the market for VOP programs. This is largely due to the costs involved in setting up and administering a VOP program. *Staffing Industry Review* (1997) estimates that 85–90 percent of the estimated 3,750 VOP sites operating in the US in 1997 were handled by national firms.

VOP relationships have developed over time in Silicon Valley. Initially VOP agreements were made for a one-year period. Until recently, VOP agreements were limited to this time period, but renewals now can extend for longer periods, sometimes ranging as high as seven years. Increasingly, some temporary help firms are asking for longer-term commitments from their clients when they first come in, given the high start-up costs. As the partnership between the VOP supplier and client develops, the volume of and variety of placements typically expands. As the vendor gets to know the client better, they can identify additional areas where they can supply staffing while also providing a wider range of services.

While there is no data source quantifying the number of high-tech firms in Silicon Valley with VOP agreements with temporary agencies, interviews with human resource personnel suggests that the use has expanded significantly in recent years. For instance, in a telephone survey of the 25 largest private sector employers in Silicon Valley, most of whom are high-tech firms, research staff at Working Partnerships found that 22 out of the 23 who answered the survey said they currently use temporary agencies regularly, and ten said they had on-site agreements with at least one agency (personal communication).

Vendor-on-premise arrangements in Silicon Valley began predominantly in less-skilled occupations in the mid 1990s, primarily in the clerical and production workforce. In the 1990s, however, IT and technical positions had become an increasingly important component of these VOP agreements, creating new challenges for the industry:

> Vendor on premise agreements are just beginning to happen for technical placements in Silicon Valley in the last couple of years. Now, every RFP that I'm involved in involves some technical site services. Customers have started collapsing the two purchasing decisions [clerical and technical]. Now they think that since it worked in clerical, it can work in technical placements. The reality is there is a big difference between clerical and technical site services. One technical service provider typically can't provide a large portion of technical needs, whereas in clerical employment, an Adecco, Manpower, or any other major temporary agency

can easily find 80 percent of a firms clerical needs. (Interview, on-site manager for major temporary help firm, July, 1999)

To meet the demands of these VOP contracts, the major temporary firms have developed extensive "secondary sourcing" arrangements. This involves a series of relationships with other temporary agencies, usually smaller, more specialized companies, who can be called on to fulfill the terms of the contract when the primary firm is unable to fill the demand. The CEO of one temp firm in Silicon Valley that employs 500 people at a time estimated that 40 percent of her business was in such "secondary sourcing" arrangements:

> We serve as a secondary source for some of the major temporary agen-
> cies who have entered into major contracts with their clients. We back up
> [Agency 1] at Intel, we back up [Agency 2] at Tandem Computers. We
> back up [Agency 3] at Novell, [Agency 4] at Cisco and [Agency 5] at
> Intel. The major companies call on us when they've guaranteed to pro-
> vide a certain number of people and aren't able to provide them. For
> instance, the temp firms may be given 24–48 hours to fill a certain order
> – say a couple hundred people to do data processing – and if they can't
> find the people, they'll come to us for help. (CEO of locally owned tem-
> porary help firm, May 1996)

The growth in VOP programs, along with these secondary sourcing arrangements, has thus provided a tremendous boom for specialized consultant brokerage firms in the region.

Consultant Brokerage Firms

High-tech consultant brokerage firms in Silicon Valley act essentially as temporary help firms that specialize in the placement of highly skilled information technology professionals for both contract (temporary) and permanent positions with their client firms. In both cases, consultant brokers in Silicon Valley are distinct from traditional consulting firms, which typically have a core of permanent staff and the firm makes money by marketing the expertise of their staff to clients for contract jobs. In the consultant broker business, in contrast, the process is ex-actly the reverse. Firms take requests from clients to fill positions for which they may not have contractors readily available and then ac-tively recruit skilled professionals to fill those positions. As a result, they have a fluid and tenuous tie with the workforce they are placing, though they may retain informal long-term relationships with many of their more valued contractors. In this model, the industry provides an important service within the regional labor market:

> The best way to think about our industry is as a series of pipes and shunts. We get the resources where they need to be efficiently. I can think of no other system that would do this. Let's take an example of a highly placed web developer. He can charge $100/hr, but if he worked as an employee, someone would need to pay him full-time and most companies don't really need him full-time. Smaller companies need him, but may not be able to afford him. If he has to market his own services, he's going to spend 30 percent of his time marketing his services. He's going to have to increase his hourly rate to cover that time, and not get himself in front of as many clients as he could otherwise. He can now go to 20 agencies, we can each get to 10 companies. He can be in front of 200 companies like that [snap] and the company that needs him the most will get him. I don't think you could design a more efficient, cost effective system. (Owner, contractor broker firm 1, June, 1999)

The business of consultant brokers in Silicon Valley has its origins in the 1970s and has clearly grown in recent years. While there is no specific data source identifying employment in consultant broker firms,[4] executives within the industry perceive a rapid expansion in both the number of competitors and the number of people doing contract work. One of the most comprehensive listings of recruiting firms listed more than 800 firms in the Silicon Valley area in 1999.[5]

The nature of contracting in Silicon Valley has changed substantially in the last twenty years. When the oldest consultant brokerage firms in the Valley got their start,[6] contracting was seen as an undesirable employment option with less secure opportunities and thus reserved for people with only marginal attachment to the labor market:

---

4   Recruiting firms may be classified in a variety of SIC codes, including temporary help supply, engineering and management services, computer and data services (software), and other professional or business services. Contractors placed through recruiting firms may be classified as self-employed, employees of the contract firm, or placed as employees of the client firm, depending on the particular arrangement.
5   Available at http://www.dice.com/recruiters/companies/regions/ncalif-ab.shtml
6   Older-established firms in the valley include: Computer Resources Group, founded in 1972, Gentry Inc; founded in 1975; and Lloyd-Ritter Consulting, founded in 1978.

For the first three to four years, everyone I talked to I had to explain what contracting was, why they would want to use contractors versus permanent. Many people don't realize that many of the early contractors were women – their benefits were covered by their husbands, and they enjoyed the contract aspect of it. The first nine to ten people that we hired [when we started in the 1970s] were all women ... Men tended to see this as too insecure, feeling they had bills and obligations. Contracting was too uncertain and they weren't interested. (Interview, Owner, contractor broker firm 1, July, 1999)

As contractors came to be more accepted by employers, the remuneration they received increased and more people became interested in being contractors. Contracting became more widely accepted and even desirable among a significant portion of skilled personnel in the high-tech industry. In a recent study of 52 technical contractors in the Silicon Valley, for example, Kunda, Barley, and Evans (1999) found that most contractors felt they benefited from being exposed to a greater number of work situations, experienced more variety in their own work, and were able to pursue interesting projects and opportunities. The contractors were fully aware of some down sides to contracting, including social isolation and insecurity, but the majority still preferred it to the options they saw as available in more "permanent" employment.

As the labor market for skilled information technology professionals tightened in the second half of the 1990s, consulting opportunities became available for a growing portion of the workforce. In earlier years, consultants tended to be more experienced workers with extensive contacts in the industry and a broad range of skills and experience. They tended to pursue consulting work as a permanent employment strategy, rather than pursuing contracting between more permanent jobs. As the skill sets have changed, however, and consulting opportunities have increased, people with even less experience in the industry have also turned to contracting work:

We used to only place people with ten years of work experience and we only worked with professional contractors – not people who were just between permanent jobs. That used to be the core – you needed more senior people, with a broad skills base, in order to find contracts. I used to advise [potential contractors] to get more skills and experience until they had at least ten years of experience. Then we dropped that figure to five years. I can remember my shock when a client said they were willing to pay some outrageous price for someone with a BS in computer science and two years of experience. Two years! But actually, for some of the new technologies, if you've been out of school for more than four years, you don't even have the skills since it wasn't taught. (Owner, contractor broker firm 1, June, 99)

The expansion in the number and diversity of people who are employed through consultant brokers has been made possible in part by the rapid development of the World Wide Web. This has made it easier to reach a larger number of potential recruits in a shorter period of time, increasing the number of potential requests that brokers are able to take:

> Back 27 years ago, I had every name and phone number of our contractors memorized . . . Now, most of our filling comes from the internet, not from word of mouth. We used to think that we did really well to get 200 résumés in a month. Now we can get over 200 a day. This does create a problem in reviewing all those résumés. Recruiters spend hours over their terminal, even after doing as tight a search as possible, narrowing it down to who to call. (Owner, contractor broker firm 1, June, 1999)

While consultant brokers place people in a wide variety of firms, ranging from small start-ups to the largest high-tech firms, an increasing portion of their business is being channeled through large temporary help firms with VOP agreements. As VOP agreements have expanded from clerical and light-industrial positions to include more skilled technical and professional positions, consultant brokers have increasingly had to shift from relationships with client human resource managers to building relationships with the temporary help firms. The skills required in technical placements, however, are much more specialized and complex, requiring VOP providers to depend on a greater number of subcontractors than in clerical placements. A major VOP provider at one of the largest Silicon Valley firms, for example, has contracts with eight subcontractors for clerical placements, and 60 subcontractors for technical placements (interview, VOP manager). Often, the subcontractors have had direct relationships with the client firms in the past but are then told to channel their services through the VOP provider. This centralizes decision making, and prevents client managers from having to field calls from multiple agencies, or build relationships with dozens of independent recruiters. It also, however, creates tensions between the subcontracting agencies and the large temp firms, and has significantly changed the business conditions for the smaller firms:

> We see the [large temporary agencies] as gatekeepers at many of the large high-tech firms in the area. We started seeing them about four to five

years ago, first at Hewlett-Packard, and a year or two later at Cisco. We used to have great relationships with the human resource managers there, and then all of a sudden these walls came up. We realized that we just have to make relationships with the gatekeepers now and we now have a great relationship with them. It makes it more difficult, since there is another layer, but they are there to help. (Owner, contractor broker firm 2, July, 1999)

When VOPs go in, initially it is very difficult, since they are trying to get things under control. Generally when they put someone in, they've never done it before, and the first couple of years it is difficult, they err in the direction of wanting to control the situation, saying things like "we don't want you to talk to hiring managers, etc.". But once they develop a better relationship with the client company and with us, we are very trustworthy people – not everyone is, some try to get around the VOP and can't be trusted – but we play by the rules and once we develop the trusting relationship, it is OK. (Owner, contractor broker firm 1, June, 1999)

Despite the tension that sometimes exists between the VOP provider and the consultant brokers, there has been substantial growth in brokers, in part because the margins are quite high. The profit rate for a technical placement can run anywhere from 15 percent to 30 percent of the salary the contractor receives, and brokers have been known to charge as much as 200 percent above salary.[7] This rate lasts for the lifetime of the placement. For someone being placed in a six-month contract at $100 an hour, for example, a profit rate of 20 percent would translate into $20,000 for a single placement, often for a single day's work. Often consultant brokers will get their start after having gained experience in a larger temporary help firm and through VOP programs:

[People from our firm] alone have probably started 100 technical staffing agencies in the last three years – where [one of our] manager[s] would start hiring technical staff, get knowledge of what he was getting billed, leave [our company] and start his own staffing agency. The margins in the technical side of the business have been very high. (Manager, VOP program for large temporary help firm, July 1999)

The levels of competition among consultant brokers, however, can be extreme. When a VOP provider is given a request from a manager in the client firm, for example, often they will initially try to fill the

7   A 20 percent profit rate translates into roughly a 45 percent mark-up rate above salary, with the remainder going to payroll taxes, insurance, and benefits.

request from their own pool. If within 24 to 48 hours they are not able to fill the request, they will then pass on the request to their subcontractors. The VOP firm will usually send out the request to multiple consultant brokers, who are then all competing to see who can fill the position in the shortest time. Since the subcontractors receive no revenue until they place someone, the stakes can be quite high. It is a clear example of a winner-take-all market (Frank and Cook 1995).

This structure of the industry creates tremendous potential for abuse. As brokers compete in fast-paced winner-take-all markets, the temptation to gain a placement through any means necessary is high:

> Some of the smaller agencies were really gauging their customers, charging as much as a 200 percent mark-up. They would withhold evidence that they were paying their worker on a 1099 [self-employed] basis, not a W-2 [employee], so they could charge a higher mark-up. They would be involved in third party relationships, such as a company getting H-1B visas for their contractors. The programmer would be making $25 an hour, and I'm being billed $100. A piece of that $75 spread is going to the agency, and a piece through an H-1B company. These are unfair business practices, designed to take advantage of an uneducated user. I was responsible for uncovering . . . a lot of these practices, but when I went to speak with agencies . . . [they reacted] as if this was totally norm, and they were shocked that I would find out and treat it as a problem. I'm no Mother Teresa, but this kind of practice shocked me. (Manager, VOP program, large temporary help firm, July, 1999)

Common business practices that are considered unethical include: actively recruiting current employees of active clients to become contractors; inducing other contractors to leave an assignment before it is completed; submitting a contractor who has already been submitted to the client by another firm; misrepresenting contractors' skills or experiences; presenting a résumé to a client prior to obtaining the consultants approval; and misrepresenting billing rates or charging exorbitant rates. Nonetheless, the Bay Area actually has a reputation for being one of the cleaner places to be in the consultant broker business. The dense social networks and extensive professional associations of professional contractors helps ensure that unethical practices on the part of brokers can result in a bad reputation that quickly spreads through these professional networks. According to one of the founders of the Northern California chapter of the National Association of Computer Consultant Businesses (NACCB):

The Bay Area is one of the cleanest places to be a contractor . . . When NACCB tried to write national bylaws, they couldn't just take our Northern California ethics, because other areas said they'd go out of business if they agreed to those principles. I believe the reason it worked here is that those of us who are the largest and best known earlier on started educating clients about what they should demand of their agencies. Now, in the Bay Area, a double submission is anathema – some companies even have a policy to not consider someone who is a double submission. (Owner, contractor broker firm 1, June, 1999)

Despite being the premier industry association, both nationally and regionally, there are only 40 local members of the NACCB Northern California chapter, despite the hundreds of brokers that exist in the area. This suggests that while the more prominent agencies may try to achieve more ethical standards, many others are likely to succumb to the incentives to place contractors by any means necessary.

Some have argued that the rise of electronic recruiting and the Internet is likely to reduce the intermediary role of recruiters. If employers can reach contractors directly through recruiting on the Web, the argument goes, there will be less of a need to depend on intermediaries. In practice, however, the mushrooming of potential candidates actually increases the importance of intermediaries in sifting through the potential candidates to identify those that would be appropriate for particular positions. The knowledge brokers have of their clients and contractors, along with the relationships they've built, still provides an important value in the labor market:

The Internet has made it much easier for us to search for people, but it has also make it easier for everyone else to search too, which increases the competition. It allows our clients to go directly to our people, but that is very labor intensive and they don't have the relationships that we do. Half of the people we place every month we know well. They're reliable and we can vouch for them. If our clients put out an ad, they may get 300 résumés but they still don't know who the people are. It is still a high-touch industry. That's what the clients are paying for, and the internet has emphasized the importance of these relationships even more. (Owner, contractor broker firm 2, July ,1999)

Thus, the growth in the World Wide Web has not only not undermined contractor brokers, it has in many ways reinforced their services. The expansion of the Internet has also contributed to a rapid growth in a range of Web-based intermediaries.

Web-based Intermediaries

The World Wide Web has become a major means by which many firms try to identify and recruit potential employees and many workers try to identify and evaluate potential job opportunities. Much of this activity involves direct ties between potential employers and potential employees. Individuals are able to search for job opportunities on individual company Web-sites and submit electronic résumés directly to potential employers. Employers are able to review submitted résumés quickly, evaluate individuals' on-line portfolios or individual Web-pages and contact potential employees directly via email. Nonetheless, as the volume of electronic recruiting has mushroomed, there has been a virtual explosion in various types of on-line intermediaries.

The on-line recruiting industry includes a variety of mechanisms, including a range of formal job boards, third party recruiters, various Usenet bulletin boards and listservs, and internal posting systems for companies. Interbiznet.com, one of the leading research firms specializing in the electronic recruiting industry, estimated that recruiters posted a total of nearly 29 million job postings on the Internet in 1998. Based on a survey of 2,620 users of Web recruiting services and 2,500 job boards, they estimated that only 6 percent of these on-line job postings were on corporate websites. The vast majority, 61 percent, were circulated through usenet bulletin boards or through listservs, while a full 33 percent were on on-line job boards.

The growth in these on-line job boards is one of the most dramatic developments in labor market intermediaries. There are thousands of sites that have sprung up in the last five years, with a whole range of different structures and business models. Some, such as monster.com or hotjobs.com, are general interest sites, listing thousands of jobs in markets across the country. Others are highly specialized, focusing on special occupations. Some are stand-alone sites, while others are integrated with a variety of different services.

There is no accurate figure on the total number of on-line job search sites on the Web. *Business Week* estimated in May 1999 that there were more than 5,000 on-line job search sites, not counting employers' own Web sites (Armstrong, Zellner, and Baig 1999). The *Wall Street Journal* quotes a more conservative estimate of 2,500 (McWilliams 1999). Whether 2,500 or twice that number, they have become important sources of listing for job opportunities, and have become a standard component of many job search strategies (Crispin and Mehler 1999).

It is possible to see these on-line job search sites as nothing more significant than simply a replacement for the classified section of major newspapers. This development alone is significant, however, since it greatly cuts down on search time and allows individuals to customize searches specific to their skills or job preferences. Over the last thirty years, job seekers have increasingly turned to ads as a primary means of finding employment opportunities. Between 1970 and 1992, for example, the percentage of job seekers placing or answering ads (primarily newspaper but also other publications) has nearly doubled, from 23.4 percent of job seekers to 41.7 percent (Ports 1993). Thus the improved search capabilities of on-line classified ads alone is likely to be a significant benefit to job seekers.

The role of on-line job search sites as intermediaries, however, goes significantly beyond being simply a replacement for classified ads. The critical additional service they provide is allowing job seekers to post their own résumés on line, making it available to firms actively recruiting candidates without the worker having to engage in an active job search. These sites also can provide a range of other valuable information, including career advice, salary surveys, and information on training opportunities. They also can provide more extensive information about the company providing job listings, and some job sites also provide on-line forums for job seekers to share information about what it is like working for particular companies.

Web intermediaries do more than simply provide information. They also contribute to the very transformation of labor markets, making it easier for people to move. They can encourage job hopping among particular groups of skilled occupations (Schwartz 1999). One sign of this contribution to job hopping is survey data that shows that the majority of people using job-search Web sites are not unemployed or even actively searching for a job. According to Intebiznet.com, only 5 percent of visitors to job boards in 1998 were currently unemployed, while only another 10 percent were employed but actively looking for a new job. Another 15 percent were thinking about looking for a job, while a full 71 percent claimed to be not even thinking about looking for a job. For many of these people, searching the on-line job boards becomes a way of keeping track of changes and opportunities in their occupation and industry, benchmarking their own job against what other opportunities might exist out there. It becomes a key way that people become aware of changing skill demands in the labor market and the need to update their own skill base, which is essential for succeeding in the regional labor market:

Table 4.4 Prominent on-line job search sites used by Silicon Valley IT professionals

Ba.jobs.offered	Craiglist.com	Jobs4women.com
Bayarea.techies.com	Dice.com	Net.temps
Bayareacareers.com	Fatjobs.com	Sanjosejobs.com
Bridgepath.com	(specifically for start-ups)	Sdforum.org (tech. Specialties)
Bridgesonline.com	Hotjobs.com	Selectjobs.com
(for women)	InforworksUSA.com	Sidewalk.com
Careermosaic.com	Interbiznet.com/top100/	Siliconvalleyjobs.com
Careerpath.com	Javajobs.com (software	Stc.org (tech. writing)
Careerbuilder.com	development)	Techies.com
Careercity.com	Jobtrak.com	VJF.com (now brassring.com)
Careermagic.com	Jobengine.com	
Contract jobs.com	Jobs.com	

Source: SV Webgrrls.com, and www.careercompany.com

> I check [every week] for the job listing in my field to see what kind of skill sets they are looking for, and I make it my business to have those skill sets . . . You better like to learn in this occupation – if not, you will be in pitiful shape. Me, I love to learn, but for someone who didn't enjoy that, it would just be impossible. You'd do OK for the first six months, but if you don't keep up, you can be in the dirt really fast. (Interview, web designer, June, 1999)

Of course, on line job search sites are still predominantly used by employees in professional or white-collar occupations. There are listings of jobs available in blue-collar, assembly, warehouse-type work, but since access to the Web is still largely shaped by economic status, a smaller portion of employees searching for those types of jobs have Internet access.

Table 4.4 lists prominent job sites that are used by Silicon Valley IT professionals. This is only a partial list, and includes both sites that are specific to the Bay Area and to technology-related jobs, as well as national sites and more general occupation/industry sites that local workers use.

One of the largest general sites is monster.com. Founded in 1994 by Jeff Taylor, monster.com grew out of The Monster Board, which claimed to be the 454th commercial site on the Web. It was established in Boston as a spin-off of a high-tech recruiting agency. Taken over by international recruitment giant TMP Worldwide, it grew rapidly. Revenues for monster.com come primarily from fees paid by companies for listing job openings and for having access to the site's résumé database. Revenues from monster.com grew from $6.6 million worldwide in 1996 to $133 million in 1999. By 2001, monster.com was taking in more than $100 million in a single quarter, with revenues up more than 111 percent from the previous year. What's more, unlike many Internet companies, the site has been profitable since 1997 (Manchester 2001). By early 2001, monster.com was getting more than 5 million unique visitors a month,[8] and in early May 2001 they passed 10 million résumés in their database, up from 3.3 million the previous year. Clearly a database of résumés that large will be useful only to the extent that extensive search capabilities contribute to matching appropriate workers and employers. Thus, the growth in electronic recruiting has led to a particular culture around the use of résumés. Résumés are often scanned by software that looks for key words, thus determining whose résumé is actually looked at by human eyes and who actually gets an interview. If the résumé contains the key words that companies are looking for, it will emerge in the initial scan. Thus it is in the employee's interest to list as many key words as possible relating to the work they do. Knowledgeable job applicants will have a special section reserved for key words, frequently quite lengthy, along with the more traditional sections devoted to objective, education, work experience, skills summary, and so on.

The most prominent site in the Silicon Valley high-tech recruiting industry is dice.com. While the name actually stands for Data-processing Independent Consultant's Exchange, the gambling metaphor that accompanies the dice imagery actually captures fairly well the type of high-rolling lifestyle that high-end contractors aspire to. Dice.com was founded by two former contractors, Lloyd Linn and Diane Rickert, who first landed contract jobs in California in 1989. It started as a simple bulletin board service, in which recruiters listed available jobs for a $300 annual fee. They had immediate success: "They rented a friend's spare bedroom, borrowed a 386 16 MHZ desktop computer to run a $90 shareware product called Spitfire, bought a laptop for demos, and put an ad in the *San Jose Mercury News*. And then went off to golf that first Sunday morning. By three that afternoon, eight contractors had called in" (Teuke 1999). Within two years, they had 50 companies

---

8   According to data from Media Metrix, as reported in the company's press release announcing Q1 2001 earnings.

subscribing to the BBS, operating on eight phone lines from San Francisco. They then moved to Des Moines, their home town, and decided to go national. They switched to a new package called Major BBS, which supported X25 packet switching, and leased a data line from Des Moines to New York, with a similar set-up to San Francisco, and later Dallas, Chicago, Atlanta, Boston, and other cities. By 1994, they owned their own nationwide data network and had 120 recruiting companies listing jobs nationwide (Crispin and Mehler 1999; Teuke 1999). When the World Wide Web began to take off in 1994, they switched their service to a Web page, and their revenue doubled every year after that, reporting $8 million in sales in 1998. In February 1999, they sold the company to Earthweb for $35 million.

One interesting aspect of the dice.com model is that they initially restricted listings on their site to recruiters – companies that place a minimum of 50 percent of the employees on other companies' sites.[9] For a monthly fee ($550/month in 1999), these recruiters get unlimited posting. As of January, 2000, they had a total of over 170,000 jobs listed – a number which had doubled every year since starting on the Web. By January, 1999, they had over 2,000 recruiters subscribed to their service. Though they provide listings in many metropolitan areas now, Silicon Valley in 1999 still accounted for 20–25 percent of listings. Yet the focus of their marketing and recruiting is not on the recruiters, but on the job seeker: "if we have the job seekers, the recruiters will follow" says sales and marketing manager Jeff Dickey-Chasins (telephone interview). Job seekers can post their profile for 30 days, but then need to reenter the site to keep it active. Profiles are emailed to member employers on a daily basis. In January, 1999, the site recorded 3,140,250 detailed job views from 20,000 distinct job seekers.

Another prominent on-line job site is brassring.com, which was formerly known as the Virtual Job Fair. This site was started by Westech (now known as Brassring), a company which specializes in organizing information technology job fairs, which have become a staple in the high-tech industry on the West Coast and more recently nationwide. The company, founded by two high school friends Rod Lake and Fred Faltersack, launched their first job fair in September 1982, which drew 40 recruiting companies. Brassring now produces over ninety high-tech job fairs a year, in virtually every major high technology center in the US and more recently Europe, and thus have developed a significant

9   This policy changed in August 1999 to make it open to client firms as well.

expertise in intermediary activity. The company eventually grew to include not only the job fairs, but a free tabloid publication, *High Technology Careers*, and, since the mid 1990s, the Virtual Job Fair Web site (changed to brassring.com in 1999). As of May, 1999, the site listed 30,000 jobs, with a database of 160,000 résumés. Initially the Web site was seen as simply a value-added product for customers of the job fairs and magazine. If people are going to the job fair, it allows them to get some information on the company before they actually interview in person. Later, however, it became clear that it was a valuable career information site on its own. The site gets more than 2 million hits a week, and during at least one Santa Clara job fair, it got half a million hits in one day. Every day about 2,000 résumés get mailed to their customers. The business model is entirely based on employers paying for advertising space on the Web, just like they do at a job fair. Charges depend on whether they simply have a few job openings or whether they want to run their whole career web site on brassring.com (Eisenhart 1998).

The rise in on-line job search engines has even led to some interesting, though apparently misguided, business models, such as the creation of on-line auctions for people. The idea began when a team of professionals working at an Internet service provider (ISP) tried to auction themselves on eBay. The offer read: "Team of 16 employees from major ISP willing to leave as a group. Total minimum bid would be $3,140,000." The team didn't succeed in auctioning off their services, but their attempt led to a number of efforts to try to expand the notion of employee auctions. The largest initiative was the "Talent Market" on monster.com, which was a place where independent contractors, freelancers, and others looking for employment could auction their skills and availability to prospective employers. When it was launched on July 4 of 1999, monster.com's founder Jeff Taylor thought this was a tremendous opportunity, and indeed within five months nearly 60,000 people had put themselves up for auction. There seemed to be little interest from employers, however, and by May, 2000 the Talent Market had been removed from the monster.com web site. Another site, bid4geeks.com, was established by one of the eBay human auctioneers, John Kinsella, but the idea never caught on and the site closed down in 2000. Another model, called eLance, focuses on auctioning projects, rather than people, and has proved to be more succesful. Firms post projects, soliciting bids for them, while freelancers can also list their résumés and experience on the Web page (Eisenberg 1999).

Employer of Record

Another type of labor market intermediary that has grown in recent years is professional employer organizations (PEOs), who specialize in being the employer of record (legal employer). Though these organizations now provide some additional value-added administrative and benefit management services, their business model is largely dependent on the complex legal and regulatory environment surrounding the employment relationship in the US. Thus, before specifically examining professional employer organizations, it is important to examine in some more depth the struggles over the legal and regulatory classification of employer status. This helps provide a greater understanding of why employers, particularly small and medium companies, might want to avoid the responsibilities of being a legal employer and to take advantage of using an intermediary.

Temporary help firms and consultant brokers have been heavily involved in trying to shape legislation governing the employment relationship to their advantage. For temporary help firms, the very service of being the legal employer allows their clients to benefit from the work of the temporary employee, while not being responsible for the administrative and legal responsibilities of being an employer. This status as employer of record, however, only emerged with significant lobbying and legislative intervention. When temporary help firms first began to emerge in the 1940s, they were treated, legally, like employment agencies, collecting a one-time fee as compensation for the placement of a worker as a regular employee with another firm. In that scenario, a standard employer–employee relationship was established between the worker and the firm with which he or she is placed, and the agency stepped out of the picture. Temporary help firms, on the other hand, wanted to maintain a formal tie to the worker, as the "employer," whether the stint of employment with a particular client firm lasted a few hours, a week, or several months or years. In this way, they would provide an additional service to their clients while also profiting from the arrangement every hour that work is being performed. Their clients preferred this arrangement since they were able to utilize labor while avoiding many of the specific social, legal, and contractual obligations that are attached to employer status.

To attain this employer status, however, temporary help firms had to avoid the heavy regulation that employment agencies faced. Their goal was to pass legislation recognizing their industry as a new type of business in which they could be recognized as the employer of record. A sustained campaign in the late 1950s and 1960s at a state level allowed in many cases for temporary help firms to be exempted from regulations pertaining to employment agencies in most states. Between 1958 and 1971, all but two states (NJ and Missouri) made accommodations of one kind or another, usually through brief amendments to existing regulations exempting temporary help firms from employment agency regulations and allowing them to become the employer of record (Gonos 1997). While this arrangement has come to be seen as "natural," in fact the designation of employer status is heavily contested, and could be based on a variety of different factors (US Department of Labor 1994).

Consultant brokerage firms have also had their own set of issues related to their status as employer of record. In their case, the issues relate primarily to their liability in cases where the contractors they place are allowed to be classified as self-employed people (referred to as "1099s" after the Internal Revenue Service (IRS) form employers submit for self-employed people) as opposed to being regular employees ("W-2s"). Regular W-2 employees have their payroll taxes withheld by their employer, who acts as an agent in collecting taxes owed to the IRS and state tax authorities. Employers who do not pay these taxes are easily caught, and are subject to enormous fines and penalties. In the case of self-employed individuals, however, there is no intermediary to act as an agent. Therefore, the tax authorities must rely on the honesty of the individuals to pay their applicable taxes. The IRS is convinced that independent contractors (specifically information technology contractors) are not paying their fair share of taxes, and over time has mounted a series of efforts to recover these funds.

The Internal Revenue Code itself does not provide any clear definition or rule dealing with the issue of whether a person should be characterized for tax purposes as an employee or an independent contractor. In the absence of a statutory definition, the IRS has used the "common law" test for determining the tax status of workers. This common law test is based on a number of different factors ranging from the skill required in the particular occupation to the level of control exercised by the individual in their work. In short, it requires a significant degree of knowledge of the particular person and work situation to determine employee status under the common law, creating significant administrative work in reviewing individual cases. Thus, for administrative convenience, the IRS has generally viewed independent contractor status with hostility.

In the 1970s many independent contractors complained about being targeted for IRS audits and in response Congress passed what became known as the "safe harbor" provision, Section 530 of the Revenue Act of 1978. This allowed certain types of people to continue to be classified as independent contractors for tax purposes, even if they were classified as employees under common law provisions. This was changed, however, by Section 1706 of the Tax Reform Act of 1986, which prohibited access to this "safe harbor" provision for individuals who provide services as an "engineer, designer, draftsperson, computer programmer, systems analyst, or similar skilled worker." In essence, Section 1706 was explicitly designed to restrict the use of contractors in the high-tech industry, and it was particularly aimed at consultant brokers who act as third parties, though it is also applied to two-party relationships as well (Bird, Segal, and Yaeger 1991; Steele 1999).

The consultant brokerage industry has been heavily opposed to Section 1706 and other efforts to limit the use of independent contractors, and continues to call for the repeal of this provision. Ironically, however, the IRS crackdown on independent contractors has in fact increased brokers' business in many ways. Many client firms who in the past might have hired independent contractors directly are now requiring the contractors to go through brokers. This has also been one of the by-products of the widely known *Vizcaino* v. *Microsoft* legal case, in which a group of long-term contractors with Microsoft sued the firm for access to Microsoft's generous benefits package, including access to stock options. The court's decision in favor of the contractors resulted in Microsoft implementing a policy to make the distinction between permanent employees and contract employees even more clear, rather than reducing the number of contractors.[10]

Ultimately the complexity of employment regulation and concerns for liability have pushed employers to increasingly use professional employer organizations. While this trend is still relatively small in Silicon Valley, it is growing, and thus is worth reviewing briefly.

Professional Employer Organizations

The role of legal employer acting as intermediary has given rise to particular firms that only provide the services of being the employer,

---

10   De Haas (1998); Hoguet (1997); Short (1998).

without providing any additional recruiting assistance. This industry has come to be known as the professional employer organization industry. According to the National Association of Professional Employer Organizations (NAPEO), the number of employees under PEO arrangements in the United States has grown from approximately 10,000 in 1984 to between 2 and 3 million in 1998, rivaling the temporary help industry in size.[11] Staffing Industry Analysts, Inc., an employment industry research firm, estimates that gross revenues in the PEO industry grew from $5.0 billion in 1991 to $21.6 billion in 1997, representing a compounded annual growth rate of approximately 28 percent (Staff Leasing Inc., 1999).

The PEO industry grew out of the employee leasing industry, which emerged in the 1970s as a response to legislation requiring all employees to receive the same benefits package. Through using leased employees, employers could provide poorer benefits and pension programs to their leased employees while maintaining generous pension programs for management and key employees. Though this provision disappeared with the 1982 passage of the Tax Equity and Fiscal Responsibility Act, the trend it established toward employee leasing has continued. Over time, leasing companies have extended their services to encompass the entire human resources arena, and have established the PEO industry (Katz 1999).

PEOs differ from temporary help agencies in two fundamental ways. First, there is no either assumed or explicit time-frame limitation on people employed through a PEO. Second, contracts with PEOs are usually negotiated in such a way that the clients remain "joint employers" under legal statutes, whereas with most staffing services for shorter-term placements or contract placements the agency remains the sole legal employer while clients avoid any administrative tasks that might confuse this distinction (Barnaba 1999).

PEOs provide an integrated and, in principal, cost-effective approach to the management and administration of human resources for their clients. They do so by contractually assuming substantial employer rights, responsibilities, and risk through the establishment and maintenance of an employer relationship with the workers assigned to its clients. PEOs are increasingly trying to market their services to small and medium-sized businesses. PEOs offer to their clients and work site employees the services and expertise of a personnel department within a large corpo-

---

11   http://www.napeo.org

ration. Few, if any, small businesses can afford a full-time human re-sources staff consisting of, for example, an accountant, a human resource professional, a lawyer, a risk manager, a benefits manager, and a manager of information services. Professional employer organizations offer this expertise to their clients. In principle, by providing these services, professional employer organizations enable their clients to concentrate on their business without the challenges and distractions associated with the "business of employment." Further, costs related to monitoring of, and compliance with, employment laws are reduced, as are the often significant costs of failure to comply with such laws.

While the origins of the PEO industry lie in efforts to reduce benefits for leased employees, the industry is now trying to market its services as a potential benefit to workers. PEOs argue that they can develop economies of scale by pooling the employees of a larger number of smaller firms and thus provide more and higher-quality benefits than the employees of individual small firms would be able to access. Each individual small business's cost of establishing and administering a range of benefit plans would be prohibitive, but PEOs can sponsor and offer these plans at a more affordable cost. In addition, the NAPEO argues that in many cases employees of small businesses would not be protected by employment laws in the absence of the PEO relationship. Because work-site employees are included in the larger workforce of a PEO for purposes of determining statutory coverage, they are in many cases covered by employment laws that don't apply to employers under a certain size, typically less than fifty employees. NAPEO argues that there is a higher rate of compliance with these laws by PEOs than by their clients because PEOs provide full-time staff who are responsible for monitoring and ensuring compliance with such laws.

While the effect of PEOs on the benefits and employment conditions of workers in Silicon Valley remains unclear, it is clear that PEOs have been growing significantly in recent years and are poised to grow much more rapidly. One sign of this is that one of the fastest-growing staffing services firms in the region is a firm that now primarily markets itself as a PEO, despite origins in the temporary help industry. The combination of services seems to be a major attraction to clients:

- Barrett Business Services – is a human resource management firm, providing a broad array of professional employment organization services. It was founded in the 1950s as a temporary help agency, but began providing PEO services in the 1990s, and now markets itself primarily as a PEO or comprehensive human resource management firm. The company operates through a network of 30 branch offices in Oregon, California, Washington, Maryland, Idaho, and Arizona. The majority of their staffing services revenue (67 percent) comes from light industrial work, with another 19 percent from technical services. They had approximately 20,000 staffing employees as of the end of 1998, with three offices in Silicon Valley (Barrett Business Services 1999).

• Another prominent PEO in the region is Trinet VCO, based in San Leandro. This company caters to venture start-up firms, specializing in high-quality benefits packages and HR management services for small and medium firms in rapidly changing and growing hightech industries. In 1998 they serviced more than 8,000 employees in eight major technology markets around the US. The company was founded in 1988, and by 1998 had grown to have over $20 million in revenues. Between 1992 and 1998 their revenue grew at a 75 percent annual compound rate. In 1999, they were listed for the fifth consecutive year on *Inc.* Magazine's list of the 500 most rapidly growing privately held firms in the country. Only 2 percent of Inc. 500 companies sustain the growth required to be listed for five consecutive years.

Thus, while still small in number in Silicon Valley, PEOs seem to be growing rapidly and are likely to become an increasingly important part of the way labor markets are structured in the area.

Conclusion: The Labor Market as Business Opportunity

The expansion of this diverse set of private sector intermediaries indicates that there is a wide range of business opportunities in the functioning of the labor market itself. The firms described above mediate between workers and employers in the process of job matching and brokering employment relationships. The revenue in all of these business models comes from the demand side of the labor market, from employers who are willing to pay for the services these intermediaries provide. These intermediaries are therefore primarily oriented toward meeting the needs of employers rather than meeting the needs of workers. Nonetheless, the business models would not be viable unless workers were willing to use these intermediaries as well. Clearly, in some cases workers feel pushed into using these intermediaries because they lack significant alternatives. Evidence on the use of temporary agencies, for instance, has demonstrated that the majority of temporary workers would prefer permanent employment but are unable to find it. The rapid growth in temporary employment is primarily driven by employers restructuring their hiring practices rather than an increase in workers' desire for temporary employment (Golden and Appelbaum 1992). Nonetheless, workers' use of intermediaries is not driven just by a lack of other alternatives. In many cases, private sector intermediaries provide services to workers that they find valuable, either by reducing the time and difficulties in searching for a new job or because they prefer the employment conditions they receive through these intermediaries (as in the case of contractors). Ultimately, in an environment where the rapid change in work requirements and employment conditions is unlikely to slow down, the opportunities for viable intermediary business models is likely to continue to expand.

5

Labor Market Intermediaries – Membership-based

There's a great deal of practical experience that is required to be a senior System Administrator – not just being trained. You have to understand the idiosyncratic way that computers behave in the wild.

Hal Polmeranz,
Board Member
System Administrators' Guild (SAGE)

Capital doesn't have a monopoly on entrepreneurialism and innovation. We intend to show that labor has that potential also.

Amy Dean
Business Manager and Chief Executive Officer
South Bay AFL-CIO Labor Council

The second broad category of labor market intermediaries are those whose organizational base is rooted in the membership of individual employees. This category includes professional associations, guilds and guild-like associations and various union initiatives. These organizations have become increasingly important in shaping the labor market experiences of workers in Silicon Valley in recent years. These organizations' activities, ranging from creating job listings and organizing networking opportunities to providing skills training and building learning communities, involve actively engaging as intermediaries in the labor market. Their strategies help build ties between workers and employers, and shape the nature of that relationship in ways that aim to improve the labor market outcomes of their members. Membership-based intermediaries are rooted in particular occupations. The skills, knowledge base, work practices and labor market experiences associated with each occupation provide organizational coherence and shape the structure and activities of the association. Many of the occupations in Silicon Valley face rapidly changing skill requirements and high levels of volatility in employment conditions. In response, these membership associations have arisen as a means to provide improved career opportunities for their members.

Membership-based associations have certain characteristics that make them distinct from private sector and public sector intermediaries. First, since they are rooted in employee membership, they are oriented toward the supply side of the labor market – advocating for the needs of their membership and generating greater opportunities for workers in the labor market. Second, since they are rooted in a particular occupation, they have a detailed and nuanced understanding of both the formal and informal skills required to perform the work in that occupation. Those intermediaries that are able to combine this understanding with effective means of identifying and anticipating changes in the industry can be very effective in providing ongoing skills development opportunities for their membership. Third, their relationship with employers is generally weak, particularly when compared with many of the private sector intermediaries. The strength of the ties with employers varies significantly, however, depending on the particular organization or association. Finally, most of these organizations operate on minimal budgets. They have not generated the revenue streams that private sector nonprofit organizations have and they do not receive significant public sector funds. Their resources are generated from member dues, some fees for services, and lots of volunteer labor. This limits the scope of what might otherwise be an even more significant impact on labor market outcomes.

Membership-based intermediaries in Silicon Valley can be thought of as existing on a continuum, based on the extent to which they actively advocate for their members in the labor market. At one end of the spectrum are professional associations that act primarily as an information intermediary, providing networking opportunities and linkages between employers and workers in particular occupations, and helping provide guidance on changes in skill requirements and industry trends. In the middle are a range of professional associations and guild-type unions that also provide information to help their members advocate for themselves individually in the labor market. These associations may provide training in individual negotiating strategies, and detailed salary information based on surveys of the profession, and ultimately try to empower workers through strengthening their information, knowledge, and skills in negotiating. At the other side of the continuum are organizations that play an active, direct role in advocating for their members. This may take the form of collective bargaining in a multiemployer relationship, as in the case of unions in the construction industry. It may also take the form of advocating for legislation, codes of conduct, or developing corporate campaigns. Whatever the particular strategy, the goal for these organizations is to improve conditions of employment for their members explicitly by altering the conditions of employment of firms, not on an individual, but on a collective basis (Bernhardt et al. 2001b).

This chapter analyzes the activities of these membership-based intermediaries in Silicon Valley. The first section provides a general discussion about the increasingly blurred boundaries between professional associations and new forms of unionism, providing a context for examining specific intermediaries in Silicon Valley. The subsequent section consists of case studies of particular membership-based intermediaries in Silicon Valley, in each case describing the history of the organization and the services they now provide. The specific organizations that are examined include: five professional associations (the System Administrators Guild, the HTML Writers' Guild, the Silicon Valley Web Guild, Silicon Valley Webgrrls, and the Society for Technical Communication); and four union initiatives (the National Writers' Union effort to organize technical writers, the Graphic Artists Guild, the United Association of Plumbers, and the efforts of the South Bay AFL-CIO Labor Council to organize temporary clerical workers). Since each of these organizations is rooted in a particular occupation, in each case the conditions of work and employment in the particular occupation are discussed.

Blurring Boundaries

Historically, professional associations and unions have represented significantly different portions of the workforce, and pursued different organizational strategies for improving the livelihoods of their members. Professional associations originated in highly skilled occupations, and defended their members' status through the creation of monopolistic practitioners groups with restrictive criteria for membership – criteria that was sometimes just self-regulated but often backed up through state regulation. Unions, in contrast, were focused on blue-collar and other working-class occupations, and defended their members' status through organizing and instituting collective bargaining arrangements with employers. With the changing occupational structure of the workforce and shifting work and employment patterns, however, these differences have narrowed in recent decades. Workers in a much wider range of occupations have created professional associations, while unions have increasingly organized in white-collar and professional occupations. Professional associations have increasingly taken on more advocacy functions and addressed employment conditions, while many union initiatives are recognizing value in collective associations even in the absence of any goal of a collective bargaining arrangement with employers.

Professional Associations

Traditional professional associations arose in a series of occupations – physicians, lawyers, engineers, administrators and executives – that are widely recognized as having certain characteristics that distinguish them from other occupational categories, including:

- a claim to represent, to have a level of mastery over, and to practice a particular discipline, skill, vocation or "calling";
- advanced learning, usually represented by higher education qualifications, showing an ability to learn and amass knowledge;
- high-level intellectual skills, showing an ability to grasp new events quickly and to respond effectively;
- independence and discretion within the working context, showing allegiance to an ethical framework and often to specific codes of practice which govern relationships between the profession, the professional, his/her clients, and the wider society. (Middlehurst and Kennie 1997)

Even in classic professions, however, these occupations did not attain professional status without a struggle. Instead, the social status and financial rewards that professionals enjoy were obtained through long periods of collective mobilization and the exercise of political power (Larson 1977). The current status of these occupations continues to be shaped by a complex interplay of market dynamics and political struggles. This status is heavily contested, both within particular professions and between competing occupations in the labor market (Derber 1982; Derber, Schwartz, and Magrass 1990). Recent unionization efforts by members of the medical profession, concerned about threats to their independence and professional status, highlight the fact that there is no linear movement toward increased professionalization, and that occupational status depends critically on changing power dynamics in the labor market (Riccardi 1999; Yellin 1999).

In occupations that lack the status of engineers, lawyers, or doctors, such as many technical or craft occupations, the struggle for improved social status and financials rewards is both more difficult to achieve and less stable once attained. Yet membership in associations in these "semiprofessions" remains both an individual strategy for people to improve their career opportunities and a collective strategy to improve the status of the occupation as a whole.

There is a range of factors that shape the extent to which different professional and technical occupations are able to gain improved social status, including: the nature of the knowledge and skills required to perform the work; the system for entering and practicing in the occupation (certification and licensing); and the nature of employment relations in the occupation. Though part of the social status of people in traditional professions is linked to the specialized knowledge they have, how access to that knowledge is socially organized is also critical. The truly high-status occupations are those which are able to organize themselves to limit the supply of skills and knowledge. Doctors, for example, monopolize not only their practice of medicine, but their licenses and the sale of medical drugs by legal prescriptions. If medical knowledge were not so strongly monopolized, the prestige and rewards of doctors would be much less. Thus, the formation of a monopolistic practitioner group has historically been a central component of occupations gaining professional status. These groups are able to determine the nature of knowledge required for the occupation, formally certify those who are fit to practice, and limit practice to those who have been appropriately certified.

In semiprofessions, however, it is much harder to create a truly monopolistic practitioner group and thus more difficult to raise the status of members of the occupation through this strategy. As a result, professional associations in these occupations tend to be more decentralized and democratic, placing less emphasis on the certification of their members and more emphasis on actively intervening in the labor market on behalf of their members (Collins 1990). This trend is particularly visible in the professional associations formed by mid-level workers in information technology industries who face a particular set of issues in trying to mobilize to maintain or improve their economic and social status. Their capacity to cope with rapidly changing technology and to deal with uncertainty is a crucial part of their power in the labor market. This kind of power, however, is less tangible than institutional bases in truly self-regulating professions. Information technology workers derive considerable status from being associated with cutting-edge technological and economic change, but at the same time they are constantly being market tested for the relevance of their skills and the organizational problems they claim to be able to solve (Fincham 1996). Creating a monopolistic practitioner group in this context is nearly impossible. Ultimately, the ability of mid-level workers in information technology industries to attain and retain their high status in the labor market requires dealing with rapid change. It requires the ability to stay on top of industry trends and changing skill demands, to find access to multiple employment opportunities when needed, and to build career mobility over time across multiple organizational contexts. Workers in these occupations solve these problems of maintaining the market relevance of their skills by taking advantage of networks of information exchange in communities of workers who share similar types of expertise. Groups of users become resources for each other in maintaining knowledge about skills that are in demand.

Workers in these occupations have organized associations to help formalize and strengthen this process of informal information sharing. These associations rarely focus on licensing or certifying members or otherwise restricting access to the occupation. Instead, they focus on networking, providing various services to their members, and helping their membership anticipate and capitalize on changing industry trends. To do this requires building closer ties with employers than traditional professional associations (in which members are often self-employed) and frequently providing placement services for their members. These associations recognize that their members are by and large in employment situations where they are being paid by an employer, rather than being self-employed. They thus also have various activities and services aimed at strengthening their members' ability to negotiate a strong contract for themselves. In essence they more actively play an intermediary role in the labor market than do traditional professional associations.

It is important to note that this activity is increasingly focused on a regional, rather than a national or state, level. Organizing regular monthly meetings, social events, and other opportunities for face-to-face interaction is a crucial part of building regular, active participation in professional associations. This helps build the "weak ties" that are so crucial in job-access and career paths (Granovetter 1973). Many of these professional associations exist only at a local level, while others have strong local chapters networked in a national and even international structure.

Changing Union Structures and Strategies

While professional associations have moved toward taking a greater role as intermediaries in the labor market, so have unions. Unions obviously have a long history in this country, but the dominant form of unionism has changed and their relative strength has ebbed and flowed over time. Prior to the 1930s, craft unions and less formal, community-based unions played the greatest role in representing workers' interests. Craft-based unions in many occupations were able to set standards of fair rates that their members individually demanded from their employers. Community-based unions, such as the Knights of Labor and the Industrial Workers of the World (IWW), had a broad social-movement character, building on community solidarity to defend workers' interests across a broad spectrum of industries (Montgomery 1987; Craver 1993). Since the 1930s, however, industrial unionism has become the dominant form of unionism in this country. This model emerged out of the organizing strategies of the Congress of Industrial Organizations (CIO) in the 1920s and 1930s, and became embodied in labor legislation with the 1935 Wagner Act. Organizing in the core of the growing mass production enterprises, workers in the CIO argued the importance of representation on an industry-wide basis, with collective bargaining carried out between company leaders and leaders of appropriate unions. At the core of this strategy is an assumption of long-term stable employment with a single employer who largely controls the conditions of employment. Workers and their unions agreed in practice to negotiate primarily over issues of compensation and work practices, leaving to company management the larger, more strategic issues of corporate investment, technological development, and other issues of competitive concern in the market.

Collective bargaining in this model, especially as it became entrenched into labor law, is based on individual work sites or with single employers. This structure of representation worked fairly well in large manufacturing industries, where a majority of workers were organized. Pattern bargaining among unionized firms, along with efforts of non-union firms to match union compensation packages (partly in order to avoid unionization), meant that in practice workers were often represented similarly across whole industries. Stable markets in mass-production enterprises, and the well-developed internal labor markets that existed in many firms, provided a solid support for union structures.

In the current economy, with high levels of volatility, uncertainty, complex networking, and outsourced production arrangements, representation that is based on a single worksite or single employer is highly inadequate for defending workers' interests. For workers who move frequently from employer to employer, or whose working conditions are not primarily determined by a single employer (such as temporary workers, and many workers in subcontracting relationships), there are few opportunities in the current industrial relations system for adequate representation.

In response, unions have been experimenting with a range of innovations that extend beyond bargaining over wages and working conditions in a single enterprise, to becoming involved in issues of labor supply, labor quality, placement, and career advancement. The initiatives include alliances with employers and community groups, as well as other unions. They can focus on strengthening internal career ladders, as well as on creating new external career ladders within an industry and across industries and expanding labor involvement in job matching as well as the design and delivery of training. Prominent examples include the following:[1]

- The Wisconsin Regional Training Partnership (WTRP) was founded in 1992 and includes more than forty mostly unionized firms employing about 60,000 workers in the Milwaukee areas. The partnership includes several industrial unions, including the Machinists, Steelworkers, Auto Workers, and Electrical Workers. The major focus is on training and performance improvement, including basic skills, process or problem-solving skills, and job-related technical skills. WTRP also provides employment-linked training for dislocated workers, and offers youth apprenticeships for high school students (Herzenberg, Alic and Wial 1998; Parker and Rogers 1995).
- The San Francisco Hotels Partnerships was started in 1993, and includes San Francisco hotels and union locals affiliated to the Hotel Employees and Restaurant Employees Union and the Service Employees International Union. Training efforts have focused on improving process systems, such as methods for doormen handling

---

1   AFL-CIO Working for America Institute (2000).

baggage for large tour groups, and improved individual skills. Training in English as a second language for housekeeping staff is seen both as a means for improving customer service as well as providing opportunities for individuals to move into better-paying, front-office, customer-interaction positions (Dresser and Rogers 1997; Herzenberg, Alic, and Wial 1998).

- The Garment Industry Development Corporation (GIDC) is a nonprofit public–private partnership in New York City that was founded in 1984 with the cooperation of the International Ladies' Garment Workers' Union (ILGWU). It provides a combination of technical assistance to firms and skills training to workers in an effort to simultaneously upgrade the New York garment industry and to create improved working conditions for garment workers in the area. (http://www.gidc.org)

These initiatives create intermediaries between workers and employers that deal with a whole range of work and employment related issues. In many ways these initiatives are similar to the structure of unions in construction trades, where hiring halls and apprenticeship training programs have been common for many years. In industries where "project-based" employment is the norm, such as in the television and movie production industry, an active intermediary role for unions is accepted practice (Gray and Seeber 1996). The fact that these initiatives are emerging in other industries, however, indicates the growing recognition among unions that standard industrial-model unionism is no longer adequate for addressing the labor market concerns of a wide range of the American workforce. The result is a growing role of unions as intermediaries in the labor market (Wolf-Powers 1999).

Silicon Valley Membership-based Intermediaries

The increasing convergence of professional associations and unions can be readily seen in the activities of membership-based intermediaries in Silicon Valley. Professional associations have a high level of visibility in the region's information technology industries. There are dozens, if not hundreds, of professional associations and similar users groups that make up the dense network of occupational relations in Silicon Valley (see table 5.1).

While professional associations have been prominent in the Valley, unions have been much less visible. Unions have a strong presence in

Table 5.1 Partial list of professional associations active in Silicon Valley

Association	Mission statement/Brief description	Year founded	Membership
American Marketers Association – Silicon Valley chapter (www.svama.org)	Sponsors meetings, workshops, and seminars where members meet and exchange ideas with leading innovators and thinkers in business, research, and academia. Also provides a forum to expand personal and professional contacts by networking with Silicon Valley marketing professionals	1980	400
Association for Computing Machinery – Bay Area chapter (www.sfbayacm.org)	Local chapter of one of the oldest educational and scientific computing societies. Hosts monthly meetings and networking opportunities	1947	80,000 national
Association for Information Technology Professionals (www.aitp.org)	National association that began in the 1950s with machine accountants in Chicago. Evolved into the AITP in 1996. Has local chapters around the country, including San Jose.	1996 (with roots to 1951)	
Association for Women in Computing – Bay Area chapter (www.linkville.com/awcmeet.html)	Dedicated to the advancement of women in the computing fields. Local chapter hosts monthly meetings, produces a newsletter, provides job listings, and hosts job fairs and professional conferences	1978	
Bay Area Association of Database Developers (www.baadd.org)	Promotes career potential of database developers through meetings, seminars, communication, publications, and other program activities	1985	100
Bay Chi (computer and human interaction) (www.baychi.org)	BayCHI is the San Francisco Bay Area chapter of the ACM Special Interest Group on Computer–Human Interaction (SIGCHI). They host their meetings at Xerox PARC		
BayLISA (www.baylisa.org)	The Bay Area Large Installation Systems Administration Users Group provides monthly meetings for members to stay up on changes in the industry, to network and improve their career opportunities. It is the local chapter of SAGE	1991	~150

Association	Mission statement/Brief description	Year founded	Membership
Black Data Processing Association – Bay Area chapter (www.bdpabac.org)	Local chapter founded in 1990. Focus on increasing opportunities for African American professionals in information technology industries. Monthly meetings in Oakland and Cupertino. Also sponsors high-school internship program.	1990	
Chinese Institute of Engineers (CIE/USA) (ww.cie-sf.org)	Promotes communication and interchange of information among Chinese engineers and scientists	1979	1,000
Chinese Software Professionals Association (www.cpsa.com)	Promotes technology collaboration and facilitates information exchange in the software profession	1988	1,400
Graphic Artists Guild of Northern California (www.gag.org/sanfran)	Promotes the economic interests of member artists. Committed to improving conditions for all creators of graphic art and raising standards for the entire industry	1995	3,000 (national)
Help Desk Institute – Silicon Valley chapter (www.svhdi.com)	Formed to provide training, educational materials, and a networking forum for Help Desk/Support Center professionals		
HTML Writers Guild (www.hwg.org)	World's largest international organization of Web authors with over 98,000 members in more than 130 nations worldwide. The HWG assists members in developing their skills, and compiles information about standards, practices, techniques, competency, and ethics as applied to web authoring		
Internation Association of Business Communicators – Silicon Valley chapter (www.gryphon-communications.com/sv-iabc/)	Offers a range of programs for career development and technical advancement, including monthly meetings, professional development services, job listings		260 local, 13,700 worldwide

Organization	Description	Year founded	Members
International Webmasters Association – Silicon Valley chapter (www.iwa-siliconvalley.org)	Brings together people who are involved in all disciplines of Webmastering, at the local and regional levels. Provides professional development and educational resources	1998 (SV Chapter)	12,000 (inter-national)
Monte Jade Science and Technology Association (MJSTA) (www.montejade.org)	Promotes the cooperation and mutual flow of technology and investment between Taiwan and the United States	1989	150 corp., 300 individuals (West Coast)
Network Professionals Association – Silicon Valley chapter (www.svnpa.org)	For networking professionals who design, implement, and maintain computer networks. They work to advance the network computing profession by educating and providing resources for its members	1990	7,000 (National)
Professional & Technical Consultants Association (www.patca.org)	Professional association of independent consultants and principals who work in small consulting firms. Based in Silicon Valley	1975	400
Silicon Valley Association of Software Entrepreneurs (www.svase.org)	Facilitates the creation of new computer software business ventures, improves the financial performance of existing ventures, and promotes and supports the commercialization of computer software technologies		
Silicon Valley Chinese Engineers Association (SCEA) (www.scea.org)	Network of Mainland Chinese engineers to promote entrepreneurship and professionalism among members and establish ties with China	1989	400
Silicon Valley Indian Professionals Association (SIPA) (www.sipa.org)	Forum for expatriate Indians to contribute to cooperation between United States and India	1991	1000

Association	Mission statement/Brief description	Year founded	Membership
Silicon Valley Linux Users Groups (www.svlug.org)	A users group that started as part of the Silicon Valley Computer Society. Promotes networking and information sharing related to LINUX, and free or low-cost implementations of UNIX	1988	
Silicon Valley Web Guild (www.webguild.org)	Dedicated to the education and professional development of the San Francisco Bay Area Webmaster community	1995	900
Silicon Valley Webgrrls (www.svwebgrrls.com)	Face-to-face networking group that provides support, information, and resources for women in new media	1996	1000
Society for Technical Communication (stc.org/region8/svc/www/)	An individual membership organization dedicated to advancing the arts and sciences of technical communication	1971 (with earlier roots)	2,000 local, 22,000 national
System Administrators Guild (www.usenix.org/sage)	Aims to advance the status of computer system administration as a profession, establishing standards of professional excellence, developing guidelines for improving the technical and managerial capabilities of members of the profession, and promoting activities that advance the state of the art or the community	1992	~5000 (national)
The Indus Entrepreneur (TiE) (www.tie.org)	Fosters entrepreneurship by providing mentorship and resources.	1992	560

(*Sources*: Saxenian (1999), interviews, http://ittalent.com/assocs.htm)

the public sector (Johnston 1994) and in many traditional industries (hotels, transportation, defense, food) but they have had little direct representation in information technology industries. Efforts to organize unions in high-tech industries that have been based on an industrial model of unionism have almost universally failed. The rapid changes in the workforce, and complex network production relations, have made it nearly impossible for traditional organizing strategies to be effective in the industry (Benner 1998).[2] Some nontraditional organizing efforts, including the Service Employees International Union's prominent "Justice for Janitors" campaign in the early 1990s, have been successful in organizing contract service workers in the industrial agglomeration (Corporate Watch 1997; Kadetsky 1993). By and large, however, there is little union representation in the information technology sector. Nonetheless, several small efforts that are organized on an intermediary model have grown and are proving successful in improving their members' employment opportunities while becoming valued intermediaries in the labor market.

The following sections examine the particular activities in these areas of a number of professional associations and union initiatives. In each case, the discussion is organized first around a description of work and employment conditions in the occupation, followed by a description of the organization itself. This in turn is followed by a discussion of the organization's activities in three areas: employment brokering; training and skills developments; and their impact on employment conditions. The case studies include five professional associations, in three different occupations, and four union initiatives. These particular organizations were chosen to reflect a range of skill and pay levels, and include a variety of organizational strategies. Table 5.2 provides a schematic of the particular occupations and organizations that are described in the following sections.

In analyzing in detail the origins and activities of these various associations, I am not simply trying to present detailed case studies. Instead, through these descriptions I hope to convey two central points. First, that despite the wide range of activities and histories, all of these membership associations play an important role in shaping labor market practices and outcomes for their members. This makes them both important as labor market intermediaries, and makes them distinct from

2 Other factors that have made organizing difficult include an ethnically diverse workforce, male-dominated unions not taking into account gender concerns, and lack of commitment of adequate resources and personnel to organizing.

Table 5.2   Membership-based intermediaries examined in following sections

Occupation	Organizations
Professional associations	
System administration	System Administrators Guild
Web design/HTML/coding	HTML Writers Guild
	Silicon Valley Web Guild
	Silicon Valley Webgrrls
Technical writers	Society for Technical Communication
Union initiatives	
Technical writers	Technical Writers' Trade Group of the National Writers Union
Graphic artists	Graphic Artists Guild
Plumbers	United Association/Pipe Trades Training Center
Temporary clerical workers	South Bay AFL-CIO Labor Council

private sector and public sector intermediaries. Second, that the character of their structure and activities is primarily shaped by being rooted in an occupational community. This occupational community provides important organizational strengths and contributes to their effectiveness in the labor market, but also means their potential is limited in occupations that lack a coherent community.

Case Study 1: System Administrators

Systems or network administration is a complex occupation requiring a variety of skills. The best systems administrators engage in a wide range of activities: they wire and repair cables, install new software, repair bugs, train users, offer tips for increased productivity across areas from word processing to CAD tools, evaluate new hardware and software, automate a myriad mundane tasks, and increase work flow at their site. In general, systems administrators enable people to exploit computers at a level which improves their individual productivity and gains leverage for the entire organization.

The work is thus highly skilled, and requires constant learning in a range of hardware and software issues. Systems administration draws on knowledge from many fields and has only recently begun to be taught at a few institutions of higher learning.[3] Without formal training programs, most current systems administrators come from a wide range of backgrounds. Most have college degrees of one sort or another and often their experience is in other technical, math, or statistics related fields. Many people fall into the occupation by chance, having worked on computer systems in college, or having learned computers as a sideline while pursuing other interests. Other people come to the occupation "up through the ranks," having worked as lower level operators working on tape drives, or computer back-up systems, or other technical work, and slowly advancing their skills to other areas. There is a lot that can't be taught in formal courses that is passed on through "oral tradition" and experience. Many of the skills can only be learned on-the-job and systems administrators often develop those skills through "apprenticing" themselves informally to a more experienced mentor.

The lack of specific training in system administration, and the extent of informal apprenticeship training, often make it hard for employers and hiring managers to accurately assess the skills of applicants. Thus, like in many information technology occupations, reputation and social networks make a huge difference in hiring practices. Employers (and vendors) have increasingly pushed for certification of skills as a way of developing more obvious indicators of applicants' skills. The substance and structure of such credentials, however, has now become an area of conflict and discussion in the occupation.

The demand for systems administrators is growing rapidly, along with the dramatic increase in the number and size of distributed networks of computers and workstations in recent years. Understanding of the profession of systems administration on the part of employers, however, has not kept pace with the growth in the number of systems administrators or with the growth in complexity of system administration tasks. Both at work sites with a long history of using computing resources and at work sites into which computers have only recently been introduced, systems administrators face perception problems that present serious obstacles to their successfully carrying out their duties. Thus, one of the key challenges systems administrators face is in communicating their work practices to employers, as well as other employees they must interact with.

3   Certification programs for system administrators have now been developed at a few institutions in the Bay Area, including De Anza College and University of California Berkeley.

Background of SAGE

The System Administrators Guild (SAGE) has its origins in a large trade association called USENIX. USENIX is the Advanced Computing Systems Association, founded in 1975 to bring together engineers, scientists, technicians, and systems administrators who "are at the cutting edge of the computing world." USENIX sponsors numerous national conferences a year on various topics related to information technology development, one of which is large installation[4] systems administration (LISA). These LISA conferences began in 1986, and have been held every year since, and currently draw over 2,000 people.

During the 1991 LISA conference, a group of system administrators from the Bay Area decided to form an organization devoted exclusively to systems administrators, which came to be known as BayLISA. They formed this users group because they were looking for a forum for networking on a regular basis to help them stay up on technical issues, and to provide each other with moral and practical support:

> BayLISA came together partially as a support group. It was important in helping us all to understand what we were going through. It was really frustrating for people at that time how little systems administration was appreciated. You could be working for a company doing absolutely critical work, and the manager still wouldn't understand what you're doing or what the value of your work is. BayLISA was a support group of people who could remind you that no, you're not insane. (Hal Polmeranz Interview)

The core of people who formed BayLISA also were critical in the formation the following year of the Systems Administrators Guild (SAGE) as a national organization with local chapters. SAGE was organized in order to advance the status of computer system administration as a profession overall. To achieve this goal, they work to establish standards of professional excellence and recognize those who attain them, develop guidelines for improving the technical and managerial capabilities of members of the profession, and promote activities that advance the state of the art in the community. SAGE was founded as a special interest group within USENIX, but over time SAGE has come to increasingly dominate USENIX functions as well, with SAGE members now making up over 50 percent of the total USENIX membership.[5] BayLISA is now the Bay Area chapter of SAGE.

---

4   Defined as larger than one hundred computers.

Employment Linking

BayLISA's monthly meetings provide an important venue for linking employers and employees. The monthly meetings remain the core of their linking activities. The meetings are always preceded by an organized social time, and then a formal open forum, prior to the presentation of the evening's topic. The open forum was originally reserved for technical issues, but it rapidly became clear that people were more interested in using it as an opportunity to announce job opportunities and for people to announce their availability for work. Recruiters regularly attend the meetings and use them as an opportunity to find prospective candidates and to build relationships with them.

Meetings are held at local company facilities, and companies are allowed to be sponsors. Of the ten local sponsors, at least five provide system administration consulting and outsourcing services, while most of the rest provide software or other products of interest to system administrators. Allowing corporate sponsorship and involvement in meetings creates for members a direct connection with employment opportunities while giving employers a connection to a pool of skilled system administrators.

Training and Skills Development

Like most professional associations in Silicon Valley, the core of BayLISA's involvement in training and skills development takes place through their monthly meetings. These meetings always include an outside speaker, talking about important new trends or topics in the area of systems administration. Examples of topics in 1999 included:

- security issues for LDAP (Lightweight Directory Access Protocol), a new software protocol for locating resources on a network;
- managing networks through mergers and acquisitions;
- challenges of training advanced system administrators in cross-operating systems and large installation techniques;
- Techniques for fighting SPAM and other email abuse.

In addition to the formal presentation, a great deal of informal

---

5 As of 7/1/99, total USENIX membership was 8,799, while 4,904 of this number were also part of SAGE (Polmeranz interview).

information sharing takes place in these meetings. People with problems or issues are able to find other people to share them with and to
talk about potential problems. Meetings tend to average about 60 people, but for particularly popular topics, they can reach a hundred and
fifty to two hundred.[6]

Impacting Employment Conditions

BayLISA's strategy to improve employment conditions for systems administrators is similar to the process followed by many more classic professional associations – develop self-monitored criteria for certifying
systems administrators and advocate to have those criteria adopted by
the industry at large. Certification includes an evaluation of skill requirements, testing methodologies, implementation logistics, and managing
a certification program. These efforts, however, are at a very early stage,
and it is unclear, given the pace of change in the industry, whether they
will have much success. The certification initiative, though emerging from
the BayLISA chapter, is organized at a national level, where SAGE has
been engaged in a long debate about the issues of developing appropriate certification systems. There already exist some certification programs
in the industry, primarily developed by companies, and SAGE is attempting to take a more proactive role in ensuring that its members' interests
are reflected in this process. Table 5.3 provides some examples of industry certification, along with SAGE commentary.

The goal of SAGE certification is to provide a program that is a product of the practitioners. Their hope is that through creating their own
certification program, they can do the following: provide employers,
who are not often knowledgeable about system administration, with
an objective standard of evaluation; provide system administrators
with a way of objectively evaluating their own skills; and provide a
basis for educational programs that is less expensive than a college degree but still provides some of the same advantages.[7]

6   Attendance and interest in BayLisa more generally has been declining in recent
years, which gives an indication of the difficulties of sustaining a professional association in the context of rapid change in the occupation. Systems administrators
in BayLISA have predominantly been focused on UNIX, and to a certain extent
Windows NT-based networks. In recent years, however, LINUX has become more
popular as a network system platform. A new association, the Silicon Valley Linux
Users Group (www.svlug.org), has emerged, whose monthly meetings typically
generate 300–500 people.
7   http://www.usenix.org/sage/cert/index.html

Table 5.3 System administrator certification programs

Certification	SAGE commentary
Microsoft Certified System Engineer	The target of much scorn, this program has evolved significantly over the years, and the current version is respected by even some SAGE members (who wish to remain anonymous)
Cisco Certification	Vendor specific but well regarded as challenging and meaningful
Sun Solaris Certified System Administration	Also vendor specific
Learning Tree System Administrator Certification	A vendor generic program which relies on courses, not testing

Source: Sage Certification Committee, in organizational newsletter. http://www.usenix.org/sage/cert/index.html

Case Study 2: Web Design/Internet Professionals

The occupation of web designers and other Internet professionals provides an interesting case in Silicon Valley for a number of reasons. First, it is a very new occupation, having only emerged as a prominent occupation since the development of the World Wide Web. Second, the occupation combines both technical knowledge and creative talent, which provides opportunities for people with a wide range of interests and skills. Specific Web jobs may emphasize either technical skills, such as integrating a Web page to a database, or creative skills, such as designing the user interface. Third, within information technology industries it is a relatively accessible occupation. The skills required in the occupation are such that it is possible to start out in the field with little more knowledge than the ability to be comfortable with a computer and to manipulate software. This is not to suggest that the occupation is unskilled – to advance in the field clearly requires a much greater knowledge of multiple software packages along with HTML programming, a demonstrated ability to constantly learn new techniques, and the ability to be focused and responsible in a hectic, deadline-driven environment. Entry-level positions, however, are available after a relatively short training period. Finally, because of the rapid growth in the World

Wide Web, the demand for Internet professionals has been extraordinarily high in the area.

There are three prominent professional associations of Web designers in the Valley, each with a significantly different background and
somewhat varying activities. One association, the HTML Writers' Guild,
is a completely virtual organization, with no local chapters and no regular face-to-face interaction. Another association, the Silicon Valley Web
Guild – the local chapter of the Association of Internet Professionals –
has very little Web interaction and depends primarily on its monthly
meetings for interaction among members. A third association, Silicon
Valley Webgrrls, combines both on-line and in-person interaction, depending a great deal on local meetings to develop networks among
members, but also using this to build a supportive on-line community.

Background

All three associations were founded during the period of rapid establishment and expansion of the World Wide Web after 1994. The first
association of Web workers to be formed was the HTML Writers Guild.
Despite having no local chapters, no regular conferences or regular
meetings,[8] it is probably the largest international organization of Web
authors, with over 123,000 members in more than 150 nations worldwide (as of April, 2001). The leadership of the guild is based in both
southern California and in Florida, but the largest portion of the membership is in Silicon Valley. The organization was started in late 1994
by a group of Web designers who had been communicating on one of
the Usenet news groups devoted to Web design. In 1994, working on
Web design as a living was a new concept – at best it had been thought
of as something systems administrators do in their spare time. They
thus founded the organization with the purpose of sharing information and knowledge, while increasing the visibility and prominence of
Web design as an occupation. The name "guild" was specifically chosen to imitate medieval guilds, reflecting the strength of sharing knowledge of a craft among a community of practitioners.

The HWG has grown so rapidly in part because there are almost no
barriers to entry into the guild. One-year trial memberships are free,

---

8 They have debated trying to set up local chapters, but don't want to compete
with the wide range of other organizations that have local chapters, including the
International Webmasters Association, the Association of Internet Professionals,
Webgrrls, and others.

and to retain membership requires simply receiving the minimum HWG correspondence: one general newsletter email a month. Full membership costs $40 a year, but in 1999 only 2,500 of the members were full members. Nonetheless, the HWG has developed a wide range of active email lists, with topics ranging from basic and advanced techniques of HTML, to business practices, standards, and ethics in the industry. There are only three part-time staff people who maintain the core functions of moderating the email lists, managing finances and membership lists, and building the organization. Their extensive Web page of resources is maintained largely by a group of volunteers.

A second association of Web workers, the Silicon Valley Web Guild, is the local chapter of the Association of Internet Professionals. Their first meeting was held in December 1996 at Netscape, as just a networking opportunity for Web masters. A hundred people attended the first meeting and the organization has grown since then to a membership of nine hundred people in 1999. The SV Web Guild, however, has a strong presence of employers within the organization itself – in fact it is almost a hybrid between a professional association and a business trade association. Their monthly meetings are held at different companies who cosponsor the meeting, providing food and meeting space for free. Companies view this as good public relations and a potential marketing tool, while also providing good links to a network of workers in high demand. Other vendors of Web-related products also participate in monthly meetings, paying $250 for a tabletop display space, or $750 for the opportunity to make a presentation to the whole group or to special interest groups.

Part of the reason for the greater corporate involvement in the Web Guild is its relationship to the national Association of Internet Professionals, of which Silicon Valley Web Guild is the local chapter. The AIP calls itself the premier professional association for those involved in the creation, maintenance, facilitation, or distribution of Internet-related content. Yet the AIP was not started by individual professionals but by a company whose rapid growth apparently was strongly linked to the adult entertainment industry.[9] AIP now has its headquarters in New

9   The company that was instrumental in founding the AIP is R. J. Gordon & Co., an electronic business services and e-commerce company based in Los Angeles. R. J. Gordon & Co. is principally known for its subsidiary creditcards.com, a processor of credit card transactions over telephone or the Internet. R. J. Gordon grew rapidly with the growth of the World Wide Web – it was named on the *Inc. Magazine* list of 500 fastest growing companies in the United State for five years in a row (1994–8). Its revenue jumped from under $5 million in 1994 to nearly $20 million in

York, has chapters all over the country, and acts much like an industry lobby organization. AIP sees its mission as providing benefits and programs that allow both its individual and corporate members to better compete in today's industry, serving as the voice of Internet professionals and industry corporations before the public, press, and within the on-line community on issues shaping the future of the Internet. There are currently over one hundred corporate members and some 12,000 individual members. Their individual membership reflects the elite character of the organization: 42 percent of their membership is senior management (defined as vice-president or above), with only 41 percent in technical/design positions that form the majority of the other associations' membership (another 10 percent are freelancers and another 7 percent are in other related sectors, such as marketing, sales, and business administration).

The third association, the Silicon Valley Webgrrls, is part of Webgrrls International, an organization that was founded in April 1995 in New York City. The national organization began relatively informally, with its founder, Aliza Sherman, and five other women meeting in a local cybercafé, to discuss their work in the Internet business. Their meetings grew rapidly and they soon founded Webgrrls International with the goal to provide a forum for women in or interested in new media and technology "to network, exchange job and business leads, form strategic alliances, mentor and teach, intern and learn the skills to help women succeed in an increasingly technical workplace and world".[10] There are more than one hundred chapters of Webgrrls, in at least 16 countries. Women are typically underrepresented in high-tech industries, and this is true of Web occupations as well. This makes advancement in the industry more difficult. As Lynda Sereno, head of the SV chapter put it, "there is a smaller "good old boy" network to get started in the industry or to move up" (interview). Thus Webgrrls was founded to provide support for women in the industry and help encourage more women to get involved in Web development. The Silicon Valley chapter of Webgrrls was started in the spring of 1997 and had over a thousand members in 2000. Like the other associations, being a member requires

1995, with much of this initial growth due to the rapid expansion of the on-line adult entertainment industry. R. J. Gordon & Co. wanted to help create an association to improve their image and make the World Wide Web more legitimate, so they put $1 million into the founding and creation of AIP (Hans Cathcart, interview).
10   http://www.webgrrls.com

no membership fee – it simply means signing on to the Silicon Valley Webgrrls mailing list. Membership is not limited to women, and monthly meetings typically have anywhere from 5 to 30 percent men attending, depending on the nature of the topic being presented.

Employment Linking

All three associations provide on-line job listing services. The HWG and the Silicon Valley Web Guild both do this through separate email lists that people can subscribe to if they are interested. Webgrrls includes messages about job opportunities along with other messages in their single email list. Interestingly, the job matching function of the HWG is relatively inactive, while that function of Webgrrls and the Web Guild is much more active. The HWG jobs list has only 20 to 40 jobs a month for their national membership. By contrast, the Silicon Valley Webgrrls list generates some 75 to 100 job listings a month just for Silicon Valley, suggesting again the importance of a regional focus in intermediary structure.

For both Webgrrls and the Web Guild, their monthly meetings also provide an important venue for employment networking. At the Web Guild meeting, they post a specific job board, where recruiters, employers, and employees list that they are searching for work or searching for employees. Webgrrls uses their monthly meetings as a way to bring new people into the occupation as well. They have "greeter grrls" who explicitly make newcomers welcome. They have also recently joined in an effort to bring more young women into the field, creating a program called MentorGirls, a cooperative venture with the San Francisco chapter, and a similar organization called San Francisco Women on the Web.[11] Their hope is that, while limited, this effort will help to create more formal mentor–apprenticeship relationships to foster improved access for women getting into the field.

Skills Training and Learning

Skills training and learning opportunities are provided by these associations in three different ways. One, organized both by Silicon Valley Web Guild and Silicon Valley Webgrrls, is through the regular monthly meetings on important topics and technical changes in the industry.

11 www.sfwow.org

A second way, organized by all three associations, is through information sharing, on-line Web references, and on-line discussion groups. A third way, engaged in only by the HTML Writers Guild, is through formal training programs.

The monthly meetings held by the Silicon Valley Web Guild and Silicon Valley Webgrrls have a similar structure. Topics are chosen based on the perceived level of interest and relevance to the membership, with input and suggestions solicited on a regular basis. Meetings are structured with explicit time set aside for networking and information sharing, which most frequently center around employment opportunities. The size of the meeting differs significantly depending on the topic being presented. For the Webgrrls, typical meetings draw between a hundred and a hundred and fifty people, but they have had meetings as large as three hundred and fifty. The most popular session in 1999 was a panel discussion on e-commerce. A similarly popular session was a panel discussion on job and career strategies. The Silicon Valley Web Guild meetings tend to be slightly smaller, drawing from sixty to a hundred people. These meetings help people build social networks that provide important technical information to members of the associations, and help them keep abreast of important changes in the industry beyond their own workplace.

All three associations provide extensive online assistance to their members. Some of this assistance is simply passive information available on their respective Web sites, on topics ranging from technical issues to salary surveys and related links. More important than the Web page, however, are the email lists or listservs. Silicon Valley Webgrrls is the most dynamic in this area. While the other two associations have a variety of different lists devoted to particular topics – e-commerce, technical development, intranets, visual design, and so on – Silicon Valley Webgrrls has a single list which all members are part of. It generates a manageable 25 to 30 messages a day, with a dynamic range of topics, interactions, and assistance. This list is a particularly important venue for people to learn new skills, especially for newcomers learning from more experienced people in the industry, in an incremental way. In one typical exchange in 1999, for example, one person asked a detailed technical question about how to create a seamless table in a Web page in which the text on one side of the table is stationary and the text on the other side scrolls. Within two hours, she got five answers back from people completely disconnected to her work situation. Members will also frequently give each other detailed immediate feedback on the artistic design of Web pages they are creating, again providing a supportive working community that stretches beyond firm boundaries. For someone just entering the field, this kind of immediate community provides an important opportunity to learn and expand their knowledge. For people constantly dealing with rapidly changing technologies, new design techniques and new software, such an immediate community of practice is invaluable for staying on top of new developments and recent trends.

The informal tone and sense of community in the Silicon Valley Webgrrls is an important part of the success and vibrancy of their association, reflected in the wide range of social and personal messages that are also sent on the list. People (mostly women) send questions asking for suggestions for local mountain bike clubs, divorce lawyers, hairdressers, housecleaners and weekend getaways. A special interest group for "Web moms" provides moral support and mutual advice for Web workers who are also mothers. The mutual support and solidarity that is evident in these exchanges makes for a sense of community that eases communication and facilitates learning.

The HTML Writers Guild does provide a service that neither of the other two associations do. They offer a series of on-line courses. In 1998, nearly two thousand people took courses, which last from 6 to 8 weeks each. In 1998, the courses accounted for approximately 25 percent of the organization's budget ($100,000/year in 1998). Courses include some of the basic topics needed to begin getting into Web writing, and also include more advanced topics (see table 5.4).

The on-line "classroom" environment is based on a threaded messaging system, facilitating discussion and feedback. Instructors provide weekly lessons, reading selections, and hands-on assignments. Students can discuss the assignments with the instructor and among themselves in the classroom area. The format has no set "meeting time," which allows students to "attend" class at a time most convenient to them, yet still provides logically organized communication between class participants. The course format allows students to see each others' work and to get regular feedback both from the instructor as well as other students. Classes are inexpensive ($25 for members, $50 for nonmembers). The courses are on-line, which can make learning difficult for some people and lacks valuable face-to-face interaction. On the other hand, they provide for maximum flexibility in hours of instruction, with students being able to take them whenever and wherever is most convenient for them.

Table 5.4 Sample of courses offered by HTML Writers' Guild

Business Writing Basics	Using Adobe Photoshop 4/5
Active Server Pages for Non-Programmers	Practical Web Management: Creating an Effective Web Site
Designing for Universal Accessibility with HTML 4.0	Creating Web Graphics with Paint Shop Pro
Working with Dynamic HTML	Layout in HTML: Workshop on Tables and Frames
Using Macromedia Dreamweaver	
Introduction to HTML 4.0	Introduction to Access 97
Introduction to JavaScript	Practical Web Management: Creating an Effective Web Site
Introduction to Cascading Style Sheets	
Beginning Programming with Perl	

Source: http://www.hwg.org

Employment conditions

The three associations' efforts to improve the labor market status of their members are relatively limited. The HTML Writers' Guild is classified as a 501(c)3 nonprofit organization for educational purposes, as opposed to a 501(c)6 nonprofit professional association. Therefore its activities are primarily devoted to educational activities and it is somewhat more limited in the extent to which it can advocate for its membership. The AIP is pursuing a certification program, along the lines of a more traditional professional association, in an effort to improve standards in the occupation. As of August 1999, however, only six companies or programs had received accreditation through AIP's program at the technician level 1 (the only accreditation rating they had developed at that point).[12] Webgrrls assists members to improve employment conditions in the occupation through providing advice online, primarily related to career options (for example, advantages of working in a start-up or an established firm; feedback on résumés,) and negotiating strategies (including pointers to salary surveys). In general, though, these organizations largely take the demand side of the labor market as given.

---

12 This included a wide range of topics in the following general categories: Internet Basics, Protocols, Internet Clients, Development, Networking, Internet Security, Internet Servers, Business Terms and Concepts, and Design Terms and Concepts.

Case Study 3: Technical Communicators

The job of technical communicators is to produce written manuals or visual representations in order to document how to use technology or new technological tools. Technical communicators must be able to convey scientific and technical information precisely, accurately, and clearly. The work involves close communication with engineers and others developing new technologies or technological tools. The work is also closely tied to the producer development cycle, so in many environments it can by fast paced and highly stressful. With the expansion of technology into every avenue of daily life, at work and at home, the need for clear, concise, and accurate documentation is becoming increasingly important. This rapid advance of technology also means that organizations have to constantly retrain their staff to use new equipment and software. This has led to a rapid expansion of demand for technical documentation to accompany the training programs.[13] The pay in the occupation is above average, reflecting the skilled nature of the work. In 1999, starting salaries for technical writers in the Bay Area were approximately $40,000, and could rise to over $100,000 for experienced writers. The median salary in the Silicon Valley was $60,000 in 1999.[14]

STC Background

The Society for Technical Communication (STC) is a national organization with more than 20,000 members. The STC was formally established in 1971, changing its name from the Society of Technical Writers and Publishers which had been established in 1960. The Silicon Valley chapter of STC is the largest, with over 2,000 members. The core of its activity is "advancing the arts and sciences of technical communication." Members include technical writers, editors, graphic artists, multimedia artists, Web and Intranet page designers, translators, technical illustrators, and others whose work involves making technical information understandable and available to those who need it. As in many of the Silicon Valley professional associations, members include employers and recruiters as well as people working in the occupation.

13 http://techwriting.miningco.com
14 STC Annual Salary Survey for 1999, available at http://stc.org

Employment Linking

The core of STC's activities (though not the core of its stated purpose) is as a networking body to help people find employment. According to Virginia Beecher, president of the Silicon Valley chapter, "probably nine out of ten" people who join STC do so because they are looking for work (personal interview). STC provides information on employment through an on-line Web and email list, but much of the networking and job information takes place at their monthly meetings. They have a specific location at the meeting for recruiters and employers to set up information about employment opportunities and for people who are looking for work to talk to them. People attending the meeting have to pay an entrance fee,[15] but despite this over a hundred people typically attend and popular topics can draw over two hundred people. Employers and recruiters come to the monthly meetings which provide an easy opportunity for people to network and find out about employment opportunities and for employers and recruiters to have immediate access to a group of technical communicators, many of whom are looking for employment.

Their employment information Web service provides a weekly listing of job opportunities to all who subscribe. The listing is both for direct employers as well as for recruiters. Listings and access to the listings are entirely free, and the positions are both posted on to the Web site and delivered via email to anyone who subscribes, which in 1999 averaged around three hundred people.

Training and Skills Development

The monthly meetings of the STC are focused around particular topics of interest to technical communicators. They also have a range of special interest groups (SIGs), who meet on a regular basis. The special interest groups include:

- the Online and Interactive Information SIG, an informal group of people who share an interest in the growing world of electronically delivered information, including topics such as on-line documentation, user interface design, interactive tutorials, help systems, information retrieval technologies, and multimedia;

15   In 1999 this was $5 for members and $10 for nonmembers, plus an additional $7 charge for the meal.

- the Windows Help SIG which is devoted to exploring on-line help systems for the Microsoft Windows computer platform; WinHelp SIG meetings often focus on the standard Microsoft-supplied Help engine, but many other related topics are also covered;
- a Writing and Editing SIG, which tries to help improve the relationship between writers and editors;
- the Usability SIG, which brings together people who are interested in topics related to product usability;
- the Silicon Valley Internationalization and Localization SIG discusses issues related to designing products and product information for international markets.

In addition, there is a SIG on consulting and independent contracting, which provides networking and support for freelancers and independent consultants, operating largely independently of the larger group. These meetings are free, and their format differs from that of the general meeting or most other SIGs in that generally they don't have a featured speaker and they don't have theater seating. They meet in a restaurant, and primarily provide support for each other. The goal is to create a mentoring environment where less-experienced contractors can gain insights from more experienced ones.

Employment Conditions

The major weakness of STC is that they have no real presence around issues of employment conditions or employer management practices. The national office does conduct a regular salary survey, but beyond that they engage in little debate or discussion about conditions of employment in the industry.

Case Study 4: Technical Writers – National Writers' Union

The National Writers' Union provides an interesting contrast to the Society for Technical Communication. The NWU has a trade group for technical writers whose membership is made of people in the same occupation as the STC, but the group more explicitly advocates for their members' interests rather than focusing on technical communication more broadly. Technical writing has becoming a significant component of the NWU's membership in the San Francisco Bay Area. There are approximately three hundred members of the Tech Writers' Trade Group. More than 75 percent of the membership is women, reflecting the gender balance of the occupation as a whole.

The Tech Writers' Trade Group (TWTG) was started in the mid-1980s, initially by a group of techical writers who had joined the NWU but were feeling the need for greater support for their specific issues. They met initially to develop a code of conduct for techical writers. There was a lot of concern at the time about the role of recruiters in the industry who were taking their 30 to 40 percent mark-up, but providing little benefit in return:

> In the early 1980s, most of us in the writers' union never used agencies. Agencies were still providing a majority of the contractors, but we had contempt for them. The reason some people would use them was that people didn't want to market themselves or didn't have the contacts, and were willing to have the 30 percent cut because they didn't have the contact on their own. We thought this was exploitative. Essentially these agencies are doing nothing more than what a literary agency does, and a literary agent takes 10–15 percent, and does a lot more. (Interview, Bruce Hartford, TWTG co-founder)

Employment Linking

One of the first things the TWTG started was a jobs hotline to broker job opportunities for NWU members. This was seen as a way to get around recruiters by building a direct link between employers and NWU members. The jobs hotline was initially focused just on techical writers, and has always been focused on the Bay Area, though some listings are national. It differs from on-line jobs search sites in that the employee, not the employer, pays for the cost of the service.[16] Compared to the $400 and upwards fees charged by many on-line job search sites, this provides a good deal for employers. It also provides a better deal than many of the recruiter agencies for employees as well, since people who find employment through the hotline agree to pay 10 percent of their first four months income to the NWU, compared to the 30 to 35 percent life-of-contract commissions typical of most brokers and job shops.

Unfortunately, following the passage of Section 1706 of the Internal Revenue Code (discussed in chapter 4), clients have increasingly

---

16   This is true for 1099-type contract positions – for W-2 normal employment positions, employers have to pay a small fee ($65/month) to list their openings.

requested that contractors go through agencies, rather than being hired directly as independent contractors. This has cut into the business of the jobs hotline, and made it less cost effective. In addition, the high demand for techical writers means that NWU members have many other options for finding employment, which has made the job hotline less self-sufficient. It was started with a grant from the United Auto Workers (UAW),[17] but when that grant ran out it had to start becoming financially self-sufficient. To do so, they started listing journalist and other writing opportunities, not just techical writing, and listing them nationally as well.

Skills Training and Development

One of the major programs the TWTG runs is an introductory seminar on how to get into techical writing. These day-long training sessions draw sixty to eighty people and provide detailed knowledge about the occupation, skills needed, resources to get into the industry, advice on negotiating contracts, salary information, and other useful resources for career improvement. Techical writing is potentially highly remunerative and provides a relative easy entry point into the high-tech industry, since it doesn't require a technical degree. Many of the people in the occupation started as clerical or administrative staff but recognized the opportunities available in learning the technical language and how to write technical documentation. Nonetheless, the occupation is not easy to break into. It can be very high-pressured, and requires the ability to sit and write in front of a computer all day for much of the work. The TWTG estimates that only one out of five people who attend their seminar ever actually ends up in technical writing, given these difficulties.

Employment Conditions

The NWU has detailed advice for members about contract negotiation, and has a contract litigation help line. This helps ensure that contracts in the industry are helping protect workers' intellectual property, compensation rates, and other matters of concern to technical writers. The organization also will play an active, direct advocacy role on behalf of members. One recent example of this concerned the issue of overtime

17   The National Writers' Union is affiliated to the United Auto Workers.

pay. In 1997, members of the California Industrial Welfare Commission who had all been appointed by Republican Governor Pete Wilson, ended daily overtime pay in California.[18] Daily overtime pay was restored by an action of the Democratic State Legislature in 1999. In response, however, the high-tech recruiting industry, led by the Northern California Chapter of the National Association of Computer Consultant Businesses (NACCB), led an initiative that was targeted at exempting highly skilled employees in the information technology industry from the daily overtime law, thus ending their daily overtime pay. The Tech Writers Subgroup of the NWU organized a coalition of groups, working with the California State Labor Federation (AFL-CIO), and ultimately reached a compromise with the recruiting industry that specifically protected overtime pay for technical writers.[19] This example of direct advocacy on behalf of their membership emerges out of their union affiliation, and was far beyond what the Society for Technical Communication was willing to do officially, despite the significant economic impact for their membership.[20]

Case Study 5: Graphic Artists

Graphic artists produce visual artwork using a combination of computer and hand-driven tools. Specific occupations include illustrators, graphic designers, computer and website designers, cartoonists, animators, textile designers, and so on. Historically, much of the work was done by hand, using a variety of different media, but these occupations have faced dramatic changes in recent years with the rapid development of computer-based design and the World Wide Web. To be successful as a graphic artist today, computer skills are essential, with software programs such as Quark, Adobe Illustrator, and Adobe Photoshop now being primary tools for the majority of people in the trade.

Employers tend to be advertising firms, graphic design firms, book publishers, magazines, and the public relations departments of major

---

18   Prior to this action, employers had to pay time-and-a-half for work exceeding eight hours a day, and double time for work exceeding 12 hours in a day.
19   The legislation that ultimately passed, SB88, removed overtime pay for all workers earning over $41 an hour unless they were specifically protected by the special clause protecting technical writers.
20   Information from interview, Andreas Ramos, Tech Writers Sub-Group.

corporations. With the rapid expansion of the World Wide Web in recent years, the demand for graphic artists has increasingly moved to the Internet, and the occupation overlaps significantly with many of the Web workers described in previous sections. Employment is often on a project-by-project basis, with high levels of contract employment or self-employment. Even for graphic artists in long-term, regular employment, changing technology, clients, and projects make for a work environment frequently characterized by rapid change.

Background

The Graphic Artists Guild began in Detroit in 1967 when a group of illustrators in a local ad agency originated what they thought would be a typical strike to gain union recognition. The ad agency was able to break the strike by getting their artwork through mail order, and thus the members began to restructure the organization in more of a guild format, focusing on services to members that could be provided even in the absence of a collective bargaining agreement. Graphic artists in other cities began to organize other local chapters shortly thereafter, and in 1971 New York became the second city to become chartered as a local member. Other cities followed: Atlanta (1978); Boston (1980); Indianapolis (1982); Vermont (1983); central Florida (1986); Albany (1988); Chicago (1993); Seattle (1994); and Northern California (1995). The guild currently has a membership of over three thousand.

For most of its history, GAG has been an independent union, but there have been frequent internal debates about affiliating with a large union that is part of the AFL-CIO. The advantage of affiliating with a larger union is the ability to get more resources for organizing, but many members had concerns about maintaining their autonomy and the possibility of having to pay higher membership dues.[21] In 1995, GAG began serious affiliation negotiations with various unions and ultimately decided, in March 1999, to affiliate with the United Auto Workers/ AFL-CIO. According to National Guild President Polly M. Law:

> This agreement is the result of nearly 20 years of research, study and negotiations. The Guild has been seeking an affiliation partner that can

---

21 Annual membership in the GAG is pro-rated depending on one's income – $120 for those earning under $12,000 a year, up to a maximum of $270 – whereas union dues frequently can be 1½ percent of total salary, which is significantly more.

strengthen our position as advocates for the rights of visual creators, while still guaranteeing the Guild's independent identity. In the UAW, we've found just such a partner. We're tremendously excited to be joining forces with a strong, democratic union, untainted by corruption or scandal, with the foresight to embrace non-traditional, independent workers like ourselves. (GAG/UAW press release, 23 March, 1999)

Despite now being affiliated with the dominant union federation in the country, GAG has had very little focus on collecting bargaining. In fact, in their 34-year history, they've had only one collective bargaining agreement, which was reached in 1995 and covered graphic artists employed at WNET, a publicly funded television station in New York.[22] Most of the activities of GAG are focused on a variety of services for members that help them improve their working conditions and career opportunities. The lack of a collective bargaining agreement means that essentially GAG has to convince its membership every year that being part of the organization is worth it, which helps ensure that the organization is responsive to changing needs of their membership.

The Graphic Artists Guild first became active in California in the early 1980s, but the Northern California chapter of the Graphic Artists Guild was formed only in October of 1995, and thus is still young compared to the national organization. Services to local members are primarily provided through the national offices.

Employment Linking

The central concern for GAG is helping their members find work – getting their members not just jobs, but good jobs that recognize the valuable contributions of graphic artists, financially and otherwise. Thus, part of their work is helping to market the skills and portfolios of their members to employers. Nationally, this is done through the *Graphic Artists Guild Directory of Illustration,* an advertising directory for illustrators that has free distribution to over 21,000 art directors and buyers around the world. In addition, the national Web site,[23] as well as the northern California chapter Web site,[24] have links to to the Web sites

---

22   They were also certified by the NLRB to be the exclusive bargaining agent for graphic artists at a second site – First Financial Merchandising Group in Boston – but never reached a contract.
23   www.gag.org
24   http://norcal.gag.org//index.html

and portfolios of individual members. This provides an opportunity for potential clients to readily access samples of members' work.

Skills Training and Development

The skills training and development assistance that the Graphic Artists Guild provides to its members is primarily through the provision of information about formal training programs, and through the creation of on-line forums to provide more informal feedback to members on a range of issues, including graphic design, illustration, animation, surface design, and web design. The forums are opportunities for members to get feedback on specific work they're involved in, or get more general suggestions on changing software, technology, or other trends in the field. The local Northern California chapter does hold periodic luncheon meetings, designed to bring together members to hear about topics of interest in the field, but they have been somewhat infrequent.

Improving Employment Conditions

The guild's real strength is in their efforts to improve employment conditions for their members. They see themselves as very different from other associations in the graphic design industry that focus more on design issues. The GAG, in contrast, is mandated by its constitution "to advance and extend the economic and social interest of [their] members," and to "promote and maintain high professional standards of ethics and practice and to secure the conformance of all buyers, users, sellers and employers to established standards." In short, as their Web page proclaims, they are "dedicated to the artist/designer, rather than to art/design".[25]

Foremost among the Guild's activities are their ongoing efforts to educate members and nonmembers in the industry about the business of being a graphic artist. This includes running programs on negotiation and pricing strategies, tax issues, self-promotion, time management, and all the other essential business skills that are not, by and large, taught in art school. The guild provides a means for experienced artists to share their understanding of the advertising, publishing, and corporate markets with young artists and a way for artists at every level of attainment to share concerns and information.

25 http://www.gag.org

One of the major activities of the guild is the regular production of *The Handbook of Pricing and Ethical Guidelines*. This publication, which has grown from its original 20-page pamphlet to a 280-page book that sells for $29.95, includes detailed information on a range of issues designed to strengthen graphic artists in their business practices, including: legal rights, ethical standards, grievance practices, professional issues (for example, deductibility of artwork), information on the impact of new technologies, and detailed guidelines for pricing and contract negotiations in a wide range of products and markets. Sales of this book provide one-third of the organization's operating budget. Since all members get a copy free, it is clear that the book has become a valued resource within large sectors of the industry beyond GAG's membership. It is currently in its ninth edition, and has been updated every two years.

Another key service GAG provides is helping its members negotiate their own contracts. This includes educational programs designed to increase their members' negotiating skills as well as a national contract monitoring service. A contract committee of the union provides assistance in understanding and negotiating contracts. They produce a bimonthly "Contract Monitor" email newsletter which analyzes and demystifies confusing clauses. In each issue the "Contract Monitor" reviews contracts submitted by members, supplies real-life negotiation tips, and offers interviews, quizzes, and commentary to keep its readers informed. The committee also maintains the "Contract Monitor" Web Site which lists the companies that have been reviewed and provides an easy-to-understand glossary of legalese commonly found in many contracts. The Web site details what is good and bad about each contract and highlights key concerns and issues that GAG members should be aware of in negotiating their own contracts.

The organization has also been active in protecting graphic artists in California since the early 1980s. One of their primary efforts was centered around the issue of ensuring copyright ownership rights for graphic artists in the state. Like intellectual property laws, such laws to protect artists' material are important for their economic livelihood. Generally, the artists retain the copyright, unless the company pays an extra fee to gain copyright control. But corporations frequently prefer to do "work for hire" in which the control of the copyright isn't really clear – artists are treated like employees, meaning the company retains the copyright but the employees are actually still hired as freelancers. In these situations, the artist legally retains control, but it can be difficult to enforce, and there have been numerous examples of people's work getting used without them receiving appropriate compensation. In response, in 1982, the guild succeeding in passing California's "Artists' Fair Practices" law. This law (Sect. 988 of the Civil Code) ensures that artists maintain legal ownership of their material unless they explicitly sign that right away.

Case Study 6: Plumbers and Steamfitters

When most people think of piping, they think of plumbing in a kitchen or bathroom. In Silicon Valley, though, the core of the industry involves the complex systems found in high-tech manufacturing and office buildings. An estimated 85 percent of the work of the pipes trades in Silicon Valley is in high-tech related industries – bio-tech, pharmaceutical, or micro-electronics. These facilities have a labyrinth of pipes delivering up to a hundred chemicals, all of which need to be extremely pure and many of which are quite dangerous. Silane, for example, burns immediately when it is exposed to air and burns so cleanly you don't see a flame. If it gets loose in a building, it will literally melt it (Mitchell 1993). The chemicals require different kinds of pipe, which must be extraordinarily smooth so that gases and liquids don't loosen tiny fragments which might contaminate the final product. Contractors and workers go to great lengths to prevent contamination, including sometimes wearing "bunny suits" similar to those used in semiconductor clean rooms. A single fingerprint inside one of these pipes can decrease the purity of the chemicals and reduce the all-important quality yield significantly.

The air conditioning systems also have to be well maintained and highly accurate. Filtering out dust particles and maintaining constant levels of humidity and temperature can make a huge difference in purity levels and quality control in microelectronics fabrication and assembly. Thus, the skills involved in piping installation are quite significant, and have changed along with the rapid changes in technology in the industry.

Background

The United Association of Plumbers, Steamfitters and Refrigeration-fitters (UA) Local #393 is the union representing commercial plumbers in the area. Prior to the 1950s, there were few commercial construction

jobs in the Valley, since the region was still dominated by the fruit can-
neries and orchards in the area. The union has grown rapidly, however, along with the region's growth, with membership expanding
particularly rapidly in the 1970s and 1980s. Membership in 1999 was
approximately 1,200 working members, of which 370 were apprentices.
The union also represents an additional 400 people who are retired,
and has a fluctuating number of additional "travelers," who are typically members of other UA local unions in other parts of the country
where work is less available.

The UA established an apprenticeship program in the area in 1941,
and established the Pipe Trades Training Center in 1961. The training
program that is run out of this center is a critical part of the union's
success, and provides a significant incentive for employers in the region to use union labor. Despite the heavy anti-union sentiment in information technology industries, high-tech firms have been willing to
work with union contractors because of the skilled work they provide.
According to Tom Fisher, Curriculum Coordinator:

> Intel complained to us a number of years ago that it costs three times as
> much to hire a plumber here as Ireland, and twice as much as in their
> facilities down in the desert. They built similar plants in each location,
> and the one here was more costly since we had to do all the initial engi-
> neering and installation. Even with that, and with our three-times labor
> cost factor, the plant that makes more money, dollar for dollar invested,
> is Santa Clara. It went in right the first time. The guys knew what they
> were doing. When they turned it on, everything worked, no leaks. Purity
> was up where it was supposed to be, and it comes out that these pain in
> the neck union people actually are worth it. (Interview, May 1999)

Wages for union plumbers are quite high, with full journeyman's wages
at $42 an hour in 2000, with total compensation (including pension and
other benefits) reaching $53 an hour. The union's apprenticeship sys-
tem includes a five-year training program open to anyone who is able
to pass a written exam of basic math and spatial relationship skills.
Entry-level wages for apprentices with no experience start at $15 an
hour, and rise regularly every six months up to the full journey scale at
the end of five years.

Employment Placement

Like most construction unions, the UA operates a hiring hall, placing
union members in jobs with contractors in the region. Contractors call

in with requests for people with specific skills or certifications, and these positions are filled on a first-come, first-served basis by members with the appropriate qualifications. Thus placements are not made on a seniority system, as in some hiring halls, but are made broadly on the basis of skills. There is a list system, which gives priority to local members[26] over "travelers," but within that all members with the same formal qualifications are treated equally. There is also a system for placing apprentices, and contractors are expected to hire one apprentice for every three journeymen hired. In practice, there is little need to enforce this. Contractors frequently like to hire apprentices, at least in part because their wages are lower and often the skill levels are not that far behind journeymen, especially if they are in their second year or more. There is lots of work that apprentices can do well while working for less money than journeymen.

Training and Skills Development

The UA has developed a remarkable training program. The Pipes Trades Training Center was established in 1961 in response to the recognized need for training in the piping industry. The center is now a 56,000 square foot facility with 28 classrooms where both journey and apprentice level courses are taught. The center's administration is coordinated by a joint labor management agreement, which has equal representation from the UA Local #393, and employer trade associations representing more than two hundred contractors in the area. The center has over fifty instructors. Many are UA members, but others are practitioners in the chemical, electrical, mechanical, or computer engineering industries.

Funding for the center is provided by contributions from Local #393 members. For each hour a member works, a portion (currently $1.00) is contributed to the center. This is over seven times the national average of union-member contributions to plumbers' training programs. In 1998–99, that resulted in $2.6 million for training in Santa Clara County alone. The center is affiliated with Foothill/De Anza Community College District and offers fully accredited courses. The center provides classroom and hands-on training in a variety of technical skills, including: welding, high purity and ultra-pure piping systems, mobile clean room, industrial controls, computer energy

26 Defined as working in the union local for four years.

management systems, and a range of other related programs. The facilities are highly sophisticated, with cutting-edge equipment to provide state-of-the-art training. High-tech installations focus on high-purity piping, ultra high-purity water systems, high-purity gas systems, clean rooms and environmental chambers, and scrubbers. The training is not limited to apprentices and, given the nature of change in the industry, there is a great need for continual training of journeymen plumbers as well. Over 1,100 members received some journey level training in 2000.

Training also includes the latest regulations and safety procedures. Many of the gases and other chemicals used in semiconductor, PCB fabrication, and certain bio-tech/medical systems are extremely toxic. The training ensures that workers have the skills they need to safely perform their work. The Toxic Gas Ordinance, for instance, established a class rating for all hazardous materials, with stringent requirements for the handling of the most hazardous materials. The union also played a key role in ensuring environmental safety and occupational health by helping to get the Toxic Gas Ordinance passed in various jurisdictions. The TGO is a regulating code that has been adopted by most local governmental agencies in the San Francisco Bay Area for the use, distribution, handling and dispensing of toxic gases. By ensuring that their members are fully familiar with this ordinance, it has also become a way of helping ensure the maintenance of union labor in the construction of high-tech piping systems.

Employment Conditions

The UA has a Master Contract that specifies in detail all the conditions of employment and compensation in the industry. This contract is negotiated regularly with four different employer associations (Northern California Mechanical Contractors Association, the Santa Clara Valley Contractors Association, the Plumbing, Heating and Cooling Contractors of the Greater Bay Area, and the Industrial Contractors' Association). The NCMCA accounts for approximately 40 percent of hours, the SCVCA another 50 to 60 percent, and the remaining two are very small. The relationship with the contractors is quite cooperative, and there have been only rare incidences of serious conflict during contract negotiations. This is due in part to the fact that many of the contractors themselves are either current or former union members – as much as 90 percent at times in the past, and currently about 75 percent. As a result, the contractors have an intimate knowledge of the skills and experience of union members and recognize that, for the highly skilled work required in many of the commercial construction projects in the area, utilizing the skills of union members is essential.

Case Study 7: Temporary Clerical Workers

The associations examined so far are all in occupations which require a certain amount of training and are in high demand in the labor market. Most membership-based intermediaries are in occupations with a significant occupational cohesion, in which workers have an identifiable skill set and common experience in the labor market. It is much harder to develop effective intermediary organizations for lower-skill workers. The lack of substantial occupation-specific skills and experience makes it difficult to maintain organizational coherence. Furthermore, without the leverage of significant skill levels, employment linkage and training programs are less effective and to improve employment conditions requires greater levels of more traditional labor organizing and political intervention. As a result, there are few membership-based intermediaries in lower-skilled occupations in Silicon Valley.

One significant initiative, however, is an effort to build effective intermediary assistance for temporary clerical workers in the valley. As mentioned in the previous chapter, clerical occupations still constitute the majority of placements by temporary help agencies in the region, and employment in these positions is both precarious and low paid. Working Partnerships Temporary Worker Project is an effort to assist temporary clerical workers in the Valley through combining advocacy efforts with the placement and training services of an intermediary.

Background

Working Partnerships Temporary Worker Project has its origins in the efforts of the AFL-CIO Central Labor Council (CLC) in San Jose to build a broad program to increase the presence of the labor movement in the region as a whole. Since the early 1990s, the CLC has actively expanded their efforts in organizing, educating, and mobilizing community support for workers' rights while giving labor a stronger voice in the political arena (Dean 1998). To reach out in new directions, the CLC launched Working Partnerships USA, a nonprofit research, education and policy institute that was established in 1995. The overall goal of the organization is to bring a wider range of voices to the table around questions of regional economic development, and to develop effective responses to the changing structure of production in information technology industries. The activities of Working Partnerships USA break down into three broad areas: research and policy development; education and training; and developing new models of employee representation.

The organization's research program has focused on identifying and documenting issues that working families in the area are facing, including contingent employment, declining wages amid growing inequality, and economic insecurity.[27] This research agenda has been strategically connected to a range of public policy initiatives, including efforts to increase accountability of corporate subsidies, promote a living wage in San Jose, reform the redevelopment agency activities and develop a community economic blueprint. These policy initiatives have helped increase the visibility of the labor movement as a strong voice for *all* working families, regardless of whether they are union members or not, and have helped build deeper political relationships with a variety of other constituencies. Combined with the Labor Council's more traditional role in electoral politics, they have helped place the labor movement in a significant role in shaping political direction in the region and representing the interests of working families as a whole.

The organization's broad education and training initiatives have focused on the creation of a Labor–Community Leadership Institute. This is a nine-week course, run in cooperation with San Jose State University extension, focused on the political economy of Silicon Valley. It provides participants with a deeper understanding of economic changes in the region and of the political institutions (both formal and informal) that help shape the region's development. Part of each class is organized around a class project which has been integrated with policy initiatives, such as a Living Wage ordinance or restructuring the Redevelopment Agency. This provides participants with opportunities to get directly involved in advocacy initiatives. The course is run in an active, participatory manner, using the principles of popular education while promoting economic literacy (Freire 1970). Recruitment for the course has targeted five main constituencies in the region: labor, community-based organizations, religious/faith-based communities, small business, and the public sector (including both elected officials and civil

---

27   Benner (1996a), Benner (1996b), Benner, Brownstein, and Dean (1999).

servants). The relationships built through the course and through alumni activities help to build bridges across constituencies while helping to create more common understandings of the issues different constituencies are facing and dealing with.

The Temporary Worker Employment Project emerged as an effort to develop new models of employee representation in the region's highly flexible labor markets. The project includes two components: Working Partnerships Staffing Services, a placement agency that puts workers in jobs that pay a living wage and offer greater access to benefits and skills training; and Working Partnerships Membership Association, an association that brings temporary workers together for a variety of common interests.

Employment Linking

The staffing service provides a worker-centered alternative to for-profit temporary agencies. As a nonprofit organization, it can charge employers competitive rates, while taking less of a mark-up and paying workers a higher hourly wage. It also prioritizes working with employers who have demonstrated experience in helping move temporary workers into more permanent positions with real career opportunities. They market their services to employers based on the extra "investment" they make in the personnel they place through access to training and provision of benefits.

Training and Skills Development

The organization focuses on helping workers develop career ladders by linking training programs with new employment opportunities across multiple firms. From basic administrative tasks, people can move into more sophisticated software manipulation, Web-page design and HTML skills, or even programming, depending on the participants' interests. The goal is to create real advancement opportunities from entry-level clerical positions for the participants, many of whom start at the very bottom of the labor market. Many of the participants have never graduated from high school or lack the basic skills needed to survive in the job market, while others have successful work experience but have been displaced through layoffs.

The training component has been built in cooperation with Mission Community College, one of the most prominent community colleges in the Valley. The training program is designed to be open entry, open exit so people can come in and out as needed. It is essential for workers to have the flexibility to gain training as needed, and to take advantage of employment opportunities when they become available, without sacrificing skills development. The goal of the program is that, as the membership base of the organization grows, a joint council will be developed between employees and employers to help review and modify the training standards over time, to make sure they meet the needs of workers and employers.

In addition to the computer and administrative skills training courses, the program also provides training and assistance to workers in other areas, including financial planning, "know your rights" legal training, ergonomics training, and access to legal assistance. Regular monthly meetings provide an opportunity for networking and information gathering. Such "secondary" training, information gathering and networking is often essential for people to be successful in the labor market in the long term.

Employment Conditions

Advocacy efforts are a crucial component of this initiative, with the goal of upgrading conditions in the temporary help industry in the region as a whole, not just for its members. This is being pursued through developing a Code of Conduct for temporary help agencies. Both temporary agencies and clients are encouraged to sign the Code of Conduct, which outlines basic protections for workers who would otherwise be extremely vulnerable. The process of developing this Code of Conduct is as important as the content itself. The initial draft of the Code was developed through consultation with a national network of organizations working on temporary employment.[28] The final version, however, has been developed through consultations with a wide-range of local organizations, along with the input of a local advisory board that includes a broad cross-section of community leaders from labor, business, faith and community-based organizations. Again, this participative process is important for building deep support for the initiative. Particular temporary agencies and their clients that refuse to sign the Code of Conduct will be targeted for public protests, highlighting problems workers in those conditions face.

---

28   The National Alliance for Fair Employment, http://www.fairjobs.org

Conclusion: Building Community-based Careers

The professional associations and union structures reviewed here have grown rapidly in Silicon Valley in recent years. They provide an important service for their members and represent an effort of workers to organize collectively to improve their standing in the labor market. These models, however, are significantly different than traditional professional associations or industrial union models. Significant components of their efforts include the following.

- *Focus on regional labor market:* These organizations play a significant role on a regional scale, helping break through fragmentation and isolation of individualized employment relations, while also providing more flexibility and opportunities for face-to-face interaction than national structures. The regional structure of the organization is important for building solidarity among members, while developing a sophisticated knowledge of labor market opportunities.
- *Occupationally and sectorally specific organization:* These organizations are not based in a single work site or a single employer, instead cutting across multiple employers within an industry, but still with enough cohesiveness around an occupational or sectoral identity to provide a basis for solidarity among workers.
- *Strong focus on career development*: These organizations are focused on improving workers conditions over time through assisting in employment linkages, skills development, and training.
- *Combining advocacy and services.* Organizing and service provision are not two opposed strategies. The advocacy agenda helps build public presence and power in the industry, while basic services (including placement services and provision of inexpensive health care) provide important assistance to workers in need. They go hand in hand.

These initiatives have grown up with little financial resources, based primarily on the volunteer labor of their members and through limited membership dues. Yet in many cases, even with these limited resources, they are helping members build success careers. By strengthening networks among people in similar occupational communities, they are helping to mitigate the risk of the high turnover and volatility inherent in information technology industries. In the process, rather than building careers based within a single firm, members are building careers through their occupationally based community networks.

Yet these membership-based intermediaries also provide services to employers, who find them to be useful channels for recruiting workers in particular occupations or with particular skill sets. Furthermore, to the extent that these intermediaries improve the knowledge and skills of workers in the regional production complex, employers benefit, in the form of a more skilled workforce, without having to invest in much internal training. What makes the membership-based intermediaries distinctive is their focus on particular occupations and the strength of their ties with workers in the region's labor market.

6

Labor Market Intermediaries—
Public Sector

The nature of industry in the Valley is constantly changing, and employers just can't tell you what skills they're going to need two years from
now ... In the past, the skills that employees had lasted longer, maybe
8–10 years. Now a current skill set might be valuable for only 18 months.
Michael Curran
Director NOVA Private Industry Council
Sunnyvale, CA

The previous two chapters have discussed the functions of both private
sector and membership-based intermediaries in Silicon Valley. Private
sector intermediaries have grown as firms have recognized increased
opportunities for profit by using intermediaries. Membership-based
intermediaries have grown as workers have recognized productive intermediary strategies for improving their prospects in a volatile labor
market. Intermediaries in both categories, of course, have been shaped
in part by government regulation, but by and large these private sector
and membership-based intermediaries have arisen in a bottom-up manner, without significant government encouragement or support. There
are, however, a number of public sector programs and publicly funded
educational institutions that directly play an intermediary role in the
labor market. In recent years, these programs have expanded their activities and grown more explicit in building their role as intermediaries.
This chapter examines three broad types of these public sector intermediaries which together cover the broad range of public sector programs
that act as intermediaries in the labor market.

First, there are a variety of institutions that make up the workforce
development "system." In their efforts to link disadvantaged workers
to employment opportunities these programs have always had some

role as intermediaries in the labor market. In recent years, however, these frequently fragmented programs have become increasingly integrated into a "one-stop career center system" aimed at improving their effectiveness as intermediaries. Two components of these changes are particularly significant: first, these services are becoming more available to the entire workforce, rather than being reserved for specific subsectors of the labor market; and, second, they are attempting to more closely link training with career mobility. Both these trends suggest the greater integration of these public sector intermediary programs into the very structure of the regional economy and labor market. In Silicon Valley, this trend is best exemplified by the NOVA Private Industry Council (PIC), one of the earliest efforts in the nation to develop a one-stop career system.

A second broad type of public sector intermediary is education-based institutions providing adult education and customized job training for employers. Historically, the education system has been distinct from the workforce development system, focusing on a broader set of education goals primarily oriented toward new entrants to the labor market. Employment training programs, in contrast, acted more as a "second chance" system providing occupation-based training for particular groups of people. In the last twenty years, however, education-based initiatives have played a greater role in retraining older workers and in expanding their ties with employers. This includes developing specialized curriculum development and training programs geared specifically for employers' needs, and providing a wide range of on-site custom training for employers. These trends blur the distinction between "education" and "job training" programs, and position educational institutions as more active intermediaries in the labor market. The University of California-Santa Cruz Extension system and various customized training programs of the far-reaching and highly valued community college system are the best examples of this trend in Silicon Valley.

The third category of publicly funded intermediaries is community and nonprofit organizations that engage in job training and placement activities. Most of the funding for these programs comes from federal and state workforce development grants, and thus they are closely integrated into the growing one-stop career center system. Certain community-based organizations are exemplary, however, in the strength of their ties in particular communities of disadvantaged workers. Being strongly integrated into social networks in poor communities can be extremely valuable for improving the effectiveness of intermediaries in improving labor market outcome for disadvantaged workers. The most prominent example in the Silicon Valley is the Center for Employment Training.

All three categories of public sector intermediaries differ from private sector or membership-based intermediaries in the primary goal that drives their activities. Rather than being driven by a profit motive, or by the goal of improving labor market outcomes for their membership, public sector intermediaries are ultimately driven by (at least in principle) their contribution to the public good. This means their structure and activities are somewhat insulated from direct market competition and volatility in Silicon Valley, and somewhat shaped by political dynamics, legislative mandates, and program priorities developed primarily in Washington DC and the State Capital of Sacramento, often far removed from the local context. As such, they have to be understood in the context of broad state and federal changes in these publicly funded programs rather than simply in response to local economic dynamics. At the same time, these organizations are also partially rooted in the regional economy and thus respond to the local demands of business, the character of the workforce, and the nature of the local labor market.

Workforce Development System

Since their beginning, public sector training programs have acted as intermediaries in the labor market through trying to find employment opportunities for disadvantaged workers and providing them with the training they need to obtain that employment. Unfortunately, most programs have had only limited success. In a review of a wide range of evaluations of training programs, Grubb (1995) concludes: "A large number [though not all] of job training programs lead to increased earnings, and the benefits generally outweigh the costs – [but] the increases in earnings are moderate by almost any standards, insufficient to lift those enrolled in such programs out of poverty" (Grubb 1995: section IV, p.1). There are a variety of reasons for this disappointing record, ranging from poor pedagogy and the short-term nature of much of the training, to poor placement rates and political interference. In recent years, however, there has been a growing consensus within the workforce development community that among the most important reasons for this poor performance was the relative isolation of these programs from employers and their lack of connection to good jobs with clear paths of mobility (Osterman 1999). In other words, they have not been very effective intermediaries, relying simply on training to improve the labor market outcomes of disadvantaged workers rather than actively brokering employment opportunities for those workers as well.

In recognition of this weakness, there has been a restructuring of workforce development programs in recent years, with the goal of developing stronger ties with employers and streamlining the fragmented service delivery structure toward becoming a more effective intermediary in the labor market. Many of the programs in Silicon Valley have been at the forefront of these changes, helping to inform national policy and providing examples of innovative intermediary structures. While the impact of such reforms nationally remains to be seen, the experience of intermediaries in Silicon Valley suggests that developing and strengthening the intermediary structure of public workforce development programs is an important part of improving their performance.

Understanding the public workforce development "system" in Silicon Valley, as in the rest of the US, is difficult and complex. There are a wide variety of federal and state funded programs that provide training and placement services, and they are poorly integrated with each other. One major source of job training funds is federal training programs aimed at economically disadvantaged workers, including adult, young, and older workers, and at those who have recently been laid off from their work.[1] A second significant source of funding comes through various welfare assistance and welfare-to-work programs. A third set of training programs has developed as the result of specifically identified problems or targeted communities, such as programs to assist workers displaced by the North American Free Trade Agreement (NAFTA), or programs for military veterans (who often face particular barriers to employment). A fourth major source of funds in California is the Employment Training Panel, which was founded in 1982 to provide training funds to employers to upgrade the skills of their incumbent workforce. The result of these various funding streams and purposes is a wide range of training programs that often have little relation to each other. A study by the GAO of just federally-funded employment and training programs found a total of 163 programs, spending $20.4 billion in 1995 (US General Accounting Office 1994). Furthermore, these programs frequently use a range of public, private and nonprofit vendors and training providers to deliver

---

1 These programs were initially brought together in 1973 under the Comprehensive Employment and Training Act (CETA), which was superceded in 1983 by the Joint Training Partnership Act (JTPA), and again in 1998 by the Workforce Investment Act, which actually went into effect on July 1, 2000.

services, including community-based organization, unions, private firms, nonprofit organizations, high schools, community colleges and technical colleges. The result is hardly a cohesive workforce development system, but rather "a non-system with a bewildering variety of purposes, services, and funding" (Grubb 1996: 9).

It is beyond the scope of this chapter to examine the ways that all of these various programs operate in Silicon Valley and how they have been effected by changing labor market dynamics. Instead, I will focus on the activities of NOVA, which coordinates a range of training programs in the region and which has gained the greatest prominence within the workforce development system as an intermediary.

NOVA had its origins in the Joint Training Partnership Act (JTPA) of 1983. It was founded as one of two Private Industry Councils in Silicon Valley, covering the northern part of Santa Clara County. Private Industry Councils were created by the JTPA to oversee the distribution of funds and the administration of training programs. The JTPA marked a significant break from previous federal training programs, particularly in its efforts to increase local involvement in setting priorities for training programs and overseeing the provisions of these services. Such local setting of priorities and oversight was seen as essential for improving the effectiveness of training provision, since labor markets are highly differentiated at a local level. Local service delivery areas (SDAs) were created to help determine policy priorities, and Private Industry Councils (PICs) were created, with the responsibility of policy guidance and program oversight of JTPA funds. The membership of PICs was mandated to include representation from public, private and nonprofit sectors, with the private sector having more than 50 percent representation. When the JTPA was superceded by the Workforce Investment Act (WIA) of 1998, this local governance structure, now renamed Workforce Investment Boards (WIBs), was maintained as an important component of the new system. Under both the JTPA and the WIA, these local governing bodies make important decisions about the nature of services provided while establishing methods for subcontracting with other groups to actually deliver the services.

The NOVA (NOrth VAlley) PIC is one of two PICs that were established in Silicon Valley.[2] The second one, actually named the Silicon

2 When the JTPA was superceded by WIA in July, 2000, NOVA essentially maintained the same organizational structure, becoming certified as the new Workforce Investment Board for northern Santa Clara County. The Silicon Valley PIC, in contrast, which had previously been administered by Santa Clara County, was taken

Valley PIC, is larger both in terms of funding and in terms of its service area, which covers the central and southern portions of Santa Clara County, including the City of San Jose. It is larger because the area it represents includes more poor neighborhoods and thus a larger population eligible for publicly funded training. NOVA, in contrast, is located in an area with fewer disadvantaged workers but one that is more directly shaped by dynamics in the high-tech industry. It is in an area that was at the heart of the emergence of the semiconductor industry in the 1960s and has been the core of high-tech innovation since then. Partly as a result of this, NOVA PIC is more developed in its role as an intermediary in the labor market and has been highly innovative in the development of its programs and funding base.

NOVA has been very explicit in its strategy of being a labor market intermediary. They have not tried to solve the problems of particular groups of disadvantaged workers. Instead they have tried to build a network of service providers providing complimentary services, positioning themselves as an intermediary between employers, job seekers, and education institutions, to provide the information and services required to meet the needs of the labor market:

> The key in our model is learning how to invest in the network, not in ourselves. The strength and size of the network is what determines the success of the program . . . The task we have at hand is way beyond any one of our resources to do it, left alone, way beyond our information banks and abilities. What causes the network to expand is the ability and the necessity of not having enough information yourself, but having part of the answer, and it only makes sense when you put it with someone else in the puzzle. The model of a stand alone program with all the resources under one roof is no longer viable. (Inteview, Mike Curran, Director, NOVA PIC, May 21, 1999)

NOVA argues that they have had to develop this intermediary structure in part because of the nature of the industry in the area, which "means being prepared to deal with constant change [as] companies ramp up or downsize almost daily [and] new technologies pop up, seemingly overnight, and skills become obsolete. Jobs open and close at a rapid pace as companies shut down one division to concentrate on another".[3] This volatility in employment means that both employers and employees are

---

over administratively by the Economic Development Department of the City of San Jose. As a result, it went through a significant amount of restructuring.
3   www.novapic.org

in greater need of intermediary services, and there are greater opportunities for intermediaries to be successful.

NOVA developed this intermediary model through a variety of different programs which now go far beyond the typical JTPA/WIA funding stream and beyond the boundaries of the six-city consortium[4] which set it up in the first place. While PICs were typically set up as bodies to manage workforce development funds primarily through the Joint Training Partnership Act, NOVA PIC in fact in 1998/99 got only $1.5 million out of $14 million in funds from the JTPA. The remainder of their funding came from some thirty to thirty-five other sources of funding, which they have accessed in an entrepreneurial manner. This includes state funds on welfare-to-work programs, company donations, federal government funds for displacement related to NAFTA, other Department of Labor funding programs, and private foundation funding as well.

One area that they have developed particularly strongly is the area of research on labor market dynamics. Like many PICs in California, they produce regular occupational outlook handbooks which analyze trends in wages, skill requirements and hiring practices in 25 high-priority occupations in the region each year. This program is not unique to the NOVA PIC, and is in fact part of a state-wide project called the California Cooperative Occupational Information System. What make NOVA unique, however, are the ways they have extended their analysis of local labor markets beyond this system.

The problem with standardized occupational outlook reports is that they give little feel for the institutional context governing employment relations, possible career ladders, or how individuals get into these occupations. To respond to these problems, and to better understand local labor market dynamics, NOVA developed an extensive series of customized studies aimed at understanding labor market dynamics in particular industries and sets of occupations. These studies complement the quantitative analysis that forms the core of occupational outlook handbooks with detailed interviews with employers and training providers in particular industry clusters.[5] The goal is to provide a more

4   Based in Sunnyvale, its jurisdiction includes six cities in northern Santa Clara County (Sunnyvale, Cupertino, Mountain View, Los Altos, Santa Clara, and Palo Alto) that are the heart of where the high-tech industry originally developed in Silicon Valley.

5   Specific publications produced in this series have examined careers dynamics in the bioscience, software, telecommunications, semiconductors, multimedia, health care, service, high-tech manufacturing, and construction industries. http://www.novapic.org/nova/empserv3.html#whitepapers

nuanced and detailed understanding of future trends in the industry
and the direction of changing labor force requirements. This analysis
of trends in the labor market becomes a living record of trends in the
labor market:

> We've found a lot of customer value in our LMI+ studies because it is not
> just aggregation of data, it is the anthropological side – what is the real
> story here. The data becomes less relevant over time, but the story be-
> comes a foundation, and has a value ten years from now. With the story
> there from the past, you can catch up much faster on the current reality,
> which is impossible with just the data. (Interview, Mike Curran, Direc-
> tor, NOVA PIC, May 21, 1999)

Not only have they developed these detailed industry cluster studies
but NOVA has also leveraged this in-depth knowledge of occupational
trends in industry clusters toward identifying career ladders for disadvantaged workers. With funding from the Packard Foundation, they
provided a detailed guide to career ladders for welfare recipients initially in four counties (San Mateo, Santa Clara, Santa Cruz, and Monterey)
with plans to expand to other counties as well.[6] The project provides
practical, tangible reference tools for both economically disadvantaged
job seekers and service providers, to understand opportunities for mobility and career advancement in various occupations. The project rec-
ognizes that to help low- and poverty-wage workers become self-reliant
requires much more than funneling individuals into low-skill, minimum-
wage jobs, and instead tries to provide the tools and resources to identify real career ladders in a highly volatile labor market.

Their goal in providing these intermediary services is not simply to
provide resources to particular groups of workers, as is specified in
most job training funding programs, but instead to provide information that is generally applicable to the labor market as a whole. This
information-channeling function has become highly respected by companies and business in the area. This is reflected in the fact that events
which launch the release of a new study are typically attended by more
than four hundred people, and their publications are regularly distributed to thousands of Silicon Valley firms and workforce development
professionals.

Perhaps the best example of NOVA's intermediary efforts, however,
is their one-stop career services center, "Connect!".[7] This program is a

6   http://www.careerladders.org
7   http://connect.one-stop.org

one-source service center that links together a range of established workforce and business solutions providers. The idea for the program started in early 1995 and was launched in 1997. By 1999 they had a total of 39 partners, providing a wide range of services for employers and job seekers. Along with the typical training and placement programs available for job seekers is a range of services for employers, including:

- comprehensive training, recruitment, career development, and outplacement programs;
- personalized employment services;
- unique employee retention and training programs;
- workforce diversity resources;
- full-service on-site training programs;
- on-site, custom training in leading-edge manufacturing techniques;
- custom training and business consulting services;
- in-depth labor market information;
- individualized research and document delivery;
- state-of-the-art videoconferencing, patent and trademark services;

Connect! has played an important role in shaping national reforms in the workforce development system. The one-stop career center concept has now become a core element of national reform of workforce development systems under the Workforce Investment Act of 1998. The goal of this reform is "to integrate education, job training, and employment programs, services and information to ensure they are delivered in a manner that is integrated, comprehensive, customer focused, and performance-based to meet economic and workforce preparation needs".[8] Connect! received one of the early one-stop system-building demonstration grants in 1996, and the lessons learned from their early efforts have been incorporated into subsequent one-stop initiatives elsewhere.

NOVA's innovative programs have received wide recognition and resulted in a highly successful program. Some signs of their success include the following.

- NOVA has met or exceeded all state-mandated performance goals since its founding in 1983, including achieving a 73 percent job

8   http://www.sjtcc.cahwnet.gov/sjtccweb/one-stop

placement rate for dislocated workers receiving retraining during the recession years following 1991.

- They received the President's Award for the Nation's Outstanding Training Program in 1992.
- Their youth@work program was honored by the Smithsonian Institution in 1997 as a successful and innovative use of information technology.
- They received a National Award for Performance Excellence in 1997 from the Enterprise, a quality initiative of the US Department of Labor.
- Their one-stop initiative, Connect!, was one of a few local demonstration projects to receive funding for demonstrating how to build effective local one-stop delivery systems.
- NOVA has served over 6,000 employers and 60,000 individuals.
- Their web site (novapic.org) has become a useful source of information for the workforce development community. The number of hits on the page has risen from 3,257 page requests in August 1997, shortly after it went on-line, to 10,950 one year later, to some 17,519 in March of 1999.
- Traffic at their youth@work (www.youthatwork.org) web site rose from 3,963 page requests in February, 1998 to 14,824 in June of 1999 (figures obtained from NOVA PIC technical staff).
- Since the mid 1980s, NOVA's budget has grown by an average of 25 percent a year, from less than $2 million per year to over $14 million in 1998.

It is important to recognize that the overall focus of NOVAs activities have been at fundamental odds to the way that most federal employment training has been structured. In the past, federal training dollars were designed to provide targeted assistance to a subsector of the population that face a particular set of barriers to employment. As a result they are often marginalized from employers, or are able to build ties only with employers who primarily employ low-skilled workers. The model of NOVA, in contrast, is to be more directly integrated into the core of the regional labor market:

> Think about some of the problems in relation to our funding. The best solutions for our programs are to give things away for free, and to give it out to as many people as possible. We're actually paid NOT to give things away for free, and to give it out only to a carefully targeted group of people. The best solution would be for people to be able to get the

information they need without having to wait to come to us, but we're paid to have people contact. If I have information that is useful, you're supposed to be eligible before I'm supposed to be able to give it to you. To have more responsible participants in the workforce system, our systems are paid to fragment it and not go to everyone. (Mike Curran, Director, NOVA, May 21, 1999)

By becoming valued service providers for employers across a range of industries, occupations, and skill levels, NOVA argues it is able to more effectively link disadvantaged workers to employment opportunities that provide real career opportunities. While it is beyond the scope of this book to attempt to verify the effectiveness of this argument, the theme of building close ties with employers is something that has emerged in other categories of public sector intermediaries as well, and suggests that playing such an intermediary role is a growing component of public sector training programs more generally.

Education-based Intermediaries

Since the beginning of job training programs in the 1960s, there has existed a strong distinction between "education" and "job training." In recent years, however, as educational institutions have gotten more involved in lifelong learning and taken a more active role as brokers in the labor market, this distinction is breaking down. In essence, educational institutions are taking on an intermediary role in the labor market that resembles the role that job training programs are taking.

Historically, education and job training programs have differed in at least six distinct ways (Grubb 1996):

1 Education programs are longer, while job training programs tend to be of short duration;
2 Education programs are open to the general population, while job training programs are open only to those who are eligible;
3 Most education programs take place in educational institutions that are well established and standardized, while job training services are offered in a bewildering variety of educational institutions, community-based organizations, firms, unions, private schools, and so on, making it difficult to determine how services are organized and provided;
4 Education programs are relatively standard, built around classroom instruction (including labs, workshops and other hands-on activities)

while job training programs provide more on-the-job training and
work experience, as well as counseling and life skills training;

5   The goals of education programs are typically quite broad, encompassing political, moral, and intellectual purposes as well as occupational ends, while job training programs are exclusively focused
on preparing individuals to become employed;

6   Job training has generally been a federal initiative, with some significant state funding in welfare programs, while education is more
typically a state and local responsibility.

In essence, the education system has been treated as the primary
means by which people gain the skills, knowledge, and education they
need to be both productive workers and productive citizens in society,
while the job training systems has been developed as a "second-chance"
system. Developed in an *ad hoc* fashion, job training provides additional
services and resources to people who for varying reasons face barriers
to effective employment. Educational institutions were seen as the primary institution to prepare people for the world of work, but initially
were not seen to be very effective at vocational education.

This distinction between education and training, however, is increasingly breaking down. Educational institutions are no longer limited to
educating individuals before they enter the job market. Community
colleges and university systems are taking a greater role in providing
lifelong education opportunities while offering more short-term certification courses and extension programs. They are developing more
customized training and education programs, working in partnership
with private sector firms to promote training in areas linked to employment opportunities. They are also creating more contract training
programs to capitalize on the trend toward corporate outsourcing of
training services, and playing a more active intermediary role in the
provision of corporate training. The knowledge and skills obtained by
this contract training in turn feed into the educational components of
the institutions.

The engagement of educational institutions in contract training and
adult education is in part driven by corporate trends toward outsourcing
of training functions. Though many companies consider employees'
knowledge, skills, and abilities critical to success, few view training as
a core competency. Consequently, the training function has become a
prime candidate for outsourcing. Data cited by the American Society
for Training and Development shows that though outsourcing all training delivery is rare (3 percent of firms), most companies (83 percent)

outsource at least some training. Data from the Outsourcing Institute is consistent with that finding. In 1996, more human resource development activities (84 percent) were outsourced than any other functions. Logistics and information technology were outsourced at 52 and 51 percent. The average outsourcing of other functions was 30 percent (American Society for Training and Development 1999).

In addition, the trend toward educational institutions being involved in training is being driven by the rise in employment in small firms, since smaller firms have also been shown to outsource a greater portion of their training budgets. The BLS Survey of Employer Provided Training, for instance, found that in 1994 on average, firms with more than five hundred employees spent 49 percent of their training money on outside training, while firms with 100–499 employees spend 57 percent on outside training, and firms with 50-99 employees spent 67 percent on outside training.[9] Thus, as the percentage of employment in large firms has shrunk, the potential market for external training agencies has arisen as well.

The majority of training is provided by private vendors, either specific training companies or what have come to be known as private, post-secondary schools. According to the American Society for Training and Development, public colleges only provided 10 to 20 percent of external training expenditures, while tuition reimbursements accounted for another 6 percent of training expenditure, with the bulk of the remainder going to private vendors (Bassi and Van Buren 1999). Nonetheless, the role of educational institutions in providing contract training is significant because of their links to traditional education. The skills, expertise, and knowledge of the local labor market that is gained by playing an active role in adult education and contract training can be fed back into basic educational programs to improve their curriculum as well. Even without this particular spin-off, however, it is clear that educational institutions are playing a more active intermediary role for workers of all ages, not simply providing a channel of entry for people first entering the labor market (Lynch, Palmer, and Grubb 1991). The American Association of Community Colleges estimates that the number of community colleges actively seeking to provide training to companies jumped from about 50 percent in 1990 to 90 percent in 1995 (Stamps 1995). Thus, this trend is not unique to Silicon Valley, but represents a broader, generalized trend as community colleges and other

9   http://www.bls.gov/news.release/sept1.toc.htm

adult education providers have recognized the opportunities created by this type of labor market.

In Silicon Valley, these trends are best exemplified by the education extension program of the University of California, Santa Cruz, and by the community college system. These educational institutions have become deeply integrated into the regional production complex, having well-developed relationships with employers in the area, and providing customized training for mid-career people. Their contract training programs, providing customized training to businesses in the area on a fee-for-service basis, also play a critical role in the arena.

University of California Extension, Santa Cruz

UCSC-Extension operates as an independent unit affiliated with the University of California Santa Cruz campus. It is entirely self-funding, and thus must generate its entire operating budget from the fees it charges for its courses. Yet the dean of UCSC-Extension reports directly to the executive vice-chancellor of the UCSC campus, and thus administratively it is integrated into the operations of the University. While the program has existed since 1965, for the first twenty years of its existence courses that predominated were those focused on "quality of life", such as humanities, culinary art, photography, and travel/study tours, rather than career oriented courses. Courses took place primarily in its facilities on the UCSC campus in Santa Cruz, spatially removed from the core of Silicon Valley by the mountains of the coastal range. As recently as 1989, they had no students taking classes in facilities in Silicon Valley itself.

This situation started to change dramatically in the early 1990s. UCSC-Extension first decided to move to Silicon Valley in 1987, and it was officially opened in 1988, initially just with an office for marketing and promotion but with no teaching space. It quickly became clear that the demand was significantly greater than had been anticipated and that UCSC-Extension needed to have their own classroom space. In 1991, their first classroom space opened, with 15,000 square feet in the top floor of a two-story building in Santa Clara. Within six months they had expanded to the whole building, and a year later opened another space in Sunnyvale, and later one in Cupertino. By 1999, they also ran a joint facility in Milpitas, in cooperation with Sun Microsystems. Sun has a teaching facility which they use during the day to provide

Table 6.1   UCSC Extension enrollments, 1998–99

Subject Area	Enrollment
Software	10,500
Hardware	10,300
Business	8,700
Art and multimedia	6,600
Education	5,000
Behavioral science	4,000
Humanities	2,500
Environment and bio tech	1,750
Other	3,650
Total	53,000

Source: UCSC-Extension Marketing Department.

instruction to their own employees, and UCSC-Extension uses the facilities in the evening.

Thus, by 1999, UCSC-Extension had a total of four different facilities in Silicon Valley. They provided courses for more than 35,000 different people a year, enrolled in more than 50,000 individual placements. This was up from total enrollment of only 21,000 in 1990/91. Total revenue for UCSC-Extension grew to $20 million in 1998/99, up from $4.8 million in 1990/91. The vast majority of their students were adults taking courses in career-oriented positions, primarily in software and hardware technologies, business and management, or multimedia art and design (see table 6.1). More than 80 percent of this training was taking place in facilities in Silicon Valley itself.

The student body is primarily adults seeking ongoing skills for career advancement, with 50 percent of enrollees being between the ages of 35 and 50. According to student profiles, 80 percent of these enrollees already have at least one college degree, while 59 percent have two or more degrees. A full 50 percent of tuition is paid for through the employers of enrollees tuition reimbursement programs (Clark 1999).

UCSC-Extension's rapid growth was due in part to an accident of timing. They arrived in the Valley during an economic downturn which put a large number of people out of work:

> We arrived at a time when the economy was going through an adjustment. People go back for more training when they are at risk, out of work, or things like that are happening. This was true during the military

downsizing [during the early 1990s] . . . When [the economy] firmed up
a bit, while employees stopped coming, but employers were then looking more for retraining existing workers for new jobs.[10]

Even once the economy started to recover, the demand for the type of
training that UCSC-Extension provided didn't decline. During the economic downturn, many companies in the area laid off their training
departments, which were often the first departments to be downsized.
As the economy improved, many companies did not reinvest in their
training departments to the same level.[11] The dependence on outside
trainers thus expanded significantly in the 1990s.

Partly in response to these trends, starting in 1994, UCSC-Extension
also developed a customized corporate training program. This effort
builds customized training for many firms in the area, both large and
small. The courses are custom designed, covering a range of disciplines,
and are developed in cooperation with the client firm. Specific companies in the area that have developed programs with UCSC Corporate
Training include Bay Networks, IBM, Netcom Corporation, Siemens
Business Communications, Sun Microsystems, Watkins-Johnson, and
Abbott Laboratories.

The number of people trained through this custom training program
is significantly smaller than through UCSC-Extension's regular programs. In 1999 they had approximately two thousand enrollments a
year. Total revenues in 1998/99 were $1.4 million, up from $1.2 million
the previous year. The character of the training has shifted somewhat
from the first couple years of activity as well, in part due to the tighten-
ing of the labor market. Initially their training was primarily for just-in-
time type projects, where a company was working on a new project
and needed people with the skills to work on it immediately. In more
recent years, the focus has been on long-term certification courses requiring 12-18 months for a certification with people taking courses
on site in the evening. This becomes a retention tool, as workers stay on
site but receive certification that will be more generally valuable and
recognized in the labor market.

---

10   Interview, Dale Stansbury, Assistant Dean for Economic Development, UCSC-
Extension June 1999.
11   Interview, Sandra Clark, Director, Corporate Training Programs.

Community Colleges

The community colleges in the area have played a crucial role in providing training for the region's workforce as well. Much of the training provided through the community college system, of course, occurs for people who are just moving into the labor market. For people moving from high school into community colleges and getting the training they require to enter the labor market for the first time, community colleges are best analyzed as part of the basic education system. For people who are returning to community colleges for training at a later point in their career, however, the community colleges play a crucial role as a labor market intermediary. This role has increased in recent years, and is expected to increase even more in the coming years. In addition, the community colleges in the area have all established contract training and economic development assistance departments to provide customized training and assistance to firms in the region, further expanding their role as labor market intermediaries. The workforce reached by the community college system, in comparison to the UCSC-Extension system, are people with lower levels of formal education who are accessing jobs with lower levels of remuneration.

There are three community college districts in Santa Clara County, with a total of six campuses. Table 6.2 lists these three community college districts, the associated campuses, and economic development programs associated with each district. One of the indicators of the community colleges role as an intermediary in the labor market is the growing age of their workforce. A significant number of students are adults returning to college to improve their skills or access new employment opportunities. Thus, in the fall of 1998, enrollment in the Foothill-De Anza District included 2,500 students who already had a bachelor's degree and 1,000 who already had a master's degree, up from 1,400 with a bachelor's degree and 800 with a master's two years previously (Foothill-De Anza Community College District 1999).

In addition, all the community college districts have developed extensive contract training programs, customized curriculum development, and economic development initiatives. The Business and Industry Institute (BII),[12] the contract training arm at Foothill-De Anza community college district, was established in 1981, the first community

12   http://wwwfh.fhda.edu/BII/BIIHome.html

Table 6.2 Community college districts in Silicon Valley

Foothill–De Anza Community College District

Students (%):
40,700 district-wide
  Caucasian 40
  Asian 27
  Hispanic 11
  African-American 4
  Other/non-specified 13

Campuses:
  Foothill College (Los Altos Hills)
  De Anza College (Cupertino)
Economic development programs:
  Occupational Training Institute
  Center for Applied Competitive
    Technologies
  Business and Industry Institute

West Valley–Mission Community College District

Students (%):
25,000 district-wide
  Caucasian 63
  Hispanic 12
  Asian, 9
  African-American 2

Campuses:
  West Valley College (Saratoga)
  Mission College (Santa Clara)
Economic development programs:
  Community Education
  Corporate Training
  California Procurement Training &
    Assistance Center
  Alternative Transportation
    Solutions
  Silicon Valley Small Business
    Development Center
  Workplace Learning Resource
    Center

San Jose–Evergreen Community College District

Students (%):
20,000 district wide
  Asian 46
  Hispanic 26
  Caucasian 16
  African-American 6

Campuses:
  San Jose City College (San Jose)
  Evergreen Valley College (San Jose)
Economic development programs:
  Institute for Business Performance

college contract training program in the state and one of the first in the country. Clients of BII have included many of the largest high-tech firms in the Valley.[13] They enroll between 3,500 and 4,500 a year, a number that expanded rapidly in the 1980s but has remained steady for much of the 1990s. When the program was first developed in the 1980s most of the training provided was generalized education, providing for-credit courses on employers' work sites, much of it in English as a Second Language for immigrants in manufacturing facilities. In the 1990s, however, there has been a switch to more customized, short-term, noncredit courses in business management. In the 1980s, courses were longer – classes of 48 hours, 72 hours, or even more, for credit. Courses now are shorter, generally from 4 to 16 hours of class time, and usually not for credit. Similar programs exist at West Valley/Mission (One-Source Training) and at San Jose/Evergreen (Institute for Business Performance)[14] but with less visibility and impact.

De Anza College is also the home of an innovative employment training provider called the Occupational Training Institute (OTI),[15] which has been running since 1975. OTI provides vocational training for low-income residents and displaced workers of Santa Clara County. It also services the local business community by providing free job placement services. Provisions include free training programs, including college fees, books, and training materials, and support services such as child care, meal allowances, transportation, financial aid, and tutorial services. OTI also offers job preparation skills, résumés, and interviewing techniques. Three- to nine-month programs include business, computer, health technology, and others.

Another interesting center at De Anza College is the Center for Applied Competitive Technologies. It was founded in 1989 by the California Community College Economic Development Network.[16] Housed at De Anza College, it is one of 12 regional centers in California with the mission to advance California's economic growth and global competitiveness through quality workforce training and services. They focus on customized on-site training which addresses basic training needs

13 Including Adobe Systems, Advanced Micro Devices, Alza, Amdahl, Apple Computer, Applied Materials, Ariba Technologies, Cisco Systems, CNET, Compac, Graphics Microsystems, Hewlett-Packard, Honeywell Measurex, Infoseek, National Semiconductor, Netscape, Silicon Graphics, Sumitomo Sitix Silicon, Synopsis, the McKenna Group, and Zilog, among others.
14 http://www.ifbp.org/main.htm
15 http://www.deanza.fhda.edu/oti
16 http://ednet.cc.ca.us

as well as more advanced manufacturing technologies. They focus on the industries dominant in the Valley, including biotech, telecommunications, computers, and electronics manufacturing. Their training is technically highly sophisticated, operating in essence as a manufacturing extension program for mostly small and medium-sized businesses. They operate nearly fifty multiday workshops a year, often focusing on operators in production techniques. In 1998, they reached a total of 568 companies in one form or another, either through training, running workshops, or one of their resource people providing customized assistance. The bulk of the training, however, was through workshops, and is directed to companies with between one hundred and two hundred and fifty employees.

One of the more innovative programs in the Valley was developed at Mission College as a customized certificate and degree program to train semiconductor technicians. The Semiconductor Manufacturing Technician Program was developed in partnership with several major semiconductor firms in the area, including Intel, and includes hands-on training in semiconductor fabrication, cleanroom procedures, monitoring manufacturing processes, and maintaining and troubleshooting manufacturing equipment. This training uses equipment and machines largely donated by firms in the area.

The West Valley/Mission community college district also administers one of the state's 18 community college-based small business development centers. This center, located in Sunnyvale, provides a range of services, including assistance in business planning and management, financing, accounting and marketing, as well as specialized assistance in such areas as procurement, international trade, database searches of federal technology, patent/trademark database searches, and assistance in competing for awards from the Small Business Innovation and Research Program, along with providing loans to small businesses.[17] It is co-sponsored with the US Small Business Administration and the California Trade and Commerce Agency. They gave out $6.5 million in loans to small businesses in Silicon Valley in 1997 (Economic Development Institute brochure, 1997). Having a small business development center connected with a community college helps build ties with employers that can help provide employment opportunities for community college students.

17   http://www.siliconvalley-sbdc.org/

Nonprofit/Community-based Initiatives

Nonprofit or community-based initiatives receive the bulk of their training and workforce development funding from public sources. They are seen by these funding programs as a service delivery vehicle for public sector training funds that might otherwise be directly administered by the public sector agencies. For example, the NOVA and Silicon Valley Private Industry Councils contract out about 75 percent of their funds to other agencies to actually implement the training. Nonetheless, nonprofits and community-based organizations can be more grounded in social networks of poor communities, making them more effective than many standard government training programs.

Silicon Valley has a substantial network of nonprofit and community-based organizations involved in workforce development and training. One of the premier community-based training initiatives is the Center for Employment Training, or CET. CET has gained prominence in recent years for two fundamental reasons. First and foremost is the success of its training programs. CET has consistently been one of the few workforce development programs able to demonstrate substantial impact on participants' earnings and employability, in contrast to many job training programs in which the increases in earnings have been moderate at best (Grubb 1996). A range of evaluations have shown significantly greater earnings increases for participants in CET's programs (Kerachsky 1994; Zabrowski and Gordon 1994):

- A US Department of Labor study found that CET produced about 33 percent greater annual earnings for out-of-school youth, compared to about 15 percent in the Job Corps (US Department of Labor 1995).
- A Rockefeller Foundation evaluation of four sites providing training to minority single mothers found CET trainees to have the only measurable increase in earnings, averaging about $2,000 a year (Hollister 1990).
- A national study conducted by Manpower Development Research Corporation found that CET produced an average increase of $6,700 after four years for criminal offenders and high-school dropouts, much higher than 13 other comparable programs around the country included in the study (Cave et al. 1993).

The reason CET has gained prominence is not simply the success of its programs. A highly influential analysis of the reasons for its success presented forcefully in a series of publications by Edwin Melendez, Marcus Weiss, and Bennett Harrison (Harrison and Weiss 1998; Melendez and Harrison 1998; Melendez 1996). Their argument is that CET has been so successful both because of its social movement origins in the farm-workers movement and, by extension, their strong networks within the Latino community, and because they have become integrated into the trusted recruiting networks of employers. In essence their role as an intermediary with strong ties on both sides of the labor market has been the source of their success (along with the technical skills training they provide). Certainly there are a range of other factors contributing to CET's success, including: combining training with remedial education programs; providing opportunities for real work on site (that is running their own child care center, cafeteria, autorepair shop, copying business, etc.); and the provision of social services on site, including child care immigration issues and job placement. Nonetheless, their role as an intermediary plays a critical role in their success.

Conclusion: Workforce Development Challenges

The rapid pace of change in Silicon Valley labor markets creates significant difficulties for training providers and other institutions devoted to improving employment outcomes for disadvantaged workers. The skills change rapidly, and often the formal technical skills that employers want change so rapidly that it is difficult for training providers to develop the training program in the time frame that employers want. A particularly poignant example comes from Foothill College where, in the mid 1990s, the college developed a technician training program in cooperation with one of the major semiconductor equipment manufacturers in the area. The training had to be developed on the company's work site, since the equipment the students would be training on was extremely expensive (over $1 million per machine) and the college didn't have the space even for a donated machine, and one which would soon be outdated. Within two years of starting the program, 35 people had gone through it to gain the training, but not a single one was hired by the company that had helped develop the training in the first place. The market conditions had changed, the technology had changed, and the company couldn't hire them.

Part of the problem was in the nature of the contractual relationship between the college and the company. The company was looking for customized, equipment-specific training, while the college wanted to make the training broader – so that it was relevant to a number of the semiconductor equipment manufacturers in the area, or even to broaden the curriculum to include technologies that are similar in other industries. According to the Chancellor of the college, the basic principles involved in the semiconductor manufacturing equipment industry, which involve linking hydraulic, electrical, mechanical, and computer systems, are actually quite similar to basic principles needed to understand new technologies in the beverage industry that were being requested at the same time. The Chancellor thus wanted to integrate the semiconductor equipment training with broader training that might be relevant to other industries as well, but the company's goals were related to very specific training for the workforce they needed, and they didn't want their equipment used for more general training that might benefit a broader sector of the workforce:

> There is an environment of rapid change, and the message we get from the private sector is "I want you now, get the skills I need you to have and *only* those skills, and get in here as fast as you can . . . It is no longer "come to a community college and we'll deal with the whole person and give you lifelong learning skills and train you to be a good citizen". Instead it is "get your 9-unit certificate and get out of here and get a job. That job lasts 90 days or 9 years, and then they are right back where they started . . . [Industry] has been yelling and screaming at education recently that we're not providing sufficient numbers of people. Finally I said, it's not just a pipeline issue. What you're asking me to do may be in fact antithetical to my own values, and that is give you a crew of 25–35 year olds who you can burn up, use up and discard. Maybe part of the problem is not that we're not filling the pipeline, but that you're flushing the toilet too many times. (Leo Chavez, Chancellor, Foothill-De Anza Community College District, personal interview, June 1999).

Ultimately, the problem in this case was that the training was linked with a single company. Training is more effective when it is linked in more of an intermediary role in the labor market more generally. This is a difficult task, however, for training providers to respond rapidly and flexibly to the rapidly changing skill demands. Clearly there is a strong demand for educational institutes, along with the employment development and training programs described in this chapter, to play an intermediary role in the labor market. The record on their effectiveness, however, is more mixed. Clearly there is significant room for improvement in the functioning of public sector intermediaries, but the approach to building better intermediary structures provides significant promise for improving labor market outcomes for workers.

Part III

Flexibility and Careers

7

Careers in Silicon Valley

Job security is the ability to get a job. Staff people don't have job security; you can be fired whenever the company likes . . . The social reality is, the staff person has no connections to a next job. They don't have social relationships. They're isolated. A contractor has these relationships. That's real job security.

Technical writer,
quoted in Kunda, Barley, and Evans (1999) p.37

I never chose temp work voluntarily, but I had to, since I got laid off and couldn't find permanent work. The time I've spent as a temp ruined my financial situation, my self-esteem, and destroyed any sense of my career direction. There is also a psychological damage in having to constantly "learn" the same old thing over and over. The need to constantly learn can be very stressful, and actually eats away at my creative energy, since I have to become short-term rather than long-term oriented.

Executive assistant in Silicon Valley

Up to this point, my concern has been with analyzing the nature of labor market flexibility in Silicon Valley and understanding the increasingly important role of intermediary organizations in shaping these labor market dynamics. In part I, I argued that labor flexibility is best understood by making a distinction between flexible work and flexible employment, recognizing that the forces shaping flexible employment patterns are different in important ways from those shaping flexible work practices. Rapidly changing work demands and skill requirements are primarily driven by broad forces of competition, innovation, and technological change. These forces do contribute to the

growth in tenuous, temporary, and mediated employment relationships, but flexible employment relationships are also heavily influenced by the legal, regulatory, and institutional environment shaping
employment in the US. Both flexible work and flexible employment
have contributed to the growth in labor market intermediaries, whose
activities are analyzed in part II. In the context of rapid change,
unpredictability, and heightened risk, both workers and employers
are turning to a range of third-party intermediaries to help them navigate through the complex labor market. Through reducing transactions costs, mediating risk, shaping compensation levels, and building
networks, these intermediaries have become a central feature of labor
markets in Silicon Valley.

   In this chapter I examine the implications of these flexible labor
markets and intermediary organizations for the livelihoods of workers
and, in chapter 8, for public policy. Flexible labor markets, at least certain aspects of them, are clearly a critical component of Silicon Valley's
economic success. The circulation of people and information from firm
to firm has helped foster creative innovation in product development
and process improvements. It has also helped ensure that new innovations quickly diffuse through the regional economy, contributing to the
region's pace of development. While individual firms have grown and
died, the regional economy as a whole has been able to thrive remarkably in the midst of the volatility and uncertainty that is inherent in
information technology industries. As a result, Silicon Valley has experienced more than four decades of dramatic economic growth and
played a critical global role in driving innovation, economic success,
and generation of wealth (Castells and Hall 1994; Kenney 2000; Lee et
al. 2000; Saxenian 1994).

   But what have been the implications of the structure of Silicon Valley labor markets for workers in the region? With so many people having only indirect, temporary, or tenuous ties with their employer, it is
clearly not appropriate to simply assume that the economic success of
the region's economy is translated into career success for workers in
the regional labor market. Flexible labor markets are risky labor markets, and workers in the region face high levels of uncertainty in their
employment opportunities and career paths. How do rapidly changing work requirements and temporary, mediated employment relationships shape who is able to benefit from the tremendous growth and
dynamism in the regional economy? What role do intermediaries play
in shaping success for workers in the regional labor market? What patterns of opportunity and inequality exist? What are the factors that shape

workers' ability to cope with increased risk in the labor market while developing rewarding careers?

Ideally, to fully assess outcomes for workers in these flexible labor markets it is important to understand not just patterns of jobs and wages, but also patterns of careers and earnings profiles over time (Arthur, Hall, and Lawrence 1989). The term "careers" in this context does not assume that work breaks down into neatly ordered patterns with consistent upward mobility so that engineers, programmers, and managers have careers while temporary workers, circuit board assemblers, and janitors do not. Instead, the term applies to all workers, fundamentally requiring we incorporate a time dimension into our analysis of labor market outcomes, trying to understand how work histories reflect employment stability and instability, skills and experience gained or made irrelevant, relationships nurtured or lost, risks or opportunities encountered. A focus on careers requires an understanding of relationships, both within and between firms, and cutting across work and nonwork activities (Arthur and Rousseau 1996).

Unfortunately, there are no regular labor market data sources that adequately track individuals' career paths at a regional level, making such an analysis difficult.[1] Nonetheless, through an examination of available labor market data, supplemented by a range of in-depth ethnographic and sociological studies of particular sectors of the regional workforce,[2] three basic patterns of labor market outcomes in the region are clear. First, while some workers in the regional labor market have clearly thrived, overall the region is characterized by high levels of

---

1   The way that government data sources are gathered, it is extremely difficult to gain an accurate, detailed, statistical picture of changing patterns of career paths in regional labor markets. The available statistics are inadequate for this type of analysis for at least three reasons. First, most available data on labor market outcomes are based on changing cross-sectional samples of workers. They can provide information on changes in wages over time, but do not allow researchers to follow an individual's wages or total earnings over time. Second, the few data sources that do track individuals over time are either national samples that are not large enough to make analysis at a regional level possible, or lack detailed demographic characteristics essential for interpreting changes at a regional level (for instance, basic earnings data provided through the unemployment insurance system). Finally, there are no existing data sources that look at all forms of compensation at a regional level, particularly stock options which are an important form of compensation for a growing sector of the workforce in Silicon Valley.

2   Chapple, Zook, Kunamneni, Saxenian, Weber, and Crawford 2000; Chun (2001); Douglas (1991); Engardio and Burrows (1997); Gregory (1984); Hossfeld (1998); Luethje (1998); Saxenian (1996); Saxenian (1999).

inequality along with stagnating wages for large sectors of the workforce. Second, the growth in flexible employment relationships is one significant factor contributing to increasing economic inequality in the region. In the current institutional and regulatory context, these employment relations dis-empower large sectors of the workforce, weakening their bargaining position in the labor market and making them more vulnerable to changing market conditions and technological obsolescence. The vulnerability of workers has been made particularly evident in the most recent downturn, as firms have rapidly shed workers and unemployment has grown rapidly. Third, intermediaries can play an important role in shaping labor market outcomes, but in contradictory ways, in some cases undermining career opportunities for workers and in some cases helping to build them. This contradictory role can be best analyzed by understanding the ways that each intermediary influences three fundamental factors that shape labor market outcomes: the nature and quality of people's skills; the nature and quality of people's social networks; and the type of power people have in the labor market.

Growing Inequality

For many workers, the economic boom of the 1990s created tremendous opportunities. Job growth was remarkably high, especially in the later half of the decade, averaging 5 percent a year for 1995–7. Unemployment rates in the Valley were consistently below statewide and national figures, with unemployment dipping below 5 percent in August, 1995, and below 4 percent in December 1995. By August of 1999, the unemployment rate in Santa Clara County dipped below 3 percent, and reached as low as 1.3 percent in December of 2000.

Labor markets in the region, however, were dramatically impacted by the economic slowdown that began in the second half of 2000. With high numbers of temporary and contract employees, firms did not hesitate to layoff large portions of their workforce. As a result, the unemployment rate in the region jumped dramatically, rising from 1.3 percent in December, 2000 to 5.4 percent in August, 2001. The unemployment rate jumped by a whole percentage point (from 3.3 to 4.3 percent) in the space of one month, from May to June. Silicon Valley unemployment rates remained below US and California levels through most of the 1990s, but by August 2001 they had skyrocketed to levels higher than state-wide and national levels and were expected to go significantly higher (see figure 7.1).

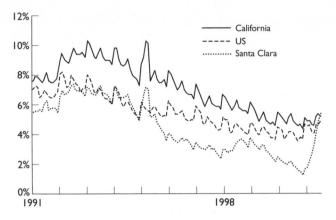

Source: http://www.calmis.cahwnet.gov/htmlfile/subject/lftable.htm
Figures are not seasonally adjusted.

Figure 7.1   Unemployment rates, Santa Clara County, California and US, 1990–2001

The tight labor markets through the latter half of the 1990s resulted in high wages for large sectors of the region's high-tech workforce. In 2000, according to Joint Venture: Silicon Valley Network, the average annual payroll in Silicon Valley, including both hourly and salaried employees, was $66,400, up 9 percent in real terms from the previous year and up more than 40 percent from the 1992 level. Silicon Valley payrolls are significantly higher than national averages – a full 84 percent higher than the national average of $36,100 in 2000. Payrolls in the leading information technology sectors were even higher: in 1999 the average annual payroll in the software cluster was $124,700, and $117,000 in the semiconductor industry (JV:SVN 2001). Average payrolls in nearly all information technology industries in the region are significantly higher than those in non high-tech industries. High levels of productivity and growth in information technology industries enable firms to pay wages significantly above the average, while strong demand for highly skilled workers tends to push wages higher as well.

There are many signs, however, that the economic benefits of the region's information technology industries are concentrated in a minority of the workforce. Annual payrolls in many nonhigh-tech sectors, for instance are quite low. In local and visitor services, for instance, a category that accounts for a full quarter of all employment in the Valley, average payroll in 1999 was only $24,000 (JV:SVN 2001). Between

Table 7.1 Change in annual average payroll and employment, Silicon Valley, 1992–8

	1992		1998		Percent change 1992–8	
	Employment	Average payroll ($)	Employment	Average payroll ($)	Employment	Average payroll
"Driving Cluster Industries"						
Software	26,715	78,693	72,320	109,220	171	39
Business services—outsourcing	50,298	25,988	84,561	28,344	68	9
Computers/Comm. contract manufacturing	22,858	47,527	35,364	54,239	55	14
Innovation related services	56,705	70,872	86,243	78,312	52	10
Semiconductors	56,681	76,094	77,698	96,339	37	27
Business services – professional	31,003	63,116	38,336	73,182	24	16
Bioscience	19,990	60,764	23,787	71,798	19	18
Computers/Comm. original equipment manufacturing	72,080	73,753	76,754	107,225	6	45
Environmental technologies	3,455	45,450	3,609	46,416	4	2
Defense/Aerospace	37,707	74,694	22,796	73,950	–40	–1
Other manufacturing industries						
Miscellaneous manufacturing	65,455	49,857	76,507	48,968	17	–2
Other major employment sectors						
Construction	38,580	46,749	61,802	49,645	60	6
Travel, tourism, leisure	24,194	21,412	35,095	28,265	45	32
Private social services	14,530	20,937	19,269	21,805	33	4
Private Hospitals	17,839	42,865	21,917	42,617	23	–1
Eating and drinking places	53,698	13,010	64,190	14,468	20	11

Other wholesale	31,662	48,423	37,600	52,489	19	8
Other private sector health services	35,569	49,405	41,010	45,066	15	–9
Other retail	82,950	25,921	94,761	27,812	14	7
Miscellaneous services	23,287	29,884	26,640	30,660	14	3
Private educational services	23,074	32,022	24,533	38,055	6	19
Finance/Insurance/Real estate	50,008	45,217	52,482	60,441	5	34
Government	111,412	40,398	115,749	43,455	4	8
Food distribution, wholesale and retail	28,716	29,566	29,960	30,072	4	2
Personal services	8,625	17,368	8,231	19,025	–5	10
Other	36,042	39,236	42,425	40,334	18	3
Total all industries	1,023,133	46,613	1,273,639	55,210	24	18

Source: Analysis of EDD ES-202 Data. Inflation adjusted 1998 dollars.

1998 and 1999, while overall wages in information technology industries rose 20 percent, in other industries they rose only 1 percent.

Low wages, however, are not limited to non high-tech sectors. For instance, out-sourcing services, a category which includes temporary help agencies and other companies providing essential services to the region's core information technology firms, was the second fastest growing sector between 1992 and 1998, yet annual payroll in this sector averaged only $28,344 in 1998. Annual payroll in contract manufacturing industries was $54,239, significantly less than that in the computer original equipment manufacturers, where annual payroll averaged over $107,000 in 1998 (see table 7.1).[3]

These averages payroll figures, however, understate the level of inequality in the region. An examination of hourly wage data in Silicon Valley, for instance, shows that those in the upper half of the labor market did quite well in the 1990s, while wages in the bottom half of the labor market stagnated. Wages at all levels declined during the economic downturn in the early 1990, but, during the boom of the late 1990s, wages in the top half of the labor market recovered more than the amount they had lost. Thus, by 2000 hourly wage rates at the 90th percentile were nearly 35 percent higher in real terms than their level in 1990, having grown from $35.62 (in 2000 dollars) to $47.98. At the 10th percentile, in contrast, the hourly wage rate in 2000 was $7.90, still more than 3 percent lower than the figure for 1990 (see table 7.2). This wage pattern in the 1990s, with wage growth concentrated at the top of the distribution and stagnating wages at the bottom, is in contrast to the 1980s, when wages grew across nearly all of the labor market, except at the bottom 10th percentile (see appendix 7.2 for full year-to-year wage changes).

With both declining wages at the bottom and rising wages at the top, income distribution in the region grew significantly more unequal in the 1990s. The Gini coefficient of wage inequality in the Valley[4], for instance, rose from 0.309 in 1989 to 0.361 in 1999. This makes wage distribution in Silicon Valley more unequal than that of the US as a whole, which had a Gini coefficient of 0.338 in 1999 (see Figure 7.2).

---

3   These figures are based on my own industry cluster analysis, using slightly different industry classifications from those used by Joint Venture Silicon Valley. See appendix 2.1 for details.
4   The Gini coefficient is a common measure of inequality, which measures the overall distribution of wages or income on a scale of 0 to 1, where a value of 1 means that one person receives all the income and a value of 0 means that all income is equally shared.

Table 7.2 Real hourly wage rates, San Jose, CA 1979–2000

Wage percentile	Hourly Wage ($2000)			Percent change	
	1979	1990	2000	79–90	90–00
90th	34.88	35.62	47.98	2.1	34.7
70th	23.13	24.71	26.97	6.8	9.2
Median	17.03	18.78	18.82	10.2	0.2
30th	13.04	13.85	13.15	6.2	−5.1
10th	8.99	8.17	7.90	−9.2	−3.3

Source: Analysis of CPS

The decline in wages for a portion of the workforce is clearly partly driven by wage declines in non high-tech industries, which still account for some 60 percent of total employment. The wage declines, however, are not limited to these sectors. Wages for production workers in the computer and electronic components[5] industries, for instance, also showed significant declines in the 1990s. The average hourly wage rate for production workers in the computer industry, for example, was $18.14 in 2001, down 12 percent from its value of $20.64 in 1990 (in 2001 dollars). The average hourly wage rate for production workers in the electronic components industry was $17.75 in 2001, down 10 percent in real terms from its value in 1990 (see figure 7.3). As might be expected, these wages declined significantly in real terms during the economic downturn that began in the second half of 2000. The downward trend, however, was consistent throughout the second half of the 1990s and simply accelerated slightly in 2001. Given that the production workforce[6] accounted for 52 percent of the total workforce in the electronic components industry, and 47 percent in all manufacturing in 1997, average wages of nearly half of all workers in the region's computer, semiconductor, and related hardware manufacturers stagnated in the 1990s. This is despite the tremendous economic boom in the last half of the 1990s, and rapidly rising wages for upper tiers of workers in the industry.

Another indicator of the limited and unequal distribution of the wealth generated in Silicon Valley's information technology industries

5 Including semiconductor and printed circuit boards.
6 As defined by the Census of Manufacturers.

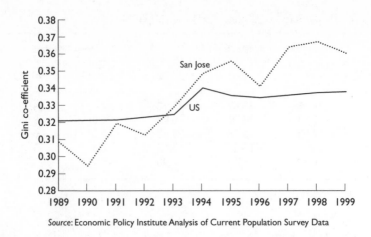

Source: Economic Policy Institute Analysis of Current Population Survey Data

Figure 7.2   Gini co-efficient of wage inequality, Santa Clara County and US, 1989–1999

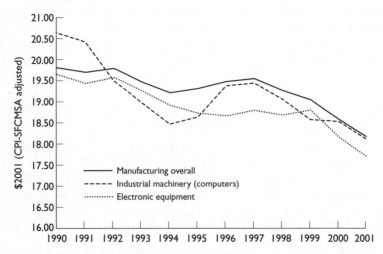

Source: California Employment development Department, Labor Market Information Division
2001 figures based on first nine months

Figure 7.3   Hourly wages for production workers, Santa Clara County, 1990–2001

is provided by comparing trends in productivity to wages. Productivity is an important measure of economic competitiveness, and manufacturing in Silicon Valley has one of the highest levels of productivity of any region in the United States. In 1997, value added per employee

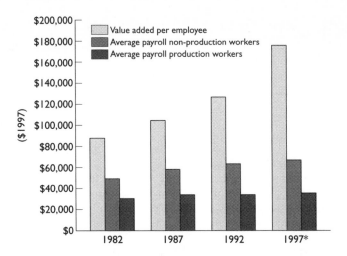

Source: US Dept of Commerce, Census of Manufacturers
*Technical note: Data for 1982–92 uses Standard Industrial Classification Codes 20–39 (Manufacturing). Data for 1997 uses the new North American Industrial Classification System Codes 31–33 (Manufacturing).

Figure 7.4   Productivity and wages in manufacturing, Santa Clara County, 1982–1997

(a simple measure of productivity) in manufacturing was $176,082 compared to a statewide average of $108,237. Improvements in productivity, however, are not being shared with the workforce within Silicon Valley. From 1982 to 1997, value added per employee in manufacturing grew by over 100 percent (a 4.7 percent annual rate increase). Yet the average wages for production workers (47 percent of the workforce in manufacturing in 1997) grew by only 16.5 percent over the whole 15-year period, while average payroll for nonproduction workers grew by only 35.6 percent (see figure 7.4).

One of the most dramatic signs of inequality in the region is the growing discrepancy between the skyrocketing compensation given to top corporate executives compared to stagnating wages of production workers in the same companies. Between 1991 and 2000 the average compensation of the top 100 executives in Silicon Valley's largest companies grew by over 2,000 percent in real terms, while the average annual income for production workers in the electronics industry declined by 7 percent. The ratio of annual income of the top 100 executives to the average production worker thus rose from 42:1 in 1991 to 956:1 in 2000 (see table 7.3).

Table 7.3 Executive compensation and production worker wages in Silicon Valley, 1991–2000

	1991	2000	% change 1991-00
Average total compensation, top 100 Silicon Valley executives	$1,603,770	$34,069,462	2024
Average annual wages production workers in electronics industry	$38,133	$35,651	−7
Ratio of average top 100 executives to average production worker	42	956	

Source: CA EDD and San Jose Mercury News

The exercising of stock options accounts for the majority of this growth in total compensation for top executives. The granting of stock options has become an increasingly widespread practice of firms in the Valley, not only to top executives but also to significant portions of their staff. Stock options enable the holder to buy stock at a preset price. As long as share prices rise at publicly traded companies, options can be tremendously lucrative. The wealth generated from this is not limited to top executives, and in fact has made a large number of Silicon Valley residents millionaires – Cisco Systems alone estimated in 1999 that 2,000 of their 19,000 employees were millionaires based on stock options (Quinn and LaFleur 1999). Stock options are, however, highly concentrated in the upper stratum of the labor market. A 1998 survey by the National Center for Employee Ownership (NCEO), for instance, found that of 20 Silicon Valley companies studied, top managers held 49 percent of all options. Senior executives in the companies held options worth $2 million, while professional and technical workers in these 20 companies received stock option packages worth roughly $58,000, and administrative assistants received packages averaging $18,000 (NCEO 1998).

It should also be noted that if the share price of the company drops below the option price, the options are valueless. Many stock options, particularly in small start-up companies, end up being worthless if the company goes bankrupt or fails. With the crash in technology and Internet stock prices in 2000, many stock options became entirely worthless. Even during the stock market boom of the late 1990s, the increasing use of stock options as compensation was not resulting in the level

Table 7.4 Top 15 metropolitan areas by average value household ownership of stocks received from employer

Metropolitan area	Percent with stocks from employer	Average stock value from employer
Anchorage, AK MSA	16	44,202
Boise City, ID MSA	14	43,210
Santa Cruz-Watsonville, CA PMSA	13	41,842
Salinas, CA MSA	12	41,415
Casper, WY MSA	13	41,371
Sioux Falls, SD MSA	14	41,370
Lincoln, NE MSA	13	40,698
Omaha, NE-IA MSA	14	40,424
Stamford-Norwalk, CT PMSA	22	40,300
Cheyenne, WY MSA	13	40,163
Billings, MT MSA	12	39,288
San Francisco, CA PMSA	21	39,075
San Jose, CA PMSA	24	39,026
Bismarck, ND MSA	13	38,992
Santa Barbara-Santa Maria-Lompoc, CA MSA	14	38,966

Source: Claritas, as reported in Quinn and LaFleur (1999)

of increased wealth in the region that might be expected from some of the popular accounts of their "widespread" use. In 1999, for instance, market research firm Claritas found that 24 percent of Santa Clara County residents hold stock received from their employers, the highest percentage of any metropolitan region in the nation, but the *value* of those stocks ($39,026) was lower than in 13 other metropolitan regions (see table 7.4).[7] Of 328 regions around the country, Santa Clara County ranked very high (3rd) in median household income in 1998, yet measured only 26th in median household wealth (Quinn and LaFleur 1999). All of this suggests that while stock options are important as a means of compensation for certain sectors of the population, their importance should not be exaggerated. The vast majority of the workforce still depends on their wages and salaries as their primary source of income.

7   Though "stocks received from employer" is not a direct measure of stock options, exercised stock options are likely to be a significant portion of this.

Factors Contributing to Inequality

Thus, an examination of cross-sectional data on employment, wages, and earnings in Silicon Valley identifies clear trends. Inequality has grown significantly in the 1990s. This trend would not be so disturbing if wages at all levels in the labor force were rising, with growing inequality simply the result of higher wage growth in upper tiers of the labor market. In truth, however, inequality is partially being driven by wage declines in the bottom half of the labor market. Furthermore, these declining wages are not limited to noninformation technology industries. Wages in many sectors of information technology industries have been declining as well, despite the tremendous economic boom during much of the decade. What are the factors contributing to this growth in inequality?

Clearly one factor is related to changing returns to education and experiences. The high demand for skilled information technology workers has driven up wages for educated workers, while wages for workers with a high-school degree or lower qualification have declined. Average wages for workers with at least some college education grew 16 percent between 1990 and 2000, while average wages for workers with only a high-school degree or less education declined by 12 percent in the same period (see table 7.5). Clearly, changing returns to education and experience can explain a significant portion of growing inequality in Silicon Valley. Though there have been no specific studies on this issue in Silicon Valley, a careful study of growing income inequality in California as a whole found that changing returns to skill, as measured by years education and work experience, could explain roughly one-third of the higher levels of inequality between 1967 and 1997 (Reed 1999).

Another factor that continues to be a major influence in shaping inequality in the region is the continued critical importance of race and ethnicity. In addition to skill levels, social networks play a critical role in shaping workers' access to employment, learning communities, and other economic resources. These networks are strongly rooted within particular ethnic communities, but these ethnic communities are often isolated from each other. Thus, for example, Chinese and Indian communities in the Valley have both been able to build strong networks and industry associations that have helped members of their respective ethnic community prosper, but there is very little interaction between the different communities (Saxenian 1999; Saxenian 2000).

Table 7.5 Average wage by education level and race, Santa Clara County, 1980–2000 ($2000)

	Average hourly wage (%)			Percent change		
	1980	*1990*	*2000*	*1980–90*	*1990–2000*	*1980–2000*
By education level						
High school or less	16.65	15.17	13.19	−9	−12	−20
More than high school	21.70	22.78	25.98	5	16	22
By Race						
White	20.46	22.00	25.47	8	17	25
Non-white	17.19	17.50	19.88	2	14	16
Overall average	19.68	20.48	22.61	4	10	15

Source: Analysis of Bureau of Labor Statistics, Current Population Survey, Outgoing Rotation Group Data. Because of small sample size, two years of data were combined, and thus the years actually represent combined averages for that year and the previous year.

Thus, racial inequality remains quite strong in information technology industries. In 1990 (the latest data available with detailed income and employment breakdowns by race and occupation)[8] whites made up 81 percent of the managerial workforce and 71 percent of the professional workforce in Silicon Valley high-tech employment. Meanwhile, in semiskilled production jobs, the largest category of blue-collar work, whites made up only 21 percent of the workforce, with Asians accounting for 40 percent and Latinos for 18 percent (see table 7.6). The average income for white men in high-tech industries in 1989 was $52,999 compared to only $30,037 for Mexican-American men, and $27,630 for Vietnamese men (see figure 7.5). Certain groups of Asians, most notably Japanese, Chinese and Indian, have reached upper tiers of the region's information technology industries. Other Asian groups, particularly Vietnamese, Filipino and Korean, remain in low-end assembly work.

Various surveys taken during the 1990s demonstrate that racial segregation has continued. According to data from the Equal Employment Opportunity Commission (EEOC), in 1996, for instance, in 33 prominent high-tech companies in the region, Blacks and Latinos were

8   At the time of writing, the employment data from the 2000 Census was not yet publicly available.

Table 7.6   High-tech manufacturing employment in Silicon Valley by race, 1990

Occupational category	Total	% White	% Asian	% Black	% Hispanic
Officials and managers	24,737	81	13	2	4
Professionals	51,468	71	22	3	4
Technicians	16,078	53	31	5	11
Sales workers	2,580	89	6	2	3
Office clerical	16,598	65	14	7	14
Skilled production	5,278	44	31	6	19
Semi-skilled production	18,591	21	40	21	18
Laborers	374	18	42	4	36

Source: US Census Public Use Microdata Sample, cited in Siegel (1994)

Table 7.7   Employment by race in 33 Silicon Valley high-tech firms, 1996

Occupational Category	Total	% White	% Asian	% Black	% Latino
Officials and managers	21,880	81	13	2	4
Professionals	63,084	71	22	3	4
Technicians	22,152	60	24	4	11
Sales workers	8,852	88	5	3	4
Office clerical	13,139	68	10	9	11
Craftsmen	2,333	66	15	4	14
Operators	14,424	34	41	7	17
Laborers	572	33	54	3	9
Service workers	213	32	14	8	45
Total	146,649	68	21	4	7

Source: Angwin and Castenada (1998), from EEOC filings obtained via FOIA request.
Data includes total employment in 33 Bay Area high-tech companies including: Adaptec, AMD, Air Touch Communications, Amdahl, Apple Computer, Bay Networks, Cirrus Logic, Cypress Semiconductor, Diamond Multi-media Systems, ESS Technology, Integrated Device Technology, Intel, Komag, Lam Research, LSI Logic, McAfee Associates, Netscape Communications, Oracle, PeopleSoft, Quantum, Rational Software, Raychem, Remedy, Sanmina, Seagate Technology, Sun Microsystems, Silicon Graphics, Sybase, Symantec, Tencor Instruments, 3Com, VLSI Technology, and Zilog.

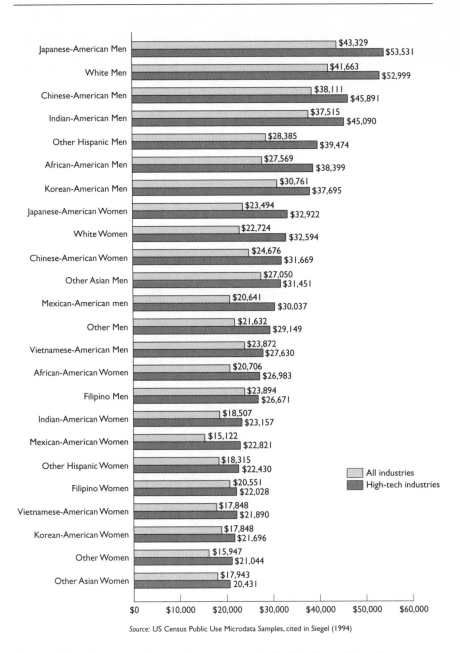

Japanese-American Men — $43,329 / $53,531
White Men — $41,663 / $52,999
Chinese-American Men — $38,111 / $45,891
Indian-American Men — $37,515 / $45,090
Other Hispanic Men — $28,385 / $39,474
African-American Men — $27,569 / $38,399
Korean-American Men — $30,761 / $37,695
Japanese-American Women — $23,494 / $32,922
White Women — $22,724 / $32,594
Chinese-American Women — $24,676 / $31,669
Other Asian Men — $27,050 / $31,451
Mexican-American men — $20,641 / $30,037
Other Men — $21,632 / $29,149
Vietnamese-American Men — $23,872 / $27,630
African-American Women — $20,706 / $26,983
Filipino Men — $23,894 / $26,671
Indian-American Women — $18,507 / $23,157
Mexican-American Women — $15,122 / $22,821
Other Hispanic Women — $18,315 / $22,430
Filipino Women — $20,551 / $22,028
Vietnamese-American Women — $17,848 / $21,890
Korean-American Women — $17,848 / $21,696
Other Women — $15,947 / $21,044
Other Asian Women — $17,943 / 20,431

All industries
High-tech industries

$0 $10,000 $20,000 $30,000 $40,000 $50,000 $60,000

Source: US Census Public Use Microdata Samples, cited in Siegel (1994)

Figure 7.5 Mean annual income by gender and ethnicity, Santa Clara County, 1989

Table 7.8 Silicon Valley high-tech workforce by race and occupational category, 1997

	% White	% Hispanic	% Asian	% Black
Total population of Santa Clara County	51	24	22	4
All high-tech firms surveyed				
White collar workforce	60	7	31	3
OEM designers and manufacturers				
Blue collar	15	23	59	4
Technicians	39	12	44	4
Contract manufacturing companies				
Blue collar	7	14	77	2
Technicians	20	6	72	3

Source: McLaughlin and Cha (1999) from EEOC Data.

significantly underrepresented, making up 4 percent and 7 percent of employees, while comprising 8 percent and 14 percent of the Bay Area labor force, respectively. Furthermore, they were concentrated in lower-skilled and lower-paying occupations, with Latinos making up 17 percent of the operators and 11 percent of the clerical staff in the high-tech firms surveyed (see table 7.7) (Angwin and Castenada 1998). Similar data from the EEOC in 1997 found the same patterns (see table 7.8).

There are clearly a range of other factors similar to nationwide trends that drive inequality in the region. These include declining unionization, eroding value of the minimum wage, increasing percentage of employment in low-wage service industries, growing immigration, and increasing globalization, which are the most prominent causes identified in national studies.[9] In addition, however, labor market flexibility and the role of intermediaries shape labor market outcomes as well, in ways that are discussed in the following sections.

Flexibility and Labor Market Outcomes

What impact has the growth in labor market flexibility had on the outcomes for workers in the region's labor markets? One clear impact of both flexible work and flexible employment has been an increase in

9   Bernstein and Mishel (1999); Levy (1998); Mishel, Bernstein, and Schmitt (2001); Moss (1999).

insecurity for workers. In the highly volatile information technology markets, workers have to continually upgrade their skills, through both formal training and informal learning. As the pace of technological change increases, workers frequently discover that their skills are valued less by employers, pushing them to return to school for significant retraining or to develop an entirely new career. Older workers are particularly impacted by this rapid change. High-tech industries tend to be dominated by younger workers, either those recently out of college or in their prime earning years. As mentioned in chapter two, wages for older workers in information technology industries actually start to decline after approximately twenty years of experience. Older workers who face layoffs often have a difficult time finding employment again, and face longer periods of unemployment while searching for new jobs. Thus, one of the by-products of rapid technological change is a long-term structural increase in the length of time people are typically unemployed.

An increase in the pace of technological change contributes to increasing length of unemployment for a number of reasons. When a firm changes technology, it may temporarily lay off workers while it closes to retool its facilities, or it may permanently lay off workers with some skills and hire new workers with different skills. Some workers, particularly those who have the hardest time acquiring new skills, may be unable to take advantage of the new job opportunities and thus face long-term unemployment. Even in cases of more incremental technological change that doesn't require retooling facilities, firms may also not consider it cost-effective to retrain some types of workers – particularly less-educated and older workers – to keep up with technological change. Firms believe it is not cost-effective to retrain older or less skilled workers, either because the retraining costs are higher or because the workers will not be on the job long enough or will not be productive enough for firms to recoup the costs of retraining. This preference not only leads to an increase in the share of the unemployed labor force made up of workers with high retraining costs, it also threatens them with permanent unemployment or at least a long period of job search before they are able to find a new jobs.

Baumol and Wolff (1998) have documented these trends at a national level. The average duration of unemployment in the 1970s for men was 13.1 weeks, while in the 1980s it was 17 weeks. The increase in unemployment is particularly dramatic for older workers, as unemployed men aged 55 to 64 were unemployed an average of 19 weeks in the 1970s, 23.8 weeks in the 1980s, and 25.3 weeks in the early part of the

Table 7.9 Mean duration of unemployment, 1970–98, period averages

	1970–79	1980–89	1990–98
Men			
Age (years)			
All men	13.1	17.1	17.3
16–19	8.3	9.3	9.7
20–24	11.6	14.5	13.4
25–34	14.0	18.3	17.1
35–44	16.8	21.1	20.1
45–54	18.0	22.7	24.0
55–64	19.1	23.8	25.3
Women			
Age (years)			
All women	10.5	12.4	14.4
16–19	7.5	7.8	9.0
20–24	9.5	10.8	11.3
25–34	10.8	12.9	14.4
35–44	12.1	14.7	17.0
45–54	13.9	16.1	18.5
55–64	16.5	17.8	20.7

Source: Baumol and Wolff (1998). Original data from US Bureau of Labor Statistics, *Employment and Earnings* (Washington DC: Government Printing Office). Figures for 1990–98 updated by author.

1990s. Related to this, and a more disturbing problem, is the increase in the number of people who face long-term unemployment. In 1993 for example, 21 percent of the unemployed were unemployed 27 weeks or more, compared to only 9 percent in 1979 and less than 5 percent in 1969.[10] (See table 7.9.)

The growth in flexible work and flexible employment relations has also served to undermine firms' investment in training. The intense pace of competition means that firms feel they have little room for the "luxury" of providing training for people without readily identifiable, valuable skills, and thus they expect to hire people with the exact match of skills required for a particular job or project. For companies with older computer programmers in need of developing certain new skills, the typical solution for many firms is to get rid of them and hire new

10   Baumol and Wolff (1998). Original data from US Bureau of Labor Statistics, Employment and Earnings (Washington DC: Government Printing Office). Note that these are national figures.

programmers instead. Most employers are reluctant to make the investment of retraining their workforce for fear that the workers will leave and take the skills with them or, even if they stay, that the demand for the skills will not remain long enough to make the investments worthwhile. The lack of retraining exacerbates imbalances between supply and demand when markets shift because employers have to wait for employees to train themselves in the new skills, typically waiting for the next generation of graduates (Cappelli 2000).

Thus, rapidly changing work requirements can create significant labor market shocks for people, increasing the risk of serious misfortune. The most negative impact of flexibility on workers' outcomes in the labor market, however, is primarily related to flexible employment, not flexible work (Masters 1999). The growth of outsourcing and the increased use of temporary employees severely weakens the ability of workers to bargain over their employment relationships, making them more vulnerable to market downturns and less likely to demand higher wages from their current employer. This is clearly evidenced in statistics on wages for temporary workers, which are significantly lower than wages of "permanent" workers with similar educational and demographics characteristics (Barker and Christensen 1998; Hudson 1999a).

Temporary workers also face serious problems in relation to occupational health and safety issues. Their legal employer, the temporary agency, is responsible for paying workers compensation insurance and for ensuring the safety of the work site. The temporary agency, however, has little or no effective control over working conditions in the work sites where they place people. In one particularly poignant example, in 1999, an assembly worker who was employed by Manpower Temporary Services in a warehouse packing Hewlett Packard printers became concerned about respiratory problems. He discovered that one of the chemicals in the ink cartridges used in Hewlett Packard printers had been linked to respiratory irritation and was a possible carcinogen. When he asked that an air quality check be conducted in the warehouse, he lost his job. He filed a complaint with the California Industrial Relations Board, which took more than twenty months to determine whether to fine Hewlett Packard, or Manpower, or both. Ultimately the California Labor Commissioner ruled that Manpower, as the legal employer, had violated the employee's right to express health and safety concerns at work. In this case, however, Manpower had no power to order an air safety check at the plant or to improve air circulation systems in the facility (Jayadev 2000).

Temporary employees are only one example of poor working

conditions facing workers in flexible employment relationships. Janitors provide a clear example of the problems that out-sourced service workers in Silicon Valley face. During the 1970s, the janitorial workforce was composed of two groups – "in-house" janitors who were employed directly by the companies for which they cleaned, and contract janitors, who were employed by private janitorial firms and contractors. In-house janitors usually had the same working benefits as other employees in their respective companies. Contract janitors generally had somewhat lower wages, but the existence of unions assured that working conditions were comparable to conditions for other unskilled occupations, and unionized janitors also received fringe benefits. By the early 1980s, however, when information technology firms began contracting out for cleaning and building maintenance services, working conditions worsened for both groups of janitors. The result in the 1990s was a three-tiered system, with reduced wages and conditions for all three tiers. The first major group consisted of janitors who worked for large unionized companies, for low wages but with access to health insurance and some other fringe benefits. The second group consisted of janitors employed by medium- and small-size cleaning contractors, most of whom were non unionized and who typically provided minimum level wages with no medical or fringe benefits. The third group was composed of self-employed contractors who informally employed a small crew of workers to fulfill their contracts. These small contractors usually clean small business offices and independent restaurants, laundries and the like, with payments in cash and working conditions that frequently violate minimum wage and health and safety standards.[11]

The institutional framework governing employment relationships provides no mechanism for contract janitors to demand higher wages from the companies whose buildings they are cleaning. These client firms are frequently highly profitable high-tech companies, but under the current labor relations system, janitors are bound to negotiate only with their legal employer – the building service firms whose profit margins are typically razor thin. This situation applies to many occupations providing services to information technology firms in the area, including security guards, cafeteria workers, and landscapers. The employment relationship for all these workers have changed, resulting in lower wages and poorer working conditions in outsourced firms, but their work itself has largely remained the same.

11   Zlolniski (1994).

Assembly workers in the region's printed circuit board industry are also highly disadvantaged by their flexible employment relations, as major hardware firms in the Valley have increasingly outsourced their manufacturing operations. This process started in the 1980s, when there was a major change in the technology of printed circuit board assembly work, with the rapid development and expansion of surface mount technology replacing the older pin-through-hole systems (Sturgeon 1999). As a result, assembly work became more automated and demand for assembly workers declined in Silicon Valley. Many assembly jobs moved overseas. The increasing sophistication of the technologies and the shortened time to market, however, has contributed to the growth of the electronic manufacturing services (EMS) industry, with major companies like Solectron, Flextronics and Sanmina growing rapidly in recent years. The importance of close communication between the engineers in these EMS firms and the original equipment manufacturers that design the equipment has prevented all assembly work from leaving the Valley, and employment in these contract assembly firms has actually grown rapidly in recent years. The work itself can be highly volatile, contributing to the insecurity of flexible work described elsewhere. The problems that emerge with the employment relationship, however, are twofold. First, to deal with the rapid fluctuations in production runs, EMS firms maintain a high level of temporary employment, typically running from 20 to 30 percent of total employment in the firm (Chun 2001; Ewell and Ha 1999; Ha 1999b). Second, these assembly workers are legally separated from the firms designing the products they are making, preventing them from receiving the generous wages and benefits packages enjoyed by many employees in these original equipment manufacturers. For example, twenty years ago Hewlett Packard managed most of their own manufacturing operations and production employees received many of the benefits of HP's famed management practices (Packard, Kirby, and Lewis 1995). Now, profit rates in EMS firms are tight, averaging 4 to 6 percent, while profit rates in Hewlett Packard and other major design firms in the Valley are 40 percent and higher. Those workers who are assembling products of the major firms in the Valley have no ability to negotiate any significant wage increases from their operations. They play a critical role in the network production systems that produce these high-value products, but are significantly disadvantaged in their employment relationship from making increased wage demands.

Thus, given the current institutional and regulatory framework surrounding the employment relationship, the growth in flexible employment has significantly disadvantaged growing portions of the workforce in the last decade. Low-wage temporary workers, outsourced service workers, and workers in complex production supply-chains all face lower wages that are in large part related to their changing employment contract. In some cases, such as the growth of the EMS industry, it could be argued that these changed employment relationships are linked with the promotion of flexible work practices and thus contribute to the pace of innovation in the Valley. In other cases, most prominently in the case of janitors in the region, the flexible employment practices provide essentially no performance improvements and result simply in lower wages for vulnerable sectors of the labor market.

Intermediaries and Labor Market Outcomes

What role do intermediaries play in shaping these labor market outcomes? It is easiest to think about this by examining the role intermediaries play in shaping three fundamental factors that broadly determine labor market outcomes:

1   The nature and quality of people's skills, information, and knowledge. This refers to both the formal education and training that workers have, and the accumulated knowledge, experience and skills that are gained in the workplace or through on-the-job learning.
2   The nature and quality of people's social networks and particularly how this shapes job-search strategies and learning opportunities.
3   The type of power people have in the labor market. Firms and individuals make decisions around work and employment in response to a complex set of forces, not simply responding to price signals from the market. The level of power workers have in the labor market and the way it is wielded can push employers to make human resource choices that reflect higher wages, better employment conditions, and a greater investment in their workforce, while it can constrain options employers may have for simply cutting costs and lowering wages.

Each type of intermediary will be briefly discussed in the context of each of these factors shaping labor market outcomes.

Skills Development

The intermediaries that play the greatest role in formal skills development are obviously the community colleges in the region. The increasing integration of the community college system with employer human resource requirements helps ensure that these training programs are oriented more toward employers' needs, thus providing more immediate employment opportunities for those people getting training. The community-based intermediaries and public sector training programs also provide training. These programs are limited, however, by having to respond to the eligibility and structural guidelines of funding agencies rather than responding directly to the needs of employers in the area. Certainly, the goal of JTPA (Joint Training Partnership Act) and more recently the WIA (Workforce Investment Act) is to provide training that meets employers needs, but historically they have demonstrated only a limited ability to do so.[12] Being constrained to work only with disadvantaged workers may strengthen the expertise of the JTPA and WIA system in understanding the problems these sectors of the workforce face, but it limits the ability to build relationships with employers at middle and upper levels of the labor market. As a result, they tend to build relationships with employers that simply provide entry-level, and frequently low-paid, employment opportunities.

For-profit intermediaries rarely provide any substantial training. At best, they provide opportunities for self-paced computer-based tutorial programs around particular software packages, typically the dominant Microsoft office software (Word, Excel, PowerPoint), along with database and desktop publishing software packages. This "training" is usually made available free. The only workers who are able to take advantage of this, however, are those who are already somewhat familiar with computers, who have the motivation to take advantage of these opportunities, and who have the time and resources to pursue these opportunities without financial support. As mentioned previously, some studies of such training programs have argued that for staffing services firms, training essentially serves as a screening device, helping them to identify workers that are likely to be successful placements, while weeding out the more difficult-to-place workers (Autor 1999; Autor, Levy, and Murname 1999).

12   Bloom, Orr, Bell, Cave, Doolittle, Lin, and Bos (1997); Grubb (1996); Lafer (1994).

Professional associations and unions, in contrast, provide a valuable infrastructure for building the learning communities that are so essential for developing and sharing both tacit and explicit knowledge in work practices. The role of these associations in ensuring rapid sharing of information and knowledge through the regional production complex has been documented, both here and elsewhere (Saxenian 1996). These associations are somewhat more limited in their provision of more formal skills training programs, though some of them do provide formal training programs.

Social Networks

Intermediaries can both substitute for social networks and build and strengthen social networks. In acting as a substitute for social networks, intermediaries may improve workers' employment opportunities if they can provide linkages to better jobs. If the linkages are to similar or poorer jobs than would be otherwise available through workers' existing social networks, their contribution is simply reducing transactions costs for workers' who may feel they have few alternatives. In acting as an organizational infrastructure for building and strengthening social networks, however, intermediaries play a critical role in shaping workers' social capital.[13] This role is particularly valuable if these social networks are both built around occupational communities, helping to facilitate the creation of learning networks, and include people from different socioeconomic levels, helping to create an infrastructure for career mobility.

Private sector intermediaries primarily substitute for social networks in the labor market, playing a critical role in helping workers gain access to employment. Skilled workers generally don't lack good social networks and the use of private sector intermediaries thus serves as a substitute for social networks in their job-search process, providing access to employment in a more rapid and efficient way than through personal contacts. For workers with poor social networks, temporary agencies may help them gain access to types of employment that they may otherwise never find. In essence, they use private sector intermediaries as a substitute for poor social networks that are

13 Putnam (2000); Wellman, Salaff, Dimitrova, Garton, Gulia, and Haythornthwaite (1996).

less effective in finding employment. The temporary agencies themselves, however, do little to help workers build and improve their own social networks. Workers are generally left to their own resources to build ties in the workplace that might lead to improved employment opportunities over time. Temporary workers in a new position often feel a desperate pressure to identify, meet and impress the "right people" in order to be able to "network" their way into better employment, but temporary agencies typically provide no assistance in these areas.

Professional associations and unions, in contrast, are good at building the infrastructure to support social networks. Through creating opportunities for workers to meet each other, share information about job opportunities, changing skill requirements, training opportunities, and so on, they provide the organizational infrastructure to support workers' long-term career advancement. They complement and strengthen workers' own social networks. They are limited, however, in the extent to which they are able to build bridges to lower levels in the labor market. None of the membership intermediaries identified were able to demonstrate long experience in providing opportunities for truly disadvantaged workers. A possible exception to this is the Working Partnerships' temporary employment program, which has shown some initial success in reaching ethnic minorities, women, and high-school drop-outs in its work. It is too early, however, to assess the extent to which this will translate into improved employment opportunities for this sector of the workforce.

The nonprofit intermediaries are the most effective in reaching truly disadvantaged workers in the labor market. In this sense, they are effective in "networking across boundaries," in a way similar to that described by Harrison and Weiss (1998). They are limited, however, in the extent to which they retain ongoing relationships with workers once these workers are no longer directly enrolled in their training programs. Thus, while they network effectively across boundaries, they do little to actually help workers build ongoing social networks. The role of other public sector intermediaries in building social networks is also mixed. Through the social interaction involved in training opportunities, workers can make important contacts, but these connections are typically short term in nature. The organizations provide no ongoing opportunities for building and strengthening social networks in the ways that the membership intermediaries do.

Labor Market Power

The third area of impact intermediaries have in shaping labor market outcomes is their effect on workers' power in shaping the nature of flexible employment relations. As Osterman (1999) describes, over the past thirty years employers have gained significant power in the labor market, while workers have become increasingly vulnerable. This situation creates opportunities for employers to use exploitative employment relations *simply because they can.* Supporting workers in the labor market is a critical way of ensuring that flexible employment is actually being used in cases that are linked with flexible work, rather than simply being a cost-cutting strategy. To be sure, empowering workers doesn't in itself promote flexible work practices, but it doesn't necessarily prevent them either, and it can help ensure that the benefits of a vibrant regional economy are shared more broadly.

In this regard, the membership associations are the only intermediaries who include empowering workers as an explicit goal of their efforts. The union intermediaries aim to do this through clear advocacy efforts, trying to explicitly alter firm hiring and employment practices. Professional associations aim to empower workers in a more diffuse way, helping raise their members' status in the labor market more broadly, and providing them with information and skills that strengthen individual's negotiations with employers.

The effect of private sector intermediaries is much more contradictory. Clearly, temporary agencies have been a key component of the decline in wages for large sectors of the workforce. Temporary workers earn lower wages and have more insecure employment, even controlling for all demographic and industry variables (Hudson 1999a; Kalleberg et al. 1997). On balance, temporary agencies must be seen as having a net negative influence on wages. Nonetheless, in tight labor markets, at least for workers with adequate skill levels, some private sector intermediaries actually can strengthen workers' ability to negotiate with their employers. The rapidity with which workers are able to find new employment opportunities means that they face little if any cost of switching jobs. They are thus much less likely to put up with unpleasant employment conditions and employers are more likely to be sure that employment conditions meet the needs of their skilled temporary workers.

Public sector intermediaries seem to do very little to empower workers in the labor market. Certainly providing access to improved skills provides greater leverage in their employment negotiations and to the extent they provide placement opportunities their impact is similar to that of private sector intermediaries. Nonetheless, these public sector intermediaries typically make no explicit effort to actively negotiate with employers on the behalf of workers, and instead exhibit a widespread willingness to accept the demand side of the labor market as given. In interviews, program managers in nonprofit intermediaries complained significantly about employment conditions through temporary agencies and poor employment opportunities in the labor market more generally, but had developed few strategies to try to change that situation.

Conclusion: Significant Problems Exist

The implications for workers' livelihoods of flexible employment and work practices are complex. Clearly many workers in the region's labor markets are doing well, and average payrolls continue to rise as the information technology industries have grown dramatically and the regional economy as a whole has thrived. It would be seriously mistaken, however, to conclude that the region's economic growth is benefiting all of the labor force. This chapter has argued that Silicon Valley's flexible labor markets are also associated with high levels of inequality and economic insecurity. Problems of navigating a career in these labor markets are not limited to low-wage workers but are also faced by many workers at middle and upper-level positions. Workers at all levels cannot depend on finding stable employment to help provide economic security, and are highly vulnerable to general economic downturns or restructuring within particular industries. In response to the volatility in the region's labor markets, workers are increasingly turning to intermediaries for help. These intermediaries in some cases undermine opportunities for upward mobility, and in other cases help build that opportunity. Both the rise in flexibility and the growth of intermediation in the labor market raise important implications for policy directed at improving labor market outcomes for workers. These are addressed in the next chapter.

APPENDIX 7.1: Silicon Valley Wage Data

Table A7.1 Real hourly wage rates by percentile, San Jose MSA, 1979–2000 ($2000)

	1979	1985	1989	1990	1991	1992	1993	1994	1995	1996	1997	1998	1999	2000	Percent change		
															1979–90	1990–2000	1979–2000
90th	34.88	33.65	35.54	35.62	35.25	32.99	34.68	34.38	33.22	35.22	39.60	40.95	39.57	47.98	2.1	34.7	37.5
70th	23.13	23.79	24.27	24.71	22.90	21.25	22.30	21.59	22.46	23.04	25.33	26.35	24.91	26.97	6.8	9.2	16.6
50th	17.03	18.20	16.79	18.78	16.92	16.24	16.34	15.22	16.38	16.79	17.71	18.52	17.07	18.82	10.2	0.2	10.5
30th	13.04	13.05	12.79	13.85	12.05	11.49	11.31	11.04	11.64	11.49	11.36	11.47	12.33	13.15	6.2	−5.1	0.8
10th	8.99	8.41	7.96	8.17	8.27	7.65	7.03	6.99	7.22	6.85	6.89	7.50	7.24	7.90	−9.2	−3.3	−12.2

Source: Author's analysis of CPS data provided by Economic Policy Institute. Figures have been adjusted for inflation using the CPS for the San Francisco CMSA as published by the California Department of Finance.

Table A7.2 Average hourly earnings by industry, production workers in Santa Clara County, 1990–2001 ($2001)

	1990 (%)	1991 (%)	1992 (%)	1993 (%)	1994 (%)	1995 (%)	1996 (%)	1997 (%)	1998 (%)	1999 (%)	2000 (%)	2001 (%)	% Change 1990–2001
Construction	32.99	32.18	32.07	31.72	32.00	31.80	31.53	31.40	31.29	30.35	29.67	28.42	−14
General building contractors	32.38	31.67	31.67	31.30	31.03	30.60	31.41	30.38	30.07	29.41	28.60	26.95	−17
Heavy construction	30.73	30.05	29.29	28.75	29.27	29.36	29.19	28.60	28.10	27.19	26.78	25.83	−16
Special trade	33.41	32.60	32.60	32.19	32.63	32.39	31.77	31.83	31.78	30.81	30.11	28.98	−13
Manufacturing	19.81	19.72	19.80	19.49	19.24	19.33	19.50	19.57	19.29	19.08	18.61	18.20	−8
Durable goods	19.99	19.91	19.99	19.68	19.40	19.46	19.71	19.81	19.51	19.29	18.78	18.35	−8
Lumber, wood, furniture	16.09	15.64	14.97	14.36	13.98	13.82	13.25	13.22	13.26	13.09	13.32	13.45	−16
Stone, clay, glass	24.17	24.32	24.34	20.81	19.43	20.52	20.93	21.61	21.30	20.76	20.23	19.31	−20
Prim. fabricated metal products	16.33	16.67	16.42	17.06	16.37	15.75	15.21	14.88	14.87	15.04	14.57	14.23	−13
Industrial machinery	20.64	20.42	19.51	18.99	18.49	18.65	19.39	19.47	19.09	18.60	18.56	18.14	−12
Electronic equipment	19.68	19.45	19.60	19.29	18.94	18.75	18.68	18.83	18.70	18.83	18.19	17.75	−10
Transportation equipment	28.73	24.71	26.19	26.44	26.14	25.54	25.74	25.00	24.87	23.91	23.02	21.80	−24
Instruments and related	19.35	19.73	20.37	21.17	22.62	24.48	25.53	26.82	27.13	26.58	25.95	24.74	28
Miscellaneous manufacturing	14.23	14.09	14.01	14.25	14.18	14.44	15.16	14.85	14.56	14.17	13.49	13.06	−8
Non-durable goods	18.79	18.52	18.80	18.35	18.39	18.63	18.15	17.84	17.68	17.40	17.13	16.78	−11
Food and kindred products	15.95	15.68	15.91	15.80	16.00	16.48	16.61	16.71	16.61	16.09	16.06	15.84	−1
Printing and publishing	24.14	23.09	22.30	21.20	20.87	21.13	20.45	19.85	19.95	19.40	18.79	18.61	−23
Chemicals and allied	20.97	21.17	22.06	23.01	23.14	24.22	23.25	21.34	21.12	20.26	19.41	18.35	−13
Rubber and miscellaneous plastics	15.37	15.70	15.66	15.25	15.64	15.95	15.75	15.72	15.69	15.37	15.17	14.92	−3
Other non-durable	18.45	18.62	18.15	17.67	17.19	16.82	16.83	16.66	16.52	16.60	16.11	15.82	−14

Source: California Employment Development Department Annual Report on Employment, Hours and Earnings.
This measures average hourly earnings of production workers by industry. Figures have been adjusted for inflation using the CPI for the San Francisco CMSA as published by the California Department of Finance. Figures for 2001 are based on first nine months of data.

8

Flexibility and Security

What am I then? What have I accomplished? Everything that I have seen, heard, and observed I have collected and exploited. My works have been nourished by countless different individuals, by innocent and wise ones, people of intelligence and dunces. Childhood, maturity, and old age all have brought me their thoughts ... their perspectives on life. I have often reaped what others have sowed. My work is the work of a collective being that bears the name of Goethe.

Johann Wolfgang van Goethe (in 1832)
Cited in College English, Vol 57, No. 7 (November 1995, p. 769)[1]

Motivated, sustained and cumulative tinkering with institutional arrangements is an indispensable tool of democratic experimentalism, of improvisational reform, of jazzlike public action . . . If American progressivism is to be reborn today and to carry forward its work, if it is to keep the religion of possibility alive and loosen the constraints that racial and gender oppression and class hierarchy impose upon our democracy, it must hear that message of democratic experimentalism more clearly.

Roberto Unger and Cornel West,
in "Progressive Politics and What Lies Ahead"
The Nation, November 23, 1998, p. 11

In December 1998, the US economy hit a milestone. It was the ninety-third consecutive month of growth, marking the longest peacetime period of economic expansion in the country's history.[2] With

---

1 My thanks to Lewis Hyde for sharing this quote with me.
2 A record that continued to expand until the third quarter of 2001.

unemployment at the lowest levels in a generation, inflation in check, and levels of productivity increases that hadn't been seen in thirty years, the US economy was at the time considered by many to be the envy of the world. Nevertheless, 1998 was also a record year for corporate lay-offs and downsizing. According to a regular survey from the outplace-ment firm Challenger, Gray & Christmas, companies announced a total of almost 700,000 layoffs in 1998 – 56 percent higher than in 1997 and the highest since the survey began in 1989, prior to the last recession. Despite the growth milestone of that year, hourly wages stagnated or fell for the bottom 60 percent of the labor market, and inequality con-tinued to grow (Mishel et al. 1999). The contrast between economic opportunity and insecurity is particularly stark in Silicon Valley, as the previous chapter shows. Prominent venture capitalist John Doerr once called the Silicon Valley led technology boom "the greatest-ever legal creation of wealth in the history of the world,"[3] and yet even at the height of an historic expansion in this dynamic region inequality in-creased, wages for a large portion of the workforce stagnated, and eco-nomic insecurity remained high.

This stark contrast – record layoffs and stagnating wages amid record economic growth – highlights one of the central paradoxes of the infor-mation economy. The development of new information technologies has made possible a period of remarkable economic opportunity, with rapid growth, new products, new markets, and the creation of tremen-dous wealth. At the same time, the volatility and unpredictability of competition is contributing to greater inequality and insecurity, pro-ducing a widespread unease about future economic opportunity (Osterman 1999; Reich 2000). The high levels of volatility inherent in an information economy were highlighted by the rapidity of the economic slowdown in the second half of 2000 and in 2001. In Silicon Valley, for example, unemployment rates more than quadrupled in the space of nine months.

Is it impossible to have greater economic security, a more equitable distribution of income and wealth, and still have innovation and rapid growth? Is insecurity a necessary consequence of an economy built around innovation and rapid change, or can we have both flexibility and security at the same time? Clearly we can do better than we are doing now. Information technology is not some independent, ineluct-able force determining in an inevitable way the structure of labor

3   Perkins and Nunez (2001).

markets. To be sure, information technology has certain characteristics that constrain our choices – like any technology it has a certain range of ways in which is can be used, altered, adjusted, and so on (Clark et al. 1988; Walker 1985). We cannot turn back the clock on processes of globalization, network production relations, the blurring of firm boundaries, or the forces of innovation that are so integrally linked with information technology. But the use of information technology is determined by decisions of organizations and individuals (Shaiken 1985; Thomas 1994; Westrum 1991). The development of technology itself is shaped by corporate power, military needs, and political imperatives (Noble 1977, 1984). Context and history are critical in shaping how technology and information technology in particular is used (Brown and Duguid 2000). Furthermore, information technology is not the only force shaping the economic restructuring of the past thirty years. Changing regulation structures play a critical role in shaping economic trajectories (Aglietta 1979; Lipietz 1987). National political structures and policies shape economic activity in fundamental ways despite economic globalization (Coates 1999; Esping-Andersen 1990). Collective mobilization on the part of workers can shape economic production in important ways (Herod 1994). Labor market regulation is an essential factor in shaping employment relationships and work practices (Kaufman 1997). Thus, the trade-off between labor market flexibility and social security – a supposed trade-off that sparked many heated debates on labor market policy in the 1980s and 1990s – is not inevitable.[4]

4   Research is finding that strict employment protection legislation, labor market standards, and social protection programs are not necessarily contrary to labor market flexibility. There are numerous ways in which security for workers can be increased without threatening, and indeed even improving, economic flexibility (Nickell 1997; Bettio and Rosenberg 1999; Blank 1994). In Blank and Freeman's (1994) words: "[there is] little evidence that labor market flexibility is substantially affected by the presence of social protection programs, nor is there evidence that the speed of labor market adjustment can be enhanced by limiting these programs" (p. 15). Strategies to simultaneously promote greater labor market flexibility and greater security for workers are being pursued through legislation at state and national level, and through promoting greater levels of negotiation between employers and workers on human resource practices (NELP 1999; Ozaki 1999; Wilthagen 1998). Other approaches that are primarily concerned with workers' security and less with economic flexibility, are focused on advocacy and organizing efforts to provide greater representation and social protections for vulnerable workers in flexible labor markets (SEIU 1993; Theodore and Mehta 1999). See also the National Alliance for Fair Employment (www.fairjobs.org) for inspiring examples of local organizing efforts in the US that have come together in a national network to confront problems of contingent workers.

Simultaneously building security for workers and effectively dealing with the rapid changes and volatility associated with the information economy, however, is not an easy task. It requires substantial changes in many of the organizations, institutions, and policies that have emerged over many decades in a more stable industrial economy.

This chapter explores two broad approaches that are particularly useful in building security for workers in the midst of rapidly changing labor markets and complex, mediated employment relationships. The first approach is rooted in the recognition of the increased importance of intermediaries in regional labor markets. Intermediaries can play a critical role for both workers and employers in shaping labor market outcomes, yet they have received relatively little attention in labor market policy, which tends to focus primarily on the supply and demand side of the labor market. The growing importance of intermediaries provides opportunities for innovative policy interventions that can assist more positive aspects of intermediary activity while hindering their more pernicious elements.

The second broad approach builds on the distinction between flexible work and flexible employment, arguing for policies and practices that can create greater employment (not job) security while also contributing to greater work flexibility. This approach is built on the recognition that the problems that workers face in flexible labor markets are primarily rooted in the increasing fragmentation and individualization of employment relations. This fragmentation decreases workers' bargaining power in relation to employers and makes them more vulnerable to employer malfeasance and labor market shocks. This individualization of employment relations is occurring at the same time that work itself is becoming more socialized. By this I mean that work activities increasingly involve social interaction: in the workplace, among teams of co-workers; across space, among colleagues, customers, suppliers, competitors, and collaborators in complex interfirm production networks; across time, through the importance of social networks and relationships for career trajectories and industrial development; and in the process of innovation, which is generated through interactive processes in which social interaction, culture, and collective identities play a critical role. Individual employment relations – which may make sense when individual labor output and contribution to overall productivity and profitability can be reliably determined – make little sense in an economic environment requiring social interaction. Furthermore, since economic success depends on encouraging sharing of information, social interaction, and collective learning processes, individualized employment relationships are frequently counter-productive to firms as well as workers. Not only do they contribute to inequality and declining wages, they also undermine long-term invest-ments in education and learning that are so essential for innovation. Instead, new employment relations need to more accurately reflect the social nature of work. This can be achieved through policy develop-ments in two areas: first, improving collective representation for work-ers, helping to create a better balance between workers' and employers' needs in the labor market; and, second, promoting more diverse and collective compensation systems, flattening out the inevitable ups and downs in earnings, and providing workers with greater resilience in the face of inevitable labor market shocks.

Both these approaches – influencing intermediaries and changing employment relationships – require changes in the concepts policy makers use for thinking about labor market policy and changes in the targets of intervention strategies. It is no longer enough to limit our approach to the traditional targets of labor market policy – firms and individuals. The increasing interconnection of economic agents, and the importance of interactive communication, requires developing strat-egies that incorporate a greater appreciation for the social nature of economic activity. It requires policies that can shape economic networks and social communities over time. The concepts explored in the fol-lowing section are offered as a useful starting-point for developing more practical policies and strategies.

New Concepts for Labor Markets in the Information Economy

Traditional approaches to labor market policy remain constrained by a set of conceptual frameworks that are rooted in an older industrial era of stable markets and mass-production industries dominated by large vertically integrated firms. In this relatively predictable environment, the goals of labor market policy were simple: create more and better jobs through improving the functioning of the labor market. In this proc-ess, there were two main targets of labor market policy: employers and workers. Approaches to employers primarily focused on legal regula-tions, including basic labor relations legislation,[5] regulations protecting

5   Still within the framework created by the National Labor Relations Act, and the Taft-Hartley Act.

workers' rights in the workplace,[6] and tax incentives to promote provision of training, health, and pension benefits and other assistance to workers. Approaches to workers focused primarily on skills training, through the range of federal, state, and foundation-funded workforce development programs (Grubb 1996) along with the creation of a legal regulatory framework providing for workers' collective representation (Gould 1993b).

The very conceptual frameworks we use in thinking about labor market policy, however, need to be reexamined. "Jobs," "work," "skills," "firms" – all these terms mean very different things now than they did thirty years ago. The information economy is resulting in significant changes in the content of work and the coordination of economic activity. To more effectively develop labor market policies in this new era, there are four fundamental changes, at least, we need to make in the conceptual framework we use for understanding and influencing labor markets. These are: a focus on industry clusters and networks, rather than firms; promoting learning rather than skills training; building communities, rather than focusing on individuals; and building careers, rather than creating jobs.

Industry clusters, not firms

Competitive success in the information economy is not achieved through the activities of individual firms. Instead, success is rooted in innovation, which is based on interactive information flows that cross firm boundaries and flow through both work and leisure environments.[7] Innovations are new creations of economic significance of various types, including new products and services, new technological capacities, and

6   The most prominent include the Title VII Civil Rights Act, the creation of the Equal Employment Opportunity Commission, the Age Discrimination in Employment Act, the Vocational Rehabilitation Act, the Occupational Safety and Health Act, and the Clean Air Act Amendments of 1977 (preventing punishment of whistleblowers). See Heckscher (1996) for a discussion of this.

7   See Amin and Cohendet (1999); Burton-Jones (1999); Eisenger (1995); Florida (1995); Glasmeier (1999); Glasmeier, et al. (1998); Hudson (1999b); Keane and Allison (1999); Keeble, Lawson, and Moore and Wilkinson (1999), Keeble and Wilkinson (1999), Kirat and Lung (1999), Laurillard (1999), Lawson and Lorenz (1999), Malecki and Oinas (1999), Maskell, Eskelinen, Hannibalsson, Malmbert, and Vatne (1998, Maskell and Malmberg (1999); Morgan (1997); Nyhan, Attwell; and Deitmer (1999); Powel (1998); Rees (2000); Saxenian (1996); Simmie (1997); Tooke (2000).

new ways of organizing production processes and the delivery of services. The processes through which innovations emerge are complex,
having to do with both the development and diffusion of information
and knowledge and the translation of this information and knowledge
into new products and production processes. The importance of innovation is most evident in knowledge-intensive industries and in
industries in which information itself is the commodity being sold. The
significance of information, knowledge production, and innovation,
however, is not limited to firms in high-tech industries or information
commodities. Indeed, innovation has been shown to be critical in a wide
range of older, low-tech industries as well.[8] Innovation is not limited to
translating sophisticated technical knowledge into new commodities
and services. Innovation takes place at all levels of a firm's activities,
may frequently involve little scientific knowledge, and can be important in a range of pedestrian activities including production processes,
logistics, marketing, sales, distribution, and industrial relations. Furthermore, innovation is not limited to advanced industrial countries,
as evidenced in the growing amount of research documenting the important role of information, knowledge, and innovation in shaping economic dynamics in Africa, Latin America, and Asia.[9]

In all of these contexts it is clear that innovation is an interactive
process (Cooke and Morgan 1998; Morgan 1997). The linear model in
which innovations are first developed in an isolated research and development unit and then translated into products for sale rarely
describes actual innovation processes. Feedback loops or reflexivity have
been widely identified as a critical component of the learning process
(Glasmeier et al. 1998; Lash and Urry 1994; MacLeod 2000). Furthermore, this process of interactivity rarely occurs within the context of a
single firm. Firms innovate through the process of interacting with a
wide range of other organizations. Through communicating with suppliers, customers, and competitors, and through building relationships
with universities, research institutes, investment firms, government
agencies, and so on, firms develop and exchange various kinds of information and knowledge that are critical to their ability to innovate.
With the growth of complex, multifirm production networks, there is a
great need to understand these connections, and the social struggles
that shape them, in a broader context, not hindered by a narrow focus

8   For example, Maskell et al. (1998).
9   Bell and Albu (1999); Chataway and Wield (2000); Ernst and Lundvall (1997);
World Bank (1998).

on the firm. In this context, firms themselves could be thought of as simply structures for the coordination of work processes along with the flows of materials and money (Klotz 1999). It is the work processes themselves, and the innovations they give rise to, that are important for economic success.

Thus, effectively shaping economic trajectories requires approaches that can affect entire production systems, rather than individual firms. This approach is now becoming firmly entrenched in economic development theory and practice as the traditional approach of providing economic subsidies and technology transfer to individual firms is becoming less effective. In its place, efforts to promote economic development are increasingly focused on broad national and regional *systems* of innovation,[10] regional *clusters* of industries,[11] and coherent "product-based subdivisions of the economy" (Storper 1997).

Labor market policy needs to develop effective mechanisms for influencing entire clusters of firms as well. Incentives need to be created to promote communication and collaboration among firms, and between firms and communities of workers. Creating such "collective actors" would help identify and solve critical problems in human resource development – problems that no single individual firm has the incentive or resources to be able to solve on their own. There are some emerging signs that such a cluster or network approach is beginning to make its way into labor market policy. One example is the recent funding initiative of the US Department of Labor to promote regional training consortia.[12] The goal of this program is to promote partnerships between companies and training providers to meet multiple needs within a regional cluster of firms. Funding is contingent upon joint projects involving multiple employers within an industry, providing some incentive for changing the behavior of multiple, rather than individual, firms. Such initiatives that address industry clusters, however, remain a minority approach within the workforce development field and need to be significantly expanded.

10 Braczyk, Cooke; and Heidenreich (1998); Edquist (1997); Lundvall (1992); de la Mothe and Paquet (1998).
11 Bell and Albu (1999); Keeble and Wilkinson (1999); Porter (1998).
12 http://wdsc.doleta.gov/sga/sga/00-102sga.htm

Learning not Skills Training

Most approaches to workforce development training pay little attention to actual learning processes. Instead, their primary focus is on training. To the extent that they address issues of learning explicitly, the
approach assumes that learning is an individual process, that it can be
separated from work activities in a classroom or training environment,
that it has a beginning and an end, and that it is largely the result of
teaching (Wenger 1998). This dominant approach to training is built
implicitly on individualistic theories of human learning and skill development that are derived from human capital theory.[13] These approaches emphasize abstract mental processes and treat skill as a
discreet, objective characteristic. They de-emphasize the social, relational
and situated base of information, knowledge, and skill, and thus do
not prove very useful for either understanding or promoting the interactive learning processes that are so central to economic success
(Anderson 1996; Hutchins 1995).

In contrast, there is a well-developed body of research and theory
on social learning processes that explicitly addresses the importance
of social interaction in the learning process.[14] These studies argue that
knowledge is acquired, developed, and applied through the interpretation of experience based on shared mental frameworks and experiences that shape individual processes of sense making and identity
formation. The artifacts of society, including the technological basis
for communication and interaction, codetermine these learning processes. Thus, the social and technological contexts in which individuals learn and work play a decisive role in the development of the
individual. "To understand how people learn is to simultaneously
understand how they are able to adapt to (and sometimes to resist)
the practices of various social institutions, and to appropriate and
operate with the technological and intellectual tools that are salient in
these environments" (Bliss et al. 1999). Thus, learning is intimately
linked with human identity formation, convention creation and cultural assets.

Furthermore, learning inevitably involves social struggles. For the
knowledge that is developed out of human learning processes to be
applied in economically productive ways, people must not only have

13   Becker (1964).
14   Bandura (1997); Bliss, Saljo and Light (1999); Wenger (1998).

knowledge, they must also feel motivated to apply that knowledge *and* have some power to help ensure its use and implementation in innovative strategies. Innovation involves change, and change may threaten the identities and commitments of others in the organization and may ultimately undermine people's own position and identity. The position of individuals within an organization shapes their ability to apply new knowledge they have gained and shapes the ability of the organization to gain from that knowledge. In other words, human learning processes are integrally linked with organizational learning processes and the exercise of power. Training that is abstracted from these concrete interactions in the workplace does little to help workers apply any additional information and knowledge they may gain.[15]

Intervention strategies to promote learning, rather than simply training, would involve at a minimum the creation of more on-the-job learning opportunities, such as through the development of mentorship relationships and stronger apprenticeship programs in a much wider range of occupations than currently exists. This would help create more environments in which learning could take place through engaging in practice and social interaction, promoting the development of both tacit and explicit knowledge rather than simply abstract individualized skills. It is also important to actively understand the work context in which workers are engaged, and to help empower them in that context, whether in their communication with co-workers or in their relation to management. Empowering workers can also contribute significantly to improved firm performance, as many employers have recognized. This is evident in the development of many (though clearly not all) "high-performance" work systems that have proved in many cases to be effective in promoting firm competitiveness (Appelbaum et al. 2000). Strengthening workers' voices can simultaneously promote more effective learning and provide incentives for more effective "high-road" competitive strategies for firms.

15 Schoenberger (1997) provides a particularly compelling analysis of this. In case studies of Xerox and Lockheed, she makes a compelling argument that the firms' structure and economic decisions are shaped in important ways by the identity, culture, and visions of the firm's CEO and other top management. She examines how this identity was built through many years of successful economic activity and how it then hindered the firms' ability to take advantage of new technological breakthroughs developed in-house, and to respond effectively to new competitors, since to do so would threaten the existing culture, identity and commitments within the firm.

Communities not Individuals

Implicit in developing an approach to learning, rather than training, is the need to focus on social interaction and communication among groups of people, rather than just individuals. In developing such an approach, it is useful to recognize the importance of "communities of practice," a concept that has emerged in the social learning literature.[16] At the core of this concept is the recognition that people learn fundamentally through their engagement in social practice, which is structured through their participation in the informal communities that get formed through the pursuit of shared enterprises over time. Participation refers "not just to engagement in certain activities with certain people, but to a more encompassing process of being active participants in the *practices* of social communities and constructing *identities* in relation to these communities" (Wenger 1998:4). Participation in communities of practice is essential for sense making (meaning) and identity formation, since it is the participation that provides the basis for making sense out of the diversity of information and knowledge that people are exposed to:

> A community of practice is an intrinsic condition for the existence of knowledge, not least because it provides the interpretive support necessary for making sense of its heritage. Thus, participation in the cultural practice in which any knowledge exists is an epistemological principle of learning. The social structure of this practice, its power relations, and its conditions for legitimacy define possibilities for learning. (Lave and Wenger 1991:98)

At the center of processes of learning, therefore, is the process by which people become part of, engage with, and contribute to the practices of these communities. Inevitably people start out as peripheral members of communities of practice. The intention of newcomers to learn is engaged by the community, and the mastery of knowledge and skills in any particular enterprise involves their moving toward fuller participation in the sociocultural practices of the community. Lave and Wenger (1991) term this process "legitimate peripheral participation" and argue that this social process "includes, indeed it subsumes, the learning of knowledgeable skills" (p. 29).

---

16   Lave and Wenger (1991); Wenger (1998).

The "communities of practice" framework has been usefully applied to understanding learning and promoting improved learning environments within the context of many single work sites and individual companies. For example, Wenger (1998) illustrates his analysis of communities of practice through examining the ways that insurance claims processors learn to be effective in their job. Orr (1996) discusses the importance of these communities of practice among photocopy repair technicians in a major photocopy company. Osterlund (1996) describes the detailed ways that interactions with multiple communities of practice contribute to the effectiveness of salespeople in a major technology firm. Wenger and Snyder (2000) discuss the challenges firms face in identifying and promoting such communities of practice while also demonstrating the beneficial outcomes of doing so.

With the rapid improvement in communication technologies, the growth in multifirm production networks, and the increasing importance of reflexive innovation processes, however, many people's day-to-day work practices are not limited to their own particular firm or work site. Work processes for many people require greater levels of daily interaction with consumers and people in other firms – customers, suppliers, collaborators, and competitors. In the process, they are forming cross-firm communities of practice that are essential for shaping economic trajectories. The challenge for labor market policy, therefore, is not to simply promote individuals' access to jobs in the labor market. Instead, the goals should be threefold. First, identify the existing communities of practice that make learning possible, both within firms and across firms, with particular attention paid to identifying occupationally based communities such as those described in chapter 5. Second, provide organizational support to help sustain and expand these communities while improving their linkages with other institutions, most particularly community college, university extension programs, and other institutions of adult education. Finally, help provide linkages for disadvantaged workers to be integrated into these communities of practice, for example through the creation of expanded apprenticeship and mentorship opportunities.

This approach is clearly a major step beyond most current labor market policies, which focus on individualized skill development, job placement and wages. Such approaches to labor market interventions, however, are emerging in some places, particularly in the community development field, as a focus on "bricks-and-mortar" approaches to neighborhood development giving way to more comprehensive initiatives focused on community-building and the promotion of social capital (PolicyLink 2000a).

Careers, not Jobs

Implicit in all these approaches is the need to focus on careers, not on jobs. Work used to be predominantly organized around relatively permanent, stable jobs, in which someone was employed for an indefinite period of time to perform a clear set of tasks outlined in a detailed job description. This standard employment relation certainly never characterized all jobs, but until recently it accounted for the dominant form of employment in most mass-production manufacturing enterprises as well as most communications, transportation, wholesale trade, and service industries such as insurance and banking, particularly for workers over 30 years old (see Hall, 1982). Furthermore, "jobs" still constitute the basis upon which nearly all labor market data on employment, occupations, wages, and so on is collected. Increasingly, however, predictable and stable tasks have been automated, and remaining work is being organized around flexible teams amid constantly shifting work demands. Job tenure and stability has declined, and workers no longer expect their current jobs to last for indefinite periods of time. Thus, there is a need to shift our analytical attention away from jobs toward careers.[17]

Trying to promote careers, rather than simply access to jobs, has already found its way into workforce development policy in theory, but remains highly problematic in practice (Giloth 2000). Part of the problem lies in the dominant quantitative approach to career development in which workforce development practitioners try to identify discrete skills and logical occupational progressions, with clearly defined movements from one job to the next. In essence, the goal in these efforts is to create a predictable institutional infrastructure across the labor market to help people move from one job to the next in a trajectory of upward mobility. Unfortunately, the rapid pace of change in the economy and rapidly changing labor markets undermine the effectiveness of efforts that are dependent on codifying particular skill sets and identifying predictable occupational trajectories. As a result of these rapid economic changes, along with the wide diversity of people's personal preferences, goals, and circumstances, individual career trajectories are typically

---

17   Arthur, Hall, and Lawrence (1989).

much more varied and unpredictable than is reflected in these ordered career ladder approaches. Instead, labor market policy needs to recognize that careers are built as much through informal learning and social networks as through developing discrete technical skills. Existing career ladder approaches are a step in the right direction, but career building programs need to pay more explicit attention to building the social networks of individuals and helping to build mentoring relationships with other people.

Intermediaries and Labor Market Policy

The conceptual approaches above, while challenging, are not impossible. They are already being adopted, at least in pieces, by various programs and organizations across the country in a bottom-up manner. These experiences are providing insights into possible changes in broader labor market policy that might help move these initiatives to a greater scale and a more broad reaching impact on labor market outcomes. One broad approach for improving labor market outcomes, built on the recognition of the increasing importance of intermediaries in the labor market, is to develop a more systematic approach toward improving the functioning of these various intermediaries.

Imagine, for a moment, what a comprehensive, "best practice" intermediary might look like. It would have strong, trusting relationships with both employers and workers, with an appropriate level of specialization in a particular occupation or industry cluster to both understand rapidly changing skill needs of employers and identify real career opportunities for workers. It would focus on building appropriate cross-firm learning environments, providing a combination of technical, communication, and problem-solving skills to help newcomers integrate into existing "communities of practice" in various workplaces. It would provide a variety of support services[18] and on-the-job assistance for disadvantaged workers to provide the additional help they need to successfully integrate into rewarding career opportunities. It would also have the leverage to change the demand side of the labor market, organizing groups of employers to improve employment relationships and work practices, while also providing greater resources to invest in the regional workforce (Benner et al. 2001; Bernhardt et al. 2001b).

18   For example, child care, transportation, counseling.

There are undoubtedly other aspects of ideal intermediary activity not touched on here, but the basic contours of a more effective intermediary system should be clear. It is probably unrealistic to expect a single intermediary to meet all of these best practices. In reality, networks of intermediaries, each specializing in a particular set of activities or services, would be more likely to be effective in reaching these best practices. The current system of intermediaries leaves a lot of be desired from this perspective. It is possible, however, to develop public policy directed at intermediaries, in essence providing support for the more beneficial aspects of their operations and implementing regulations restricting their more pernicious activities.

One approach that is frequently advocated by organizations representing contingent workers is to regulate temporary help firms and other intermediaries that act as legal employers of contract workers (for example, employee leasing firms and contractor brokers). Typically these regulations are focused on providing the same protections for temporary workers that permanent workers have in the work site. This may include such provisions as limiting the length of time someone can be employed in a "temporary status," trying to ensure equal pay for equal work, clarifying provisions for collective bargaining and co-employment status, improving access to health care, and so on (NELP 1999; Theodore and Mehta 1999). Such provisions are relatively weak in the United States, though they are somewhat stronger in Europe, where there has been a much greater resistance to employer-initiated labor flexibility (Houseman and Osawa 1995; Messmer 1994; Overman 1993).

Such regulatory efforts, however, while sometimes effective, also frequently have unintended consequences that tend to undermine their overall impact on improving labor market outcomes. A particularly poignant example emerges in the experience in The Netherlands with the passage of the Flexibility and Security Act, which took effect in January, 1999. This "Flexicurity" Act had a provision requiring temporary firms to give many of their workers permanent status after a certain period of time, requiring the firms to continue to pay these workers even if there was no work available. While this provided benefits for some temporary workers, it also led many temporary agencies to let go large numbers of their temporary workers, with trade unions reporting that temporary workers were dismissed *en masse* immediately prior to the law taking effect.[19] As Carnoy and Castells (1997) argue, the

---

19   http://eiro.eurofound.ie/1999/01/Features/nl9901117f.html
http://eiro.eurofound.ie/1999/05/Features/nl9905140f.html

demand for flexibility can be met in multiple ways, and in countries where temporary work is more regulated, firms pursue other strategies for increasing labor flexibility, such as the use of part-time or subcontracted work. Thus, strategies that aim to restrict some of the negative practices of intermediaries can be useful, but if they do not recognize the importance of flexible work in some form they are likely to be limited in their overall impact.

A more promising approach is to put significant resources into promoting the development of positive intermediary models, which with this assistance may then replace more negative intermediaries, contributing to work flexibility but also building greater labor market opportunities for workers. Of particular interest here is the potential role of membership-based intermediaries. Traditionally, unions and professional associations have had little interaction with the workforce development system. Many unions have ignored broad labor market based training, seeing it as less of a priority than wage, benefit, and internal training programs negotiated as part of collective bargaining agreements with unionized employers. Similarly, the workforce development system has largely ignored unions and professional associations as a potential source of valuable training and placement assistance (Giloth 2000). My analysis of membership-based intermediaries in Silicon Valley, however, suggests that unions and professional associations have a set of unique characteristics as intermediaries. The development of strong occupational communities makes them particularly effective at linking skills development with improved employment conditions, contributing to the competitiveness of firms in the region while ensuring that workers benefit more directly from economic growth.

The weakness of membership-based intermediaries is evident in their somewhat limited connection with more disadvantaged sectors of the labor market. Resources from federal and state workforce development funds, however, could be used to strengthen the training component of membership-based intermediaries while also providing incentives for these organizations to develop apprenticeship and mentoring programs that could help integrate more disadvantaged workers into these strong career networks. Funds could also be structured in such a way as to promote greater coordination and cooperation between the variety of different intermediaries in regional labor markets. Some aspects of this are already in place, in line with requirements in the Workforce Investment Act that one-stop career centers include a wide range of public sector programs under a single entry-point. This should be expanded, however, to include not just public sector programs but also community colleges and membership-based intermediaries, who offer valuable services and networks that many of the public sector intermediary programs lack.

Whether restricting negative intermediary practices or providing support for positive practices, the key point here is to recognize that intermediaries have become a fundamental component of the structure and dynamics of labor markets. Efforts to entirely get rid of them and build a stronger direct tie between workers and employers are likely to prove ineffective and possibly detrimental to the vitality of regional economies. The best approach is to accept intermediaries as a reality in contemporary labor markets, do our best to understand the forces contributing to their activities and the impact of their efforts, and to influence their activities in ways that lead to desired outcomes.

Labor Flexibility and a New Employment Contract

For most of the twentieth century, our notions of employment were defined by what came to be known as a standard employment contract. This contract included employment for an indefinite period of time (that is, not temporary status), working for a single employer who controlled the conditions of employment. Workers could expect steady work with predictably rising pay. Employers were legally responsible for meeting basic conditions of employment and ensuring reasonably safe work environments. Legally, this relationship is treated as a direct contract between an individual employer and an individual worker, though the US labor relations system created provisions for collective representation in negotiating the conditions of the contract. Rather than being understood as an individual employment contract, however, on a broad level the employment contract that developed during the period of stable mass production is best understood as a social compact between business, labor, and capital. Ultimately embodied in part in key New Deal era legislation[20] and in part through the practices of economic actors themselves, this compact served to socialize compensation systems in important ways through flattening wage distributions and redistributing rewards from increased productivity. In this social compact, employers provided stable work and substantial wage gains

20   The National Labor Relations Act of 1935, the Fair Labor Standards Act of 1938, and the Social Security Act of 1935, which not only established social security but also our unemployment insurance system.

in exchange for shop-floor peace, which was important for employers who needed stability to reap the productivity benefits from improvements in mass production technology. The compromise of paying higher wages ultimately helped employers as well since it helped create a large middle class, whose demand for consumer goods served as the engine of growth for thirty years after World War II. The government played a role in ensuring broad social safety-net policies which used a portion of the productivity improvements to mitigate extreme poverty while helping to stabilize demand in the economy among unemployed people and older workers. This helped contain social conflict and minimize negative impacts of cyclical downturns.

The existence of large corporations in this context helped play an important role in compressing the wage distribution, thereby reducing inequality and expanding the middle class. Large-scale organizations tended to compress wages by raising them for workers at the bottom of the scale and limiting them at the top. Compensation was not based on individual productivity levels or contributions to profitability – seniority played a greater role in determining compensation. Wages were also effectively compressed through the training practices of these large corporations. Firms recognized the importance of the firm-specific knowledge required if their workers were to be productive. New hires were thus often given lengthy training programs, with firms willing to invest in their human resources and forego immediate contributions to the firm's activities in the expectation that they would reap ample rewards over the long period of time employees would stay with the firm. Thus, compensation for newly hired employees was frequently greater than their contribution to the firms' profitability, but firms would gain in the long run from their employees' increased productivity, given compressed wage structures. In essence, these compensation systems were not based on individuals but were structured based on the relationship between different groups of workers in a firm. Meanwhile, the broad social compact helped redistribute resources in society, minimizing extremes of inequality.

Ironically, during this time that the employment contract was more socialized, work itself, at least in classic blue-collar jobs, was in many ways more individualized. The moving assembly line perfected the transfer of control over the pace and intensity of labor from the worker to the machine, and to Taylorized management practices. In doing so, it tied the worker firmly to a particular space on the shop-floor, making it difficult to have social interactions with anyone more than a few feet away on the line. Scientific management, which separated conception from implementation, meant that a large portion of the workforce was treated simply as mindless individualized labor whose activities could be controlled by managers. Work tasks were determined by long and complex job descriptions and bureaucratic rules, providing only minimal room for worker initiative, while routinized work tasks required less social interaction in the process of performing the work. Overall, then, during much of the twentieth century, labor markets in the US could be broadly characterized as individualized work practices but socialized employment relationships.

With the changes in work and employment over the last thirty years, however, we have witnessed an increased socialization of work, and an increased individualization of the employment contract. By socialization of work, I mean that the tasks involved in work, and the information and knowledge required to perform that work, rely more now than in the past on social interaction and communication. This is evident in a variety of different ways. In the workplace, work systems increasingly involve teamwork, with both project-based work and interactive processes designed to improve production systems (that is, high-performance work organization and continuous improvement programs) which require higher levels of cooperation and communication among workers. In addition, an increasing percentage of the workforce are involved in occupations that require communication with people not in their firm, frequently beyond the work site. This is clearly true in many service occupations (ranging from day care workers to retail sales clerks to high-end producer service representatives) in which workers are directly interacting with consumers and client firms. It is also true of nearly all professional and semiprofessional occupations, in which communication with a whole range of collaborators, colleagues, and customers is a critical component of work processes. Aside from the few remaining assembly-line jobs and highly Taylorized back-office processing systems, it is hard to identify occupations in the contemporary economy that don't require significant social interaction as part of the labor process. Not only are work processes increasingly dependent on social interaction, but long-term career success for workers is also increasingly dependent on social interaction through the strength and character of people's social networks. Finally, the innovation and learning that occurs in this social interaction has been identified as a critical component, if not *the* most critical component, of economic success.

At the same time that work has become increasingly dependent on social interaction, employment contracts have become increasingly individualized. The complete individualization of employment relations would involve everyone being self-employed, marketing their own portfolio of skills, experiences, and relationships to various task-performing organizations for temporary periods of time, and constantly competing for resources and personal support in an entirely market-driven process. Obviously this characterization is extreme and overstates the current situation. Nonetheless, the changes in the employment relationship discussed in chapter 1 clearly suggest that the employment contract for an increasing number of workers is moving in this direction. The number of workers covered by collective bargaining agreements in unionized firms has fallen to the lowest level since the 1930s. The number of people who are self-employed has grown. Compensation levels have become increasingly dispersed and individualized, along with a growth in performance-linked incentive systems tied to individual productivity measures. The decline in job tenure, the growth in temporary employment, and the increase in the level of job churning, all mean that individuals have highly diverse patterns of relationships with a range of different employers over a lifetime. Furthermore, the restructuring of welfare programs, the decline in assistance through unemployment insurance, and the increasingly tattered social safety-net programs all mean that workers benefit much less overall from a social wage than they did in the past.

In this context, some workers have faired well – particularly those with highly desired skills, good social networks, and the ability to negotiate decent wages for themselves. For many workers, however, despite the increased social interaction involved in work, the individualization of employment relations has resulted in lower wages and greater insecurity. Developing a new employment contract is thus essential to building security for workers in the labor market. Fortunately, promoting employment relationships that recognize the social nature of work can simultaneously contribute to economic competitiveness, as well as building security for workers, by helping to rationalize learning networks, improve incentive structures, and stabilize consumer demand.

It is useful to think about strategies for building new employment contracts in two broad areas. The first, is by reforming the industrial relations system to promote better collective representation for workers built around occupational communities and industry clusters rather than individual work sites and companies. In additional to empowering workers in the labor market, this can solve collective actor problems for employers, resulting in greater investment in human resources and the development of more effective learning networks. The second is by promoting diversified compensation systems which allow workers to be less dependent on a regular wage and thus less vulnerable to unexpected labor market shocks. This could be achieved through a variety of ways, including expanding wealth-sharing initiatives and developing public programs that provide greater wage protection, retraining, and career development resources. Combined, these could help cushion workers from the inevitable volatility in labor markets.

Reforming the labor relations system

Our current labor relations system, built from the 1935 National Labor Relations Act and subsequent amendments, assumes long-term stable ties with a single employer. For workers to gain collective representation, they must identify and (legally) defend a clear and sufficient "community of interest," and ensure that a majority of workers within that community vote for collective representation even in the face of significant employer opposition. Tremendous resources are expended by both unions and employers in simply challenging the boundaries of appropriate "communities of interest," to say nothing of the legal challenges to representation elections themselves. With rapidly changing labor markets and a constantly shifting workforce, building and maintaining significant solidarity in work site or employer-based communities of interest is extremely difficult. Furthermore, many workers, including supervisors, managers, certain categories of professional employees, and the self-employed – over 40 percent of the workforce – are now explicitly denied access to collective representation. Additional problems arise for workers in subcontracted industries, since employers face no legal responsibility for subcontracted workers, despite having significant power to influence the wages and working conditions of those workers.[21]

Rather than being based almost exclusively on increasingly ephemeral work site based communities of interest, an improved labor relations system should encourage collective representation along somewhat more stable occupational and industry lines. Charles Heckscher (1996) has laid out in significant detail many aspects of what a full system of such "associational unionism" might look like. Through

21 Carre, DuRivage; and Tilly (1994); Cobble (1994); Friedman (1994); Gould (1993a); Gould (1993b); Siegel (1994).

associations much like those described in chapter 5, workers gain collective strength, even in the absence of collective bargaining agreements and contracts, through the provision of a broad range of educational and service activities and access to legal representation to help protect workers' rights in the workplace. To be fully effective, however, such associations must also be able to enter into contractual agreements with employers – with individual companies, certainly, but more importantly with multiple employers and industry associations. This would give them greater ability to curtail bad employment practices, improve career opportunities, and negotiate improved compensation systems. Building representation along such occupational and industry lines, however, would require some significant changes in labor law. At the minimum, it would require provision for allowing pre-hire agreements and for creating incentives for promoting industry-wide bargaining, both of which are currently prohibited outside the building trades.[22] Workers should also once again have the ability to exert economic pressures on employers. Many such efforts used to be legal prior to the Taft-Hartley Act of 1947, and in fact millions of non-factory workers – teamsters, longshoremen, waitresses, cooks, musicians, and others – who successfully organized between the 1930s and the 1950s relied on pre-hire agreements, recognitional picketing, secondary boycotts, limitations on nonunion or nonunion goods and other approaches to secure bargaining rights. Making these approaches legal once again would make representation more possible for subcontracted workers as well as for more mobile professionals, consultants, and technical workers. Another legal reform that would assist collective representation is to develop mechanisms for minority representation, requiring employers and industry associations to negotiate with groups of workers even if they don't have majority representation. In essence this would help lower the bar for workers seeking assistance in negotiating better employment relationships by allowing a minority of workers to have outside support even if they are not able to convince a majority of the need for union representation.

In many cases, employers would be resistant to the expansion of collective representation, thus requiring significant collective organizing among workers in an industry cluster. In many situations, however, it is possible to develop win–win strategies in which employers also benefit from collective organization in an industry, and so might

---

22   Friedman (1994).

be less resistant to workers' collective representation. This is particularly evident in cases where unions or other workers' associations can solve collective actor problems that employers face, particularly around skills development and training. All employers like to have a well-trained workforce, but individual employers have little incentive to contribute to training on their own when high levels of turnover mean they are unlikely to reap the benefits of increased training investments. In a classic collective actor problem, what is rational from the perspective of individual firms ends up undermining skill development in the industry as a whole. This dynamic has been particularly evident in the "shortage"' of information technology workers the US experienced in the late 1990s. Many detailed examinations of this phenomenon made it clear that management practices and the institutional framework of skills development were a key part of the problem, helping to explain the ineffective response to the rapid growth in demand for information technology workers (Cappelli 2000; National Research Council 2001). Unions and other workers' associations organized on an occupational or industry level can help solve this problem by negotiating with employers to invest in regional training programs and collaborative learning networks. Workers would gain from improved career opportunities, while employers would be able to capture many of the same gains from investment in human resources in organized regional labor markets that they used to capture in internal labor markets. When unions or professional associations play a strong role in helping with skill development and promoting improved competitiveness in the industry, such win–win strategies are possible (AFL–CIO Working For America Institute 2000).

Diversifying Compensation Systems

One of the critical problems workers currently face is the increased unpredictability in earnings. Workers can no longer expect regular, gradually increasing wages. Instead, workers face more frequent periods of unemployment, and job and career shifts that may result in dramatic changes in income. Following layoffs, workers frequently are forced to accept jobs with significantly lower wages. Long-term skill obsolescence can result in declining earnings over time as well. In essence, workers face increased risk in contemporary labor markets. One of the basic principles of mitigating risk in all contexts is to diversify, and the same strategy can be useful in thinking about policies that can help workers decrease their vulnerability to unexpected labor market shocks. Promoting access to a more diverse range of compensation, including in particular greater wealth accumulation and the improvement of social wage programs, can help flatten out fluctuations in workers' income and minimize the disruptive effects of periods of unemployment.

Obviously the most direct way of expanding workers' wealth is through the expansion of stock options and employee stock-ownership plans. This has become a critical form of compensation for certain middle- and upper-level employees, particularly in Silicon Valley but elsewhere as well. Firms have found that providing stock options can help motivate employees to be more willing to engage in risky enterprises, while increasing their motivation to maximize performance. Furthermore, it allows start-up firms to attract highly experienced employees while lowering the upfront costs they might otherwise have to pay for workers in high demand. For these workers, the increased risk of working for risky enterprises is compensated for by the potential for significant returns if the firm is successful. As described in chapter 7, however, stock options are available to a relatively limited section of the workforce, and in nearly all cases are limited to direct employees. Access to stock options and other forms of employee stock ownership should be expanded and, given the extensive use of subcontracting networks and outsourcing in the information economy, indirect workers should have access to stock options as well. Firms are unlikely to do this of their own volition. Increased pressure from workers themselves would be necessary to make this happen, or some form of public intervention to provide incentives for expansion of stock options or to require that stock options be provided at least to all direct employees (perhaps in proportion to salary) if they are provided to any.

There are, perhaps, easier ways of expanding worker ownership, since workers' ownership stake in the economy doesn't have to be limited to gaining ownership shares in the firms that employ them. It can also be either more narrowly focused on particular products they have worked on or more broadly focused on access to stock ownership more generally. In terms of a more narrow focus, one clear existing example is the motion picture and television industry. Unions in the industry[23] have negotiated a compensation system with the Alliance of Motion Picture and Television Producers (the dominant employers' associa-

23 Primarily the Screen Actors Guild (SAG), the Writers Guild of America (WGA), and the Directors Guild of America (DGA).

tion) that includes the provision of "residuals". These are additional payments to workers for the exhibition of a product in media other than the one for which it was originally created (for example, movies shown on TV), or for its reuse within the same medium subsequent to the initial exhibition. Payment continues as long as the product continues to be sold. Resources from residuals rose from only $7.6 million in 1960 to $337.9 million in 1990. For actors in particular, residuals have become an extremely important source of income, accounting for 46 percent of all compensation in 1990. For actors in television commercials, who are at the bottom of the acting hierarchy and mostly only receive the minimum pay scale, residual compensation is particularly important, amounting to four times as much as initial session fees (Christopherson and Storper 1989; Gray and Seeber 1996; Paul and Kleingartner 1994). At present, the compensation system in this information-based industry is very unusual, but it is possible to envision a range of occupations and industries in which workers (organized collectively) might be able to negotiate similar residuals from employer associations more easily than broad stock options.

A broader approach, also requiring some public sector intervention, would involve increasing workers' access to stock ownership in the economy more generally. The easiest way to do this would be in relation to pension programs, through providing greater incentives to employers to contribute to 401(k) pension plans, or even requiring them to do so. Small employers in particular continue to provide much less access to employer-sponsored pension programs than large employers. There is also potential for taking advantage of economies of scale in administrative costs by encouraging the pooling of small employers in the same industry together, either through industry associations or workers associations where they exist. In addition, options for pre-tax contributions to pension plans could be expanded, and penalties for early withdrawal reduced, to enable workers to gain access to these resources prior to retirement should they need to.

There are more ambitious possibilities as well. The Alaska Permanent Fund provides a particularly innovative and interesting example that has been in operation for over twenty-five years. This fund was established through a state constitutional amendment that was approved by Alaska voters in 1976 requiring that at least 25 percent of oil revenues generated from exploiting Alaska's oil reserves and paid to the state, be deposited into a public savings account and invested for the benefit of current residents and all future generations of Alaskans. The fund pays a dividend – a share of the fund's earnings – to every

Alaskan resident each year ($1,540.88 in 1998). The dividend program was designed to provide Alaskans with a personal stake in how the fund is managed and a personal interest in protecting it.[24] The fund is based on the principle that all Alaskans should directly benefit from the exploitation of nonrenewable natural resources. This same principle underpins another more recent, more ambitious, proposal to create a national Sky Trust in which all US residents would benefit directly from ownership shares in a trust created by a tax on the burning of all carbon-based fuels (Barnes 2001). Another creative program to expand ownership stake in the economy is proposed by Bruce Ackerman and Anne Alstott in *The Stakeholder Society* (Ackerman and Alstott 1999). They propose that every US-born resident be provided with a $80,000 "stake" when they turn 18 years old, to be funded out of an annual wealth tax. The motivation for their proposal is primarily to address inequality in economic opportunity, but clearly it could also decrease workers' vulnerability to labor market shocks through expanding their wealth and thus diversifying their income sources.

Other programs to diversify workers' access to economic resources can be developed directly through reforms of public programs – expanding the "social wage" – but doing so in ways that respond to the volatility in labor markets and help workers efficiently and productively reintegrate into gainful work. One area that clearly warrants attention is the unemployment insurance (UI) system, which was designed more than sixty years ago to provide partial, temporary replacement of wages to workers during temporary cyclical downturns. On a macroeconomic scale, the UI system is probably the most effective automatic counter-cyclical program in existence, helping to maintain consumer demand during economic downturns through redirecting resources generated during economic growth periods. As the economy has changed, however, its structure has become outdated, making it more difficult for unemployed workers to benefit. The UI system assumes that layoffs are primarily temporary, not structural, and that workers will return to the same job or industry. It provides no assistance to workers wanting to develop new skills or get retraining – indeed, it discourages workers from getting significant retraining since workers lose their benefits if they are not actively looking for work, even if they are going back to school to get skills for a new career. Furthermore, the eligibility requirements for unemployment benefits exclude many

24 See http://www.apfc.org

unemployed workers, particularly those in nonstandard employment relations,[25] and by the late 1990s only 42 percent of the unemployed actually received UI benefits, down from a high of 75 percent in 1975. The benefits provided through unemployment insurance are also inadequate, typically replacing only 40 to 45 percent of a worker's wage up to a maximum benefit. Such a low replacement level provides little assistance for people trying to refine or expand their skills to meet the needs of our rapidly changing economy. Consequently, the program does little to reduce chronic and repetitive unemployment (US Department of Labor 1998). Reforms should expand eligibility, increase benefit levels, and make it easier for workers to continue to receive benefits even while also improving their skills or shifting careers. In essence, the goal should be to transform the unemployment insurance system into a "retraining and reemployment insurance" system.

A more innovative "layoff insurance" program should also be seriously considered. This concept, which has gotten support from some labor economists, is designed to compensate workers for income losses they may experience after being laid off. Since the 1980s, consistently between 45 and 50 percent of displaced full-time workers who find full-time replacement jobs within two years have earned less than they earned prior to being laid off – a full third typically earning more than 20 percent less than prior to being laid off (Hipple 1999). Layoff insurance would supplement pay for these workers for a period of time even after they got a new job, helping to make up a portion of their lost income. This would cushion the impact of the disruption and help workers plan more confidently for the future, knowing they wouldn't suddenly find themselves with much lower pay for an extended period of time. It would also encourage people in their efforts to move to a new career or industry, knowing they can supplement their lower earnings for a period of time until they gain more experience and expertise.[26]

Another source of compensation that needs improvement is the area of health care, where the current system of employer-based health insurance is particularly poorly suited to a mobile workforce and rapidly changing industries. Some 44 million Americans are uninsured, with

25 Including the self-employed, many part-time and temporary workers, and anyone who may have left a job for any reason other than being involuntarily laid off, and anyone still unemployed after the time-limit for benefits, typically 26 weeks, though it varies by state.
26 Baily, Burtless, and Litan (1993); Jacobson, LaLonde; and Sullivan (1993); Mandel (1996).

four in five working full time or living in a household where someone works full time. Workers without a long-term, stable employment relationship, including many part-time, temporary, and contract workers along with many low-wage workers, all have a more difficult time getting health care insurance. Meanwhile, the substantial administrative costs involved every time someone switches an employer wastes unnecessary resources while providing suboptimal care for large sectors of the workforce. The goal of an efficient, truly universal single-payer system may seem impossible in the current political climate. Nonetheless, health insurance coverage should not be based on one's place of work. Short of a single-payer national health system, promoting portable union benefits programs or collective programs available through professional associations would allow for the benefits of economies of scale in purchasing and administration. Many small businesses would benefit from such expanded systems as well, since they would be able to reduce administrative costs of benefits systems.

A Final Word

Obviously the reforms and new ideas outlined above are schematic and far from a complete program for addressing insecurity in volatile labor markets. Furthermore, there are a range of other policies, such as raising the minimum wage and expanding the earned income tax credit, which would be needed to fully address the problems many workers face in contemporary labor markets. Rather than develop a detailed set of policy proposals, however, my purpose has been to explore more far-reaching concepts and ideas. Labor markets in the information economy are significantly different from those that existed during the height of the industrial era. The policies, programs, and institutions that shape contemporary labor markets, however, still reflect many of their industrial age origins. Incremental reforms to these institutions may provide some help in meeting the goal of improving security for workers while maintaining the flexibility required for economic competitiveness. Such incremental reforms, however, are unlikely to be sufficient to meet the challenges we currently face. There is an urgent need for more creative thinking and the exploration of more far-reaching policies that can directly address the structure and dynamics of labor markets in the information age. If this book provides some modest contribution toward this more ambitious enterprise, it will have met its purpose.

References

Abraham Katherine. 1990. Restructuring the Employment Relationship: The Growth of Market-Mediated Work Arrangements. In *New Developments in the Labor Market: Towards a New Institutional Paradigm*, eds. K. Abraham, R. McKersie. Cambridge: MIT Press

Ackerman Bruce, Alstott Anne. 1999. *The Stakeholder Society*. New Haven: Yale University Press

AFL-CIO Working For America Institute. 2000. *High Road Partnerships Report: Innovations in Building Good Jobs and Strong Communities*, AFL-CIO Working For American Institute, Washington, DC

Aglietta Michel. 1979. *A Theory of Capitalist Regulation: The U.S. Experience*. London: New Left Books

Alchian A., Demsetz H. 1972. Production, Information Costs, and Economic Organization. *American Economic Review* 62:777–95

American Society for Training and Development. 1999. *Outsourcing Research Report*, American Society for Training and Development, Washington, DC

Amin Ash, Cohendet Patrick. 1999. Learning and Adaptation in Decentralised Business Networks. *Environment and Planning D: Society and Space* 17:87–104

Anderson John R. 1996. *The architecture of cognition*. Mahwah, NJ: Lawrence Erlbaum Associates

Angel David. 1994. *Restructuring for Innovation: The Remaking of the U.S. Semiconductor Industry*. New York: Guilford Press

Angwin Julia, Castenada Laura. 1998. Digital Divide: High-Tech Boom a Bust for Blacks, Latinos. In *San Francisco Chronicle*. San Francisco. May 4, 1998

Appelbaum Eileen, Bailey Thomas, Berg Peter, Kalleberg Arne. 2000. *Manufacturing Advantage: Why High-Performance Work Systems Pay off*. Ithaca, NY: ILR Press

Appelbaum Eileen, Batt Rosemary L. 1994. *The New American Workplace: Transforming Work Systems in the United States*. Ithaca, NY: ILR Press. ix, 287 pp.

Armstrong Larry, Zellner Wendy, Baig Edward. 1999. Now Searches Take Weeks, Not Months. In *Business Week*, May 17, 1999, pp. 76–80

Aronowitz Stanley, DiFazio William. 1994. *The Jobless Future: Sci-tech and the Dogma of Work*, University of Minnesota Press, Minneapolis.

Arthur Michael, Rousseau Denise, eds. 1996. *The Boundaryless Career: A New*

Employment Principle for a New Organizational Era. New York, Oxford: Oxford University Press

Arthur Michael, Hall Douglas, Lawrence Barbara, eds. 1989. *The Handbook of Career Theory.* Cambridge, New York: Cambridge University Press

Atkinson Robert, Court Randolph, Ward Joseph. 1999. *The State New Economy Index: Benchmarking Economic Transformation in the States.* Washington, DC: Progressive Policy Institute

Attewel P. 1987. The Deskilling Controversy. *Work and Occupations* 14:3, 323–46

Autor David H. 1999. *Why Do Temporary Help Firms Provide Free General Skills Training,* MIT Economics Department, Cambridge

Autor David H., Levy Frank, Murnane Richard. 1999. *Skills Training in the Temporary Help Sector: Employer Motivations and Worker Impacts,* Department of Labor, Employment and Training Administration, Washington, DC

Averitt Robert T. 1968. *The Dual Economy: the Dynamics of American Industry Structure.* New York: W. W. Norton. xi, 208 pp.

Baily Martin Neil, Burtless Gary, Litan Robert. 1993. *Growth with Equity,* Brookings Institution, Washington, DC

Bandura Albert. 1977. *Social learning theory.* Englewood Cliffs, NJ: Prentice-Hall. viii

Barker Kathleen, Christensen Kathleen, eds. 1998. *Contingent Work: American Employment Relations in Transition.* Ithaca, NY: ILR Press

Barnaba Constance. 1999. Want to get the best employees? Ask a PEO. In *HR Focus,* 76: 9, September 1999, p. 15

Barnes Peter. 2001. *Who Owns the Sky? Our Common Assets and the Future of Capitalism.* Washington, DC: Island Press

Barrett Business Services, 1999. Annual Report (Portland, OR: Barrett Business Services) http://barrettbusiness.com

Baru Sundari. 2001. *Working on the Margins: California's Growing Temporary Workforce.* San Diego: Center on Policy Initiatives

Baumol William, and Wolff Edward. 1998. *Side Effects of Progress: How Technological Change Increases the Duration of Unemployment.* Policy Brief No. 41 Annandale-on-Hudson: Jerome Levy Economics Institute

Baumol William, Wolff Edward. 1998. *Side Effects of Progress: How Technological Change Increases the Duration of Unemployment. Rep. Policy Brief No. 41,* Jerome Levy Economics Institute, Annandale-on-Hudson

Bassi Laurie, Van Buren Mark. 1999. *Sharpening the Leading Edge,* American Society for Training and Development, Washington, DC

Beatty Sally. 1999. Monster Game. In *Wall Street Journal,* January 25, 1999, pp. B8

Becker Gary. 1964. *Human Capital: A Theoretical and Empirical Analysis with Special Reference to Education.* Chicago, IL: University of Chicago Press

Bell M., Albu M. 1999. Knowledge Systems and Technological Dynamism in Industrial Clusters in Developing Countries. *World Development* 27:1715–34

Belous Richard S. 1989. *The Contingent Economy : the Growth of the Temporary, Part-time, and Subcontracted Workforce.* Washington, DC: National Planning Association. xiv, 121 pp.

Benner Chris. 1996a. *Growing Together or Drifting Apart?: Working Families and Business in the New Economy,* Working Partnerships USA, with the Economic Policy Institute, San Jose, CA

——. 1996b. *Shock Absorbers in the Flexible Economy: The Rise of Contingent Employment in Silicon Valley*, Working Partnerships, San Jose, CA

——. 1998. Win the Lottery or Organize: Economic Restructuring and Union Organizing in Silicon Valley. *Berkeley Planning Journal* 12

Benner Chris, Brownstein Bob, Dean Amy. 1999. *Walking the Lifelong Tightrope: Negotiating Work in the New Economy*, Working Partnerships USA with the Economic Policy Institute, San Jose, CA

Benner Chris, Brownstein Bob, Dresser Laura, and Leete Laura. 2001. Staircases and Treadmills: The Role of Labor Market Intermediaries In Placing Workers and Fostering Upward Mobility. In *Proceedings of the 53rd Annual Meeting of the Industrial Relations Research Association*, January 5–7, 2001, New Orleans, ed. Paula Voos. Champaign, IL: Industrial Relations Research Association

Benton Lauren. 1989. Industrial Subcontracting and the Informal Sector. In A Portes, M Castells, L Benton, eds. *The Informal Economy: Studies in Advanced and Less Developed Countries*. Baltimore: Johns Hopkins University Press

Bernhardt Annette, Marcotte Dave. 2000. Is "Standard Employment" Still What It Used to Be? In *Nonstandard Work: The Nature and Challenges of Changing Employment Arrangements*, ed. F Carre, M Ferber, L Golden, S Herzenberg. Champaign, IL: Industrial Relations Research Association

Bernhardt Annette, Morris Martina, Handcock Mark, Scott Marc. 1999. Trends in Job Stability and Wages for Young Adult Men. *Journal of Labor Economics* 17:4 Part 2, S65–S90

Bernhardt Annette, Morris Martina, Handcock Mark, Scott Marc. 2001a. *Divergent Paths: Economic Mobility in the New American Labor Market*. New York: Russell Sage Foundation

Bernhardt Annette, Pastor Manuel, Hatton Erin, Zimmerman Sarah. 2001b. Moving the Demand Side: Intermediaries in a Changing Labor Market. In *Proceedings of the 53rd Annual Meeting of the Industrial Relations Research Association*, January 5–7, 2001, New Orleans, edited by Paula Voos. Champaign, IL: Industrial Relations Research Association

Bernstein Jared, Mishel Lawrence. 1999. *Six Reasons for Skepticism About the Technology Story of U.S. Wage Inequality*, Economic Policy Institute, Washington, DC

Bessant John. 1989. *Microelectronics and Change at Work*, International Labour Office, Geneva

Bettio Francesca, Rosenberg Samuel. 1999. Labour markets and flexibility in the 1990s: The Europe–USA opposition revisited. *International Review of Applied Economics* 13:3, 269–79

Bhargava Hemant, Choudhary Vidyanand, Krishnan Ramayya. 2000. Pricing and Product Design: Intermediary Strategies in an Electronic Market. *International Journal of Electronic Commerce* 5:37

Bird Bruce M., Segal Mark A., Yaeger Philip L. 1991. The Classification of Technical Service Specialists for Employment Tax Purposes: Section 1706 and Beyond. *Journal of Applied Business Research* 8: 1, 64–71

Blank Rebecca, ed. 1994. *Social Protection versus Economic Flexibility: Is There a Trade-Off*. Chicago: University of Chicago Press

Blank Rebecca, Freeman Richard. 1994. Evaluating the Connection between Social Protection and Economic Flexibility. In R Blank, ed. *Social Protection Versus Economic Flexibility: Is There A Trade-Off?* Chicago, IL: University of Chicago Press

Bliss Joan, Saljo Roger, Light Paul, eds. 1999. *Learning Sites: Social and Technological Resources for Learning*: Pergamon Press

Bloom H. S., Orr L. L., Bell S. H., Cave G., Doolittle F., et al. 1997. The benefits and costs of JTPA Title II-A programs – Key findings from the National Job Training Partnership Act Study. *Journal of Human Resources* 32: 3, 549–76

Borjas George. 1988. Earnings Determination: A Survey of the Neoclassical Approach. In *Three Worlds of Labor Economics*, ed. G Magnum, P Philips. Armonk: ME Sharpe

Braczyk Hans-Joachim, Cooke Philip, Heidenreich Martin, eds. 1998. *Regional Innovation Systems*. London: University College London Press

Braverman Henry. 1975. *Labor and Monopoly Capital: The Degradation of Work in the Twentieth Century*. New York: Monthly Review Press

Bregger J. E. 1996. Measuring Self-Employment in the United States. *Monthly Labor Review* 119:1–2, 3–9

Bridges William. 1994. *JobShift: How to Prosper in a Workplace Without Jobs*. Reading, MA: Addison-Wesley

Brodsky Melvin. 1994. Labor market flexibility: a changing international perspective. *Monthly Labor Review* 117:11, 53–60

Bronstein A. S. 1991. Temporary work in Western Europe: Threat or complement to permanent employment? *International Labour Review* 130:3

Brown John Sealy, Duguid Paul. 2000. *The Social Life of Information*. Boston, MA: Harvard Business School Press

Buroway Michael. 1985. *The Politics of Production: Factory Regimes Under Capitalism and Socialism*. London: Verso

Burton-Jones Alan. 1999. *Knowledge capitalism: business, work, and learning in the new economy*. Oxford England; New York: Oxford University Press. viii, 248 pp.

Business Week. 1985. America's High Tech Crisis: Why Silicon Valley Is Losing Its Edge. In *Business Week*, March 1985, pp. 56–67

Callaghan Polly, Hartmann Heidi. 1991. *Contingent Work: A Chart-Book on Temporary and Part-time Employment*, Economic Policy Institute, Washington, DC

Capecchi Vittorio. 1989. The Informal Economy and the Development of Flexible Specialization in Emilia-Romagna. In A Portes, M Castells, L Benton, eds. *The Informal Economy: Studies in Advanced and Less Developed Countries*. Baltimore: Johns Hopkins University Press

Cappelli Peter. 1999. *The New Deal At Work: Managing the Market-Driven Workforce*. Boston: Harvard Business School Press

———. 2000. *Is There a Shortage of Information Technology Workers?*, Wharton School, University of Pennsylvania, Philadelphia

Cappelli Peter, Bassi Laurie, Katz Harry, Knoke David, Osterman Paul, Useem Michael. 1997. *Change at work*. New York: Oxford University Press. viii, 276 pp.

Carnevale Anthony, Rose Stephen. 1998. *Education for What? The New Office Economy*, Educational Testing Service, Princeton, NJ

Carnoy Martin. 2000. *Sustaining the new economy: work, family, and community in the information age*. New York, NY. Cambridge, MA: Russell Sage Foundation; Harvard University Press. xi

Carnoy Martin, Castells Manuel. 1997. *Sustainable Flexibility: a Prospective Study on Work, Family and Society in the Information Age*, OECD, Paris

Carnoy Martin, Castells Manuel, Benner Chris. 1997. Labour markets and employment practices in the age of flexibility: A case study of Silicon Valley. *International Labour Review* 136:1, 27–48

Carre Francoise, Ferber Marianne, Golden Lonnie, Herzenberg Stephen. 2000. *Nonstandard Work: The Nature and Challenges of Changing Employment Arrangements*. Madison, WI: Industrial Relationships Research Association

Carre Francoise, DuRivage Virginia, Tilly Chris. 1994. Representing the Part-Time and Contingent Workforce. In *Restoring the Promise of American Labor Law*, ed. S Friedman. Ithaca, NY: ILR Press

Carre Francoise, Joshi Pamela. 1997. *Building Stability for Transient Workforces: Exploring the Possibilities of Intermediary Institutions Helping Workers Cope With Labor Market Instability. Rep. 1*, Radcliffe Public Policy Institute, Cambridge

Castells Manuel. 1996. *The Rise of the Network Society*. Cambridge, MA: Blackwell Publishers

Castells Manuel, Hall Peter. 1994. *Technopoles of the World : The Making of Twenty-First-Century Industrial Complexes*. London, New York: Routledge. x, 275 pp.

Castells Manuel, Aoyama Yuko. 1994. Paths Towards the Information Society – Employment Structure in G-7 countries, 1920–1990. *International Labour Review* 133:1, 5–33

Castro J. 1993. Disposable Workers. In *Time Magazine*, March 29, 1993 pp. 43–7

Cave George, Bos H., Doolittle F., Toussaint C. 1993. *JOBSTART: Final report on a program for school droupouts*, Manpower Demonstration Research Corporation, New York

Chapple Karen, Zook Matthew, Kunamneni Radhika, Saxenian AnnaLee, Weber Steven, Crawford Beverly. 2000. *From Promising Practices to Promising Futures: Job Training in Information Technology for Disadvantaged Adults*, Ford Foundation, New York

Chataway Joanna, Wield David. 2000. Industrialization, Innovation and Development: What Does Knowledge Management Change? *Journal of International Development* 12:803–24

Chopra Sunil, Meindl Peter. 2001. *Supply chain management: strategy, planning, and operation*. Upper Saddle River, N.J.: Prentice-Hall

Christopherson Susan. 1990. Emerging Patterns of Work. In *Skills, Wages and Productivity in the Service Sector*, ed. T Noyelle. Boulder: Westview Press

Christopherson Susan, Storper Michael. 1989. The Effects of Flexible Specialization on Industrial Politics and the Labor Market: The Motion Picture Industry. *Industrial & Labor Relations Review* 42:331–47

Chun Jennifer. 2001. Flexible Despotism: The Intensification of Uncertainty and Insecurity in the Lives of High-Tech Assembly Workers. In *The Critical Study of Work: Labor, Technology and Global Production*, ed. R Baldoz, C Koeber, P Kraft. Philadelphia: Temple University Press

Clark Jon, McLoughlin Ian, Rose Howard, King Robin. 1988. *The Process of Technological Change*. Cambridge: Cambridge University Press

Clark Sandra. 1999. University of California Customizes Education for Silicon Valley Titans. In *Corporate University Review*. March/April 1999

Claymon Deborah. 1999. PC Makers at your Service. In *San Jose Mercury News*. San Jose, CA. August 1, 1999

Clinton Angela. 1997. Flexible labor: Restructuring the American work force. *Monthly Labor Review* 120:3–17

Coase R. H. 1937. The Nature of the Firm. *Economica* 14:386–405
Coates David. 1999. *Models of Capitalism: Growth and Stagnation in the Modern Era.* Cambridge, UK: Polity Press
Cobble Dorothy Sue. 1991. *Dishing It Out: Waitresses and Their Unions in the Twentieth Century.* Chicago, IL: University of Illinois Press
——. 1994. Making Postindustrial Unionism Possible. In *Restoring the Promise of American Labor Law,* ed. S Friedmand. Ithaca, NY: ILR Press
Collins Randall. 1990. Changing Conceptions in the Sociology of the Professions. In *The Formation of Professions: Knowledge, State and Strategy,* ed. RaMB Torstendahl. London: Sage
Cooke Philip, Morgan Kevin. 1998. *The Associational Economy: Firms, Regions, and Innovation.* New York: Oxford University Press
Corporate Watch. 1997. Organizing the High-Tech Industry: An Interview with Jon Barton. In *Corporate Watch* (http://www.corpwatch.org)
Craver Charles. 1993. *Can Unions Survive?: The Rejuvenation of the American Labor Movement.* New York: New York University Press
Crispin Gerry, Mehler Mark. 1999. *Career Xroads: The 1999 Directory to the 500 Best Job, Resume and Career Management Sites on the World Wide Web, 4th Edition.* Kendall Park, NJ: MMC Group
Davidow William, Malone Michael. 1992. *The Virtual Corporation: Structuring and Revitalizing the Corporation for the 21st Century.* New York: HarperCollins
De Haas Renate M. 1998. Vizcaino v. Microsoft. *Berkeley Technology Law Journal* 13:1, 483–99
de la Mothe John, Paquet Gilles, eds. 1998. *Local and Regional Systems of Innovation.* Boston, London: Kluwer Academic Publishers
Dean Amy. 1998. On the Road to Union City. In *Not Your Father's Union Movement: Inside the AFL-CIO,* ed. Jo-Ann Mort. London: Verso Books
Derber Charles. 1982. *Professionals as Workers: Mental Labor in Advanced Capitalism.* Boston, MA: G.K. Hall and Co.
Derber Charles, Schwartz William, Magrass Yale. 1990. *Power in the Highest Degree: Professionals and the Rise of a New Mandarin Order.* New York: Oxford University Press
Diebold Francis, Neumark David, Polsky Daniel. 1994. Comment on Kenneth A. Swinnerton and Howard Wial, 'Is Job Stability Declining in the U.S. Economy?' *Industrial and Labor Relations Review* 49:2, 348–55
Doeringer Peter B., Piore Michael J. 1971. *Internal Labor Markets and Manpower Analysis.* Lexington, MA: Heath.
Douglass Marcia. 1991. *The Myth of Meritocracy: Race, Gender, and Class in Silicon Valley.* Ph.D. dDissertation thesis. University of California, San Diego, San Diego
Dresser Laura, Rogers Joel. 1997. *Rebuilding Job Access and Career Advancement Systems in the New Economy,* Center on Wisconsin Strategy, University of Wisconsin, Madison
DuRivage Virginia. 1992. *New Policies for the Part-Time and Contingent Workforce.* Armonk: M. E. Sharpe
Economic Development Institute. 1979. *EDI in Brief – Informational Brochure* (Saratoga, CA: Economic Development Institute, West Valley-Mission Community College District)

Edquist Charles, ed. 1997. *Systems of Innovation: Technologies, Institutions and Organizations.* London and Washington: Pinter

Eisenberg Dan. 1999. We're for Hire, Just Click. In *Time Magazine*, August 16, 1999, pp. 46–7

Eisenger Peter. 1995. State Economic Development in the 1990s: Politics and Policy Learning. *Economic Development Quarterly* 9:2, 146–58

Eisenhart Mary. 1998. The View From the Job Fair: Westech CEO Fred Faltersack On Today's High-Tech Job Picture. In *Microtimes.* 178. April 22, 1998

Engardio Pete, Burrows Peter. 1997. Where immigrants find a melting pot of gold. In *Business Week*, August 18, 1997, p. 123

English-Lueck Jan. 2002. Cultures@Silicon Valley. Palo Alto: Stanford University Press

Erickcek George, Houseman Susan. 1997. *Temporary, Part-time and Contract Employment in the United States*, W. E. Upjohn Institute for Employment Research, Kalamazoo, Michigan

Ernst Dieter. 1997. *From Partial to Systemic Globalization: International Production Networks in the Electronics Industry*, Berkeley Roundtable on the International Economy, University of California, Berkeley, Berkeley, CA

Ernst Dieter, Lundvall Bengt-Ake. 1997. *Information Technology in the Learning Economy: Challenge for Developing Countries. Rep.* Working Paper No. 97–12, Danish Research Unit for Industrial Dynamics, Aalborg, Denmark

Espe Erik. 1999. Disk Drive Competition Leads to Price Cuts. In *San Jose and Silicon Valley Business Journal*, June 18, 1999, p. 8. San Jose

Esping-Andersen Gosta. 1990. *The Three Worlds of Welfare Capitalism.* Princeton, NJ: Princeton University Press

Ewell Miranda, Ha K. Oanh. 1999. Multi-Billion Dollar Industry is at Heart of Valley Growth. In *San Jose Mercury News.* San Jose, June 27, 1999

Farber Henry. 1996. Are Lifetime Jobs Disappearing? Job Duration in the United States: 1973–1993. In J Haltiwanger, M Manser, R Topel, eds. *Labor Statistics Measurement Issues.* Chicago: University of Chicago Press

Feldstein Martin. 1975. The Importance of Temporary Layoffs: An Empirical Analysis. *Brookings Papers on Economic Activity* 3:725–45

Fernandez R. M., Weinberg N. 1997. Sifting and sorting: Personal contacts and hiring in a retail bank. *American Sociological Review* 62:6, 883–902

Fincham Robin. 1996. Introduction: Problems and Perspectives for the Organised Professions. In *New Relationships in the Organised Professions*, ed. R Fincham. Aldershot: Avebury

Florida Richard. 1995. Toward the Learning Region. *Futures* 27:5, 527–36

Foothill-De Anza Community College District. 1999. *Foothill-De Anza Community College District 2005: Planning for the New Millennium*, Foothill-De Anza Community College District, Los Altos Hills

Frank Robert, Cook Philip. 1995. *The Winner-Take-All Society.* New York: Free Press

Freire Paulo. 1970. *Pedagogy of the Opressed.* New York: Herder and Herder

Friedman Sheldon, ed. 1994. *Restoring the Promise of American Labor Law.* Ithaca, NY: ILR Press

Fuller Linda, Smith Vicki. 1996. Consumers' Reports: Management by Customers in a Changing Economy. In *Working in the Service Society*, ed. C L Macdonald, C Sirianni. Philadelphia: Temple University Press

Garson Barbara. 1988. *The Electronic Sweatshop: How Computers Are Transforming the Office of the Future Into the Factory of the Past*. New York: Simon & Schuster

Gee James Paul, Hull Glynda, Lankshear Colin. 1996. *The New Work Order: Behind the Language of the New Capitalism*. Boulder, CO: Westview Press

Gertler Meric. 1992. Flexibility revisited: districts, nation-states, and the forces of production. *Transactions: Institute of British Geographers* 17:259–78

Giloth R. P. 2000. Learning from the field: Economic growth and workforce development in the 1990s. *Economic Development Quarterly* 14:4, 340–59

Glasmeier Amy. 1999. Territory-Based Regional Development Policy and Planning in a Learning Economy. *European Urban and Regional Studies* 6:1, 73–84

Glasmeier Amy, Fuellhart Kurt, Feller Irwin, Mark Melvin. 1998. The Relevance of Firm-Learning Theories to the Design and Evaluation of Manufacturing Modernization Programs. *Economic Development Quarterly* 12:2, 107–24

Golden Lonnie, Appelbaum Eileen. 1992. What is driving the boom in temporary employment? *American Journal of Economics and Sociology* 51:473–92

Gonos George. 1997. The Contest over "Employer" Status in the Postwar United States: The Case of Temporary Help Firms. *Law & Society* 31:1, 81–110

Gordon David M., Edwards Richard, Reich Michael. 1982. *Segmented Work, Divided Workers : The Historical Transformation of Labor in the United States*. Cambridge, UK: Cambridge University Press

Gould William. 1993a. *Agenda for Reform: The Future of Employment Relationships and the Law*. Cambridge, MA: MIT Press

———. 1993b. *A Primer on American Labor Law, 3rd Edition*. Cambridge, MA: MIT Press

Granovetter Mark. 1973. The Strength of Weak Ties. *American Journal of Sociology* 78:1360–80

———. 1985. Economic Action and Social Structure: The Problem of Embeddedness. *American Journal of Sociology* 91:481–510

———. 1995. *Getting a Job: A Study of Contacts and Careers*. Chicago: University of Chicago Press

Gray Lois, Seeber Ronald, eds. 1996. *Under the Stars: Essays on Labor Relations in Arts and Entertainment*. Ithaca: ILR Press

Gregory Kathleen. 1984. *Signing-Up: The Culture and Careers of Silicon Valley Computer People*. Ph.D. dissertation thesis. Northwestern University, Evanston, IL

Grubb Norton. 1995. *Evaluating Job Training Programs in the United States: Evidence and Explanations. Rep. MDS-1047*, National Center for Research in Vocational Education, Berkeley

———. 1996. *Learning to Work: The Case for Reintegrating Job Training and Education*. New York: Russell Sage Foundation

Ha K. Oanh. 1999a. 1,100 Jobs To Be Cut by IBM. In *San Jose Mercury News*, June 25, 1999, p. 1. San Jose

———. 1999b. Part is fast-growing piece of tech industry. In *San Jose Mercury News*, April 18, 1999, p. 1. San Jose

Hall Robert. 1982. The importance of lifetime jobs in the U.S. economy. *American Economic Review* 72:4, 716–24

Harrison Bennett. 1994. *Lean and Mean: The Changing Landscape of Corporate Power in the Age of Flexibility*. New York: Basic Books

Harrison Bennett, Weiss Marcus S. 1998. *Workforce Development Networks : Community-Based Organizations and Regional Alliances*. Thousand Oaks, CA: Sage Publications

Heckscher Charles. 1996. *The New Unionism: Employee Involvement in the Changing Corporation*. Ithaca, NY: ILR Press

Henderson Jeffrey. 1989. *The Globalisation of High Technology Production: Society, Space, and Semiconductors in the Restructuring of the Modern World*. London: Routledge

Henderson Jeffrey, Scott Allen. 1988. The Growth and Internationalization of the American Semiconductor Industry: Labor Processes and the Changing Spatial Organization of Production. In *The Development of High Technology Industries: An International Survey*, ed. M. Breheny. London: Routledge

Hepworth Mark E. 1989. *Geography of the Information Economy*. London: Belhaven. 224 pp.

Herod Andrew. 1994. On Workers' Theoretical (In)Visibility in the Writing of Critical Urban Geography: A Comradely Critique. *Urban Geography* 15:7, 681–93

Herzenberg Stephen, Alic John, Wial Howard. 1998. *New Rules for a New Economy: Employment and Opportunity in Postindustrial America*. Ithaca, NY: ILR Press

Hipple Steven. 1999. Worker Displacement in the 1990s. *Monthly Labor Review* 122:7

Hirst Paul, Zeitlin Jonathan. 1991. Flexible Specialization versus Post-Fordism: theory, evidence, and policy implications. *Economy and Society* 20:1

Hochschild Arlie. 1983. *The Managed Heart: Commercialization of Human Feelings*. Berkeley, CA: University of California Press

Hoguet Laura. 1997. Labour and employment: Mighty Microsoft loses Vizcaino. *International Commercial Litigation* 47

Hollister R. G. 1990. *The Minority Female Single Parent Demonstration: New Evidence About Effective Training Strategies*, Rockefeller Foundation, New York

Hossfeld Karen. 1988. *Divisions of Labor, Divisions of Lives: Immigrant Women Workers in Silicon Valley*. Ph.D. dissertation thesis. University of Santa Cruz, Santa Cruz

Houseman S., Osawa M. 1995. Part-Time and Temporary Employment in Japan. *Monthly Labor Review* 118:10, 10–18

Hudson Ken. 1999a. *No Shortage of "Nonstandard" Jobs*, Economic Policy Institute, Washington, DC

Hudson Ray. 1999b. The Learning Economy, the Learning Firm and the Learning Region: A Sympathetic Critique of the Limits to Learning. *European Urban and Regional Studies* 6:1, 59–72

Hull Glynda A. 1997. *Changing Work, Changing Workers : Critical Perspectives on Language, Literacy, and Skills*, State University of New York Press, Albany, NY

Hunt Christopher, Scanlon Scott. 1998. *Job Seekers Guide to Silicon Valley Recruiters*. New York: Wiley

Hutchins Edwin. 1995. *Cognition in the wild*. Cambridge, MA: MIT Press. xviii, 381 pp.

Ingerman Sidney. 1970. *Industrial Growth and Wage Structure Formation in the California Peninsula Aerospace Industry*. Ph.D. dissertation thesis. University of California, Berkeley, Berkeley, CA

Jacobson Louis, LaLonde Robert, Sullivan Daniel. 1993. *The Costs of Worker Dislocation*, W. E. Upjohn Institute of Employment Research, Kalamazoo, MI

Jayadev Raj. 2000. Winning and Losing Workplace Safety on Silicon Valley's Assembly Line. In *Pacific News Service*. San Francisco

Johnson J. H., Bienenstock E. J., Farrell W. C. 1999. Bridging social networks and female labor-force participation in a multiethnic metropolis. *Urban Geography* 20:1, 3–30

Johnston Paul. 1994. *Success While Others Fail: Social Movement Unionism and the Public Workplace*. Ithaca, NY: ILR Press

JV:SVN. 1995. *Integrating Silicon Valley's Defense and Commercial Economies: A Community-Based Action Plan*, Joint Venture: Silicon Valley Network, and Center for Continuing Study of the California Economy, Palo Alto

——. 1999. *Joint Venture's 1999 Index of Silicon Valley*, Joint Venture Silicon Valley, Palo Alto

——. 2000. *2000 Index of Silicon Valley*, Joint Venture: Silicon Valley Network, San Jose

——. 2001. *2001 Index of Silicon Valley*, Joint Venture: Silicon Valley Network, San Jose

Kadetsky Elizabeth. 1993. Clean Rooms, Dirty Secrets: Silicon Valley's Unseemly Underbelly. In *San Jose Metro*. San Jose, March 25–31, 1993

Kalleberg Arne, Rasell Edith, Hudson Ken, Webster David, Reskin Barbara, et al. 1997. *Nonstandard Work, Substandard Jobs: Flexible Work Arrangements in the U.S.*, Economic Policy Institute, Washington, DC

Kanter Rosabeth Moss. 1995. Nice Work If You Can Get It: The Software Industry as a Model for Tomorrow's Jobs. *American Prospect* 23, 52–8

Kaplinsky Raphael. 1987. *Microelectronics and Work Revisited: A Review*, International Labour Office, Geneva

Katz Bruce. 1999. What a PEO Can Do For You. *Journal of Accountancy* 188:1, 57–61

Kaufman Bruce, ed. 1997. *Government Regulation of the Employment Relationship*, 50th Anniversary Volume. Madison: Industrial Relations Research Association

Kazis Richard. 1998. *New Labor Market Intermediaries: What's Driving Them? Where Are They Headed? Rep.* WP03, MIT Sloan School of Management, Cambridge, MA

Keane Julie, Allison Janelle. 1999. The Intersection of the Learning Region and Local and Regional Economic Development: Analysing the Role of Higher Education. *Regional Studies* 33:9, 896–902

Keeble David, Lawson Clive, Moore Barry, Wilkinson Frank. 1999. Collective learning processes, networking and "institutional thickness" in the Cambridge region. *Regional Studies* 33:4, 319–32

Keeble David, Wilkinson Frank. 1999. Collective Learning and Knowledge Development in the Evolution of Regional Clusters of High Technology SMEs in Europe. *Regional Studies* 33:4, 295–303

Keller, John. 1981. *The Production Worker in Electronics: Industrialization and Labor Development in California's Santa Clara Valley*. Ph.D. dissertation thesis. University of Michigan

Kenney Martin, ed. 2000. *Understanding Silicon Valley: The Anatomy of an Entrepreneurial Region*. Palo Alto: Stanford University Press

Kerachsky Stuart. 1994. *The Minority Female Single Parent Demonstration: Making a Difference – Does an Integrated Program Model Promote More Jobs and Higher Pay*, Mathematica Policy Research, Washington DC

Kirat Thierry, Lung Yannick. 1999. Innovation and Proximity: Territories as Loci of Collective Learning Processes. *European Urban and Regional Studies* 6:1, 27–38

Klotz Ulrich. 1999. The Challenges of the New Economy. FIET – International Federation of Commercial, Clerical, Professional and Technical Employees

Kogan Deborah, Dickinson Katherine, Fedrau Ruth, Midling Michael, Wolff Kristin. 1997. *Creating Workforce Development Systems That Work: A Guide for Practitioners. Rep. DOL COntract No. F-4957–5–00–80–30*, Social Policy Research Associates, for the US DOL, Employment and Training Administration, Menlo Park

Kopytoff Verne. 2001. Internet Firms Vanish From Chronicle 500. In *San Francisco Chronicle*. San Francisco, May 7, 2001

Korzeniewicz Miguel, Gereffi Gary. 1994. *Commodity Chains and Global Capitalism*. Westport, CT: Praeger

Kunda Gideon, Barley Stephen, Evans James. 1999. *Why Do Contractors Contract? The Theory and Reality of High End Contingent Labor. Rep. Working Paper #WP04*, MIT Sloan School of Management, Cambridge, MA

Lafer G. 1994. The Politics of Job Training – Urban Poverty and the False Promise of JTPA. *Politics & Society* 22:3, 349–88

LaGuerre Michel. 1993. *The Informal Economy in the San Francisco Bay Area. Rep. 594*, Institute for Urban and Regional Development, Berkeley

Langberg Mike, Davis Jack. 1995. How the Valley Has Changed. In *San Jose Mercury News*, April 10, 1995, pp. 1–14G. San Jose

Larson Magali Sarfatti. 1977. *The Rise of Professionalism: A Sociological Analysis*. Berkeley, CA: University of California Press

Lash Scott, Urry John. 1994. *Economies of Signs and Space*. London: Sage

Laurillard Diana. 1999. A Conversational Framework for Individual Learning Applied to the "Learning Organisation" and the "Learning Society." *Systems Research and Behavioral Science* 16:113–22

Lave Jean, Wenger Etienne. 1991. *Situated Learning: Legitimate Peripheral Participation*. Cambridge: Cambridge University Press. 138 pp.

Lawson Clive, Lorenz Edward. 1999. Collective Learning, Tacit Knowledge and Regional Innovative Capacity. *Regional Studies* 33:4, 305–17

Lee Chong-Moon, Miller William, Hancock Marguerite Gong, Rowen Henry, eds. 2000. *The Silicon Valley Edge: A Habitat for Innovation and Entrepreneurship*. Palo Alto: Stanford University Press

Leidner Robin. 1993. *Fast Food, Fast Talk: Service Work and the Routinization of Everyday Life*. Berkeley, CA: University of California Press

Levy Frank. 1998. *The New Dollars and Dreams: American Incomes and Economic Change*. New York: Russell Sage Foundation

Levy Stephen, Arnold Bob. 1999. *California Economic Growth 1999 Edition*, Center for Continuing Study of the California Economy, Palo Alto

Lipietz Alain. 1987. *Mirages and Miracles: The Global Crisis of Fordism*. London: Verso

Lozano Beverly. 1989. *The Invisible Work Force: Transforming American Business With Outside and Home-Based Workers*. New York: Free press

Luethje Boy. 1998. *Race and Ethnicity in "Post-Fordist" Production Networks: Silicon Valley and the Global Information Technology Industry.* Presented at American Sociological Assiciation Annual Meeting, San Francisco

Lundvall Bengt-Ake, ed. 1992. *National Systems of Innovation: Towards a Theory of Innovation and Interactive Learning.* London and New York: Pinter

Lundvall Bengt-Ake , Johnson B. 1994. The Learning Economy. *Journal of Industrial Studies* 1:2, 23–42

Lynch Robert, Palmer James, Grubb Norton. 1991. *Community College Involvement in Contract Training and Other Economic Development Activities. Rep. MDS-379*, National Center for Research in Vocational Education, Berkeley

Macdonald Cameron Lynne, Sirianni Carmen, eds. 1996. *Working in the Service Society.* Philadelphia: Temple University Press

Machlup Fritz. 1952. *The Production and Distribution of Knowledge in the United States.* Princeton, NJ: Princeton University Press

MacLeod Gordon. 2000. The Learning Region in an Age of Austerity: Capitalising on Knowledge, Entrpreneurialism, and Reflexive Capitalism. *Geoforum* 31:219–36

Malberg Anders, Maskell Peter. 1999. Localized Learning and Regional Economic Development: Guest Editorial. *European Urban and Regional Studies* 6:1, 5–9

Malecki Edward, Oinas Paivi, eds. 1999. *Making Connections: Technological Learning and Regional Economic Change.* Aldershot, UK: Ashgate

Manchester Philip. 2001. World's largest electronic "job board" plans up-market move. *Financial Times.* March 7, 2001

Mandel Michael. 1996. *The High-Risk Society: Peril and Promise in the New Economy.* New York: Times Business

Manser Marilyn, Picot Garnett. 1999. The role of self-employment in U.S. and Canadian job growth. *Monthly Labor Review* 22:4, 10–25

Maskell Peter, Eskelinen Heikki, Hannibalsson Ingjaldur, Malmberg Anders, Vatne Eirik. 1998. *Competitiveness, Localised Learning and Regional Development: Specialisation and Prosperity in Small Open Economies.* New York, London: Routledge

Maskell Peter, Malmberg Anders. 1999. The Competitiveness of Firms and Regions: Ubiquitification and the Importance of Localized Learning. *European Urban and Regional Studies* 6:1, 9–25

Masters Stanley. 1999. The Role of Flexible Production in Earnings Inequality. *Challenge* 42:4, 102–17

Matloff Norman. 1999. *Debunking the Myth of a Desperate Software Labor Shortage,* House Judiciary Committee, Subcomittee on Immigration, Washington, DC

Mayer Jeffrey, Price Lee et al. 1999. *The Emerging Digital Economy II,* Department of Commerce, Secretariat on Electronic Commerce, Washington DC

McLaughlin Ken, and Ariana Cha. 1999. Divisions: Segregation Trends Emerge in High-Tech Industry, Experts Say. *San Jose Mercury News,* April 16, 1999

McWilliams Gary. 1999. . . . Find a Job: There are some 2,500 sites that promise to match you with an employer. How do you pick? In *Wall Street Journal,* Monday, December 6, 1999 pp. R16–R22. New York City

Melendez Edwin. 1996. *Working on Jobs: The Center for Employment Training,* Mauricio Gaston Institute for Latino Community Development and Public Policy, Boston, MA

Melendez E., Harrison B. 1998. Matching the disadvantaged to job opportunities: Structural explanations for the past successes of the center for employment training. *Economic Development Quarterly* 121:1, 3–11

Messmer Max. 1994. Temporary Employees Are Part of New Europe. *Peronnel Journal*

Middlehurst Robin, Kennie Tom. 1997. Leading Professionals: Towards New Concepts of Professionalism. In *The End of the Professions? The Restructuring of Professional Work*, ed. Jea Broadbent. London and New York: Routledge

Mincer Jacob. 1994. Human Capital: A Review. In *Labor Economics and Industrial Relations: Markets and Institutions*, ed. C Kerr, P Staudohar. Cambridge, MA: Harvard University Press

Mishel Lawrence, Bernstein Jared, Schmitt John. 1999. *The State of Working America, 1998–99*. Ithaca, NY: Cornell University Press

——. 2001. *The State of Working America, 2000–2001*. Ithaca, NY: Cornell University Press

Mitchell James. 1993. Union, Pipe Trades Training Center Are The Right Fit. In *San Jose Mercury News*. San Jose, July 18, 1993

Molina Frieda. 1998. *Making Connections: A Study of Employment Linkage Programs*, Center for Community Change, Washington DC

Montgomery David. 1987. *The Fall of the House of Labor: The Workplace, the State, and American Labor Activism, 1865–1925*. Cambridge: Cambridge University Press

Morgan Kevin. 1997. The Learning Region: Institutions, Innovation and Regional Renewal. *Regional Studies* 31:5, 491–503

Morrow L. 1993. The Temping of America. In *Time Magazine*, March, 1993, pp. 40–1

Moss Philip. 1999. Earnings Inequality and the Quality of Jobs. In *Corporate Governance and Sustainable Prosperity*, ed. Wamos Lazonick. New York: Macmillan and St. Martin's Press

National Commission for Manpower Policy. 1978. *Labor Market Intermediaries: A Special Report. Rep. No. 22*, National Commission for Manpower Policy, U.S. Dept. of Labor, Washington, DC

National Research Council. 2001. *Building a Workforce for the Information Economy*. Washington, DC: National Academy Press

NCEO. 1998. *Current Practices in Stock Option Plan Design: Results and Analysis of from the 1998 NCEO Survey of Companies with Broad-Based Stock Option Plans*, National Center for Employee Ownership, Oakland

NELP. 1999. *Workplace Equality for "Nonstandard" Workers: A Survey of Model Legislation*, National Employment Law Project, New York

Neumark David. 2000. *Changes in Job Stability and Job Security: A Collective Effort to Untangle, Reconcile, and Interpret the Evidence*, National Bureau of Economic Research, Washington, DC

New Ways To Work. 1991. *New Policies for Part-Time and Contingent Workers: Summary of a Conference on the Changing Workforce*, New Ways To Work, San Francisco

Nickell S. 1997. Unemployment and labor market rigidities: Europe versus North America. *Journal of Economic Perspectives* 11:3

Noble David F. 1977. *America By Design: Science, Technology, and the Rise of Corporate Capitalism*. New York: Knopf

———. 1984. *Forces of Production: A Social History of Industrial Automation*. New York: Knopf

Nonaka Ikujiro, Takeuchi Hirotaka. 1995. *The Knowledge-Creating Company: How Japanese Companies Create the Dynamics of Innovation*. New York, Oxford: Oxford University Press

North D. C. 1981. *Structure and Change in Economic History*. New York: W. W. Norton

Nyhan Barry, Attwell Graham, Deitmer Ludger. 1999. *Towards the Learning Region: Education and Regional Innovation in the European Union and the United States*, CEDEFOP–European Center for the Development of Vocational Training, Thessaloniki

Olsten Staffing Services, 1994. Annual Report. Melville, NY: Olsten Staffing Services http://www.olsten.com

Orr Julian. 1996. *Talking About Machines: An Ethnography of a Modern Job*. Ithaca: Cornell University Press

Osterlund Carsten. 1996. *Learning Across Contexts: A Field Study of Salespeople's Learning At Work*. MA thesis. Arhus University, Denmark

Osterman Paul. 1984. *Internal Labor Markets*. Cambridge, MA: MIT Press

———. 1996. *Broken Ladders: Managerial Careers in the New Economy*. New York: Oxford University Press

———. 1999. *Securing Prosperity: The American Labor Market: How It Has Changed and What To Do About It*. Princeton, NJ: Princeton University Press

Osterman Paul, Lautsch Brenda. 1996. *Project Quest: A Report to the Ford Foundation*, MIT Sloan School of Management, Cambridge, MA

Overman Stephanie. 1993. Temporary services go global. *HRMagazine* 38:8, 72–4

Ozaki Muneto. 1999. *Negotiating Flexibility: The Role of the Social Partners and the State*. Geneva: International Labour Office

Packard David, Kirby David, Lewis Karen R. 1995. *The HP way: how Bill Hewlett and I built our company*. New York: HarperBusiness

Parker Eric , Rogers Joel. 1995. *The Wisconsin Regional Training Partnership: Lessons for National Policy*, National Center for the Workplace, IIR, Berkeley

Parker Robert E. 1994. *Flesh Peddlers and Warm Bodies : The Temporary Help Industry and Its Workers*. New Brunswick, NJ: Rutgers University Press

Pastor Manuel. 2000. *Regions that work: how cities and suburbs can grow together*. Minneapolis: University of Minnesota Press

Pastor Manuel and Ana Robinson Adams. 1996. Keeping Down With the Jones: Neighbors, Networks and Wages. *Review of Regional Economics* 26:2

Pastor Manuel, Marcelli Enrico. 2000. Men in the Hood: Skill, patial and social mismatch among male workers in Los Angeles County. *Urban Geography* 21:6, 474–96

Paul A., Kleingartner A. 1994. Flexible Production and the Transformation of Industrial Relations in the Motion Picture and Television Industry. *Industrial & Labor Relations Review* 47:4, 663–78

Peck Jamie. 1996. *Work-Place: The Social Regulation of Labor Markets*. New York: Guilford Press.

Perkins Michael C., Nunez Celia. 2001. Why Market Insiders Don't Feel Your Pain. In *Washington Post*, March 15, p. A25

Perry Anne. 1992. The Evolution of U.S. Trade Intermediaries: The Changing International Environment. Westport, CT: Quorum Books

Perry Anne. 1992. *The Evolution of U.S. Trade Intermediaries: The Changing International Environment*. Westport, CT: Quorum Books

Perry George. 1972. Unemployment Flows in the U.S. Labor Market. *Brookings Papers on Economic Activity* 2: 245–78

Persky J., Wiewel Wim. 1994. The Growing Localness of the Global City. *Economic Geography* 70:129–43

Pfeffer Jeffrey, Baron James. 1988. Taking the Workers Back Out: Recent Trends in the Structuring of Employment. In B. Straw, L. Cummings, eds. *Research in Organizational Behaviour, Vol. 10*, pp. 257–303. Greenwich, CT: JAI Press

Pink Daniel. 1998. Free Agent Nation. In *Fast Company*, 12, December/January pp. 131–47

Piore Michael. 1980. *Birds of Passage: Migrant Labor and Industrial Societies*. Cambridge: Cambridge University Press

Piore Michael J., Sabel Charles F. 1984. *The Second Industrial Divide: Possibilities for Prosperity*. New York: Basic Books

Pivetz Timothy, Searson Michael, Spletzer James. 2001. Measuring Job and Establishment Flows with BLS Longitudinal Data. *Monthly Labor Review* 124:4, April, pp. 13–20

PolicyLink. 2000a. *Community Based Initiatives: Promoting Regional Equity*, PolicyLink, Oakland, CA

——. 2000b. *Perspectives on Regionalism: Opportunities for Community-Based Organizations to Advance Equity*, PolicyLink, Oakland, CA

Pollert Anna. 1988. Dismantling flexibility. *Capital & Class* 34:42–75

Porat Marc Uri. 1977. *The Information Economy: Definition and Measurement*. Washington: Office of Telecommunications, U.S. Department of Commerce

Porter Michael E. 1998. Clusters and the new economics of competition. *Harvard Business Review* 76:6, 77–90

Ports Michelle Harrison. 1993. Trends in Job Search Methods, 1970–1992. *Monthly Labor Review* October 1993: 63–7

Powell Walter. 1990. Neither Market Nor Hierarchy: Network Forms of Organization. In *Research In Organizational Behavior: An Annual Series of Analytical Essays and Critical Reviews*, ed. B Staw, LL Cummings, pp. 295–336. Greenwich, CT: JAI Press

——. 1998. Learning from Collaboration: Knowledge and Networks in the Biotechnology and Pharmaceutical Industries. *California Management Review* 40

Putnam Robert D. 2000. *Bowling alone: the collapse and revival of American community*. New York: Simon & Schuster. 541 pp.

Quinlan Tom. 1999. Seagate Wields Ax Again. In *San Jose Mercury News*. San Jose, September 15, 1999

Quinn Michell, LaFleur Jennifer. 1999. A Hard Look At Silicon Valley's Boom. In *San Jose Mercury News*. San Jose, August 15, 1999

Reed Deborah. 1999. *California's Rising Income Inequality: Causes and Concerns*, Public Policy Institute of California, San Francisco

Rees Teresa. 2000. The Learning Region? Integrating Gender Equality into Regional Economic Development. *Policy & Politics* 28:2, 179–91

Regan and Associates. 1997. *A Labor Market Analysis of the Interactive Digital Media Industry: Opportunities in Multimedia*, NOVA Private Industry Council, Sunnyvale

Reich Robert B. 2000. *The future of success*. New York: A. Knopf

Reuters. 2001. Report: Dot-com carnage continues as 55 firms close. In *San Jose Mercury News*. San Jose, May 1, 2001

Riccardi David. 1999. L.A. County Doctors Vote Decisively to Unionize. In *Los Angeles Times*, May 29, 1999, pp. A1. Los Angeles

Rifkin Jeremy. 1995. *The End f Work: The Decline of the Global Labor Force and the Dawn of the Post-Market Era*. New York: G. P. Putnam's Sons

Rogers Jackie Krasas. 2000. *Temps: the many faces of the changing workplace*. Ithaca, NY: Cornell University Press

Rose Frank. 1999. *The Economics, Concept, and Design of Information Intermediaries*. New York: Physica-Verlag

Rousseau Denise. 1995. *Psychological Contracts in Organizations: Understanding Written and Unwritten Agreements*. Thousand Oaks, CA: Sage Publications

Rubinstein Ariel, Wolinsky Asher. 1987. Middlemen. *Quarterly Journal of Economics*: 581–93

Sabel Charles, Zeitlin Jonathan. 1997. Stories, Strategies, Structures: Rethinking Historical Alternatives to Mass Production. In *World of Possibilities: Flexibility and Mass Production in Western Industrialization*, ed. C Sabel, J Zeitlin. Cambridge, UK: Cambridge University Press

Sassen Saskia. 1989. New York City's Informal Economy. In A Portes, M Castells, L Benton, eds. *The Informal Economy: Studies in Advanced and Less Developed Countries*. Baltimore: Johns Hopkins University Press

——. 1996. *Losing Control?: Sovereignty in an Age of Globalization*. New York: Columbia University Press

Saxenian AnnaLee. 1994. *Regional Advantage: Culture and Competition in Silicon Valley and Route 128*. Cambridge, MA: Harvard University Press. xi, 226 pp.

——. 1996. Beyond Boundaries: Open Labor Markets and Learning in Silicon Valley. In *The Boundaryless Career: A New Employment Principle for a New Organizational Era*, ed. MaDR Arthur. Oxford: Oxford University Press

——. 1999. *Silicon Valley's New Immigrant Entrepreneurs*, Public Policy Institute of California, San Francisco

——. 2000. Networks of Immigrant Entrepreneurs. In *The Silicon Valley Edge*, ed. C-M Lee, W Miller, MG Hancock, H Rowen. Stanford, CA: Stanford University Press

Schoenberger Erica. 1997. *The Cultural Crisis of the Firm*. Cambridge, MA: Blackwell

Schwartz Evan. 1999. Career Sites Gain Rapidly, Along With Job Hopping. In *New York Times*. New York, Monday, October 4, 1999

Seavey Dorie. 1998. *New Avenues Into Jobs: Early Lessons from Nonprofit Temp Agencies and Employment Brokers*, Center for Community Change, Washington DC

Segal Lewis, Sullivan Daniel. 1997. *Temporary Services Employment Durations: Evidence from State UI Data*. Rep. WP-97-23, Federal Reserve Bank of Chicago, Chicago

SEIU. 1993. *Part-Time, Temporary, and Contracted Work: Coping with the Growing "Contingent" Workforce*, Service Employees International Union, Washington, DC

Sevilla Ramon. 1992. *Employment Practices and Industrial Restructuring: A Case Study of the Semiconductor Industry in Silicon Valley, 1955–1991*. Ph.D. dissertation thesis. University of California, Los Angeles, LA

Shaiken Harley. 1985. *Work Transformed: Automation and Labor in the Computer Age*. New York: Holt, Rinehart, and Winston

Shapiro Carl, Varian Hal R. 1998. *Information Rules: A Strategic Guide to the Network Economy*. Boston, Mass.: Harvard Business School Press

Short Amy L. 1998. Workers misclassified as independent contractors were entitled to retirement benefits: Vizcaino v. Microsoft Corp. *Tax Lawyer* 51:2, 405–12

Siegel Lenny. 1994. *The Silicon Valley Experience: Why Labor Law Must Be Brought Into the Twenty-First Century*, U.S. Commission on the Future of Worker–Management Relations, Washington, DC

Silvestri George. 1997. Occupational Employment Projects to 2006. *Monthly Labor Review* v 120:11, 58–83

Simmie James, ed. 1997. *Innovation, Networks and Learning Regions?* London: Regional Studies Association

Smith Vicki. 1994. Braverman's Legacy: The Labor Process Tradition at 20. *Work and Occupations* 21:4, 403–21

——. 2001. *Crossing the great divide: worker risk and opportunity in the new economy*. Ithaca, NY: ILR Press

Sparke Matthew. 1994. A Prism for Contemporary Capitalism: Temporary Work as Displaced Labor as Value. *Antipode* 26:4

Spulber Daniel. 1999. *Market Microstructure: Intermediaries and the Theory of the Firm*. Cambridge: Cambridge University Press

Staff Leasing. 1999. Annual Report. Bradenton, FL: Staff Leasing Inc. (http://www.staffleasing.com)

Staffing Industry Report (1998) Volume X, No. 11 June 11, 1999 (www.sireport.com)

Staffing Industry Review. 1997. VOP Programs Proliferate. In *Staffing Industry Review*, November/December, 1997

Stamps David. 1995. Community Colleges Go Corporate. *Training Magazine* 32:12, 36

Standing Guy. 1999. *Global labour flexibility: seeking distributive justice*. New York: St. Martin's Press

Steele Dorothy L. 1999. Section 1706 Internal Revenue Code: Where it came from and where it is going (Independent contractor status for professional services). *Journal of Professional Services Marketing* 20:1, 99–114

Stepick Alex. 1989. Miami's Two Informal Sectors. In A Portes, M Castells, L Benton, eds. *The Informal Economy: Studies in Advanced and Less Developed Countries*. Baltimore: Johns Hopkins University Press

Storper Michael. 1997. *The Regional World: Territorial Development in a Global Economy*. New York: Guilford Press

Storper Michael, Scott Allen. 1990. Work organisation and local labour markets in an era of flexible production. *International Labour Review* 129:5, 573–91

Storper Michael, Walker Richard. 1989. *The Capitalist Imperative: Territory, Technology, and Industrial Growth*. Oxford, UK: Blackwell

Sturdy Andrew, Knights David, Willmott Hugh. 1992. *Skill and Consent: Contemporary Studies in the Labour Process*. London: Routledge

Sturgeon Tim. 1999. *Turn-key production networks: industry organization, economic development, and the globalization of electronics contaract manufacturing*. Ph.D. dissertation thesis. University of California, Berkeley

Suzik Holly Ann. 1999. Solectron Tells Its Tale. In *Quality*, 38:5, April 1999, pp. 53–9

Swinnerton Kenneth, Wial Howard. 1995. Is Job Stability Declining in the U.S. Economy? *Industrial and Labor Relations Review* 48:2, 293–304

Taylor Michael. 1999. The small firm as a temporary coalition. *Entrepreneurship and Regional Development* 11:1–19

Teuke Molly Rose. 1999. Dice Clicks! In *Contract Professional*. 3: 7 May 1999

Tharp Paul. 1999. .Coms Rush Super Bowl. In *New York Post*, New York, November 23, 1999

Theodore Nikolas, Mehta Chirag. 1999. *Contingent Work and the Staffing Industry: A Review of Worker-Centered Policy and Practice*, Center for Urban Economic Development, University of Illinois, Chicago

Thomas Robert. 1994. *What Machines Can't Do: Politics and Technology In the Industrial Enterprise*. Berkeley, CA: University of California Press

Tilly Chris. 1996. *Half a Job: Bad and Good Part-Time Jobs in a Changing Economy*. Philadelphia: Temple University Press

Tooke Jane. 2000. Learning Regions: The Politics of Knowledge at Work. *Environment and Planning A* 32:761–8

US Department of Labor. 1994. *Report and Recommendations: Executive Summary: Commission on the Future of Worker Management Relations*, U.S. Department of Labor, Washington, DC

———. 1995. *What's Working (and What's Not): A Summary of Research in the Economic Impacts of Employment Training Programs*, U.S. Department of Labor, Washington, DC

———. 1998. *A Dialogue: Unemployment Insurance and Employment Service Programs*, USDOL, Washington, DC

US General Accounting Office. 1994. *Multiple Employment Training Programs: Most Federal Agencies Do Not Know If Their Programs Are Working Effectively. Rep. GAO/HEHS-94-88*, U.S. GAO, Washington, DC

Veneri Carolyn. 1998. *Here Today, Jobs Tomorrow: Opportunities in Information Technology*, Bureau of Labor Statistics, Washington, DC

Walker Richard. 1985. Technological Determination and Determinism: Industrial Growth and Location. In *High Technology, Space and Society*, ed. M Castells. Berverly Hills, CA: Sage

Wallerstein Immanuel. 1979. *The Capitalist World Economy*. Cambridge, UK: Cambridge University Press

Waterman Robert, Waterman Judith, Collard Betsy. 1994. Toward a Career-Resilient Workforce. *Harvard Business Review* 72:4, 87–95

Wellman B., Salaff J., Dimitrova D., Garton L., Gulia M., Haythornthwaite C. 1996. Computer Networks as Social Networks – Collaborative Work, Telework, and Virtual Community. *Annual Review of Sociology* 22:213–38

Wells Miriam J. 1996. *Strawberry Fields: Politics, Class, and Work in California Agriculture*. Ithaca, NY: Cornell University Press

Wenger Etienne. 1998. *Communities of Practice: Learning, Meaning, and Identity*. Cambridge, UK: Cambridge University Press

Wenger Etienne, Snyder William. 2000. Communities of Practice: The Organizational Frontier. *Harvard Business Review* January–February

Westrum Ron. 1991. *Technology & Society: The Shaping of People and Things*. Belmont, CA: Wadsworth

White Dennis. 1998. *Software Industry: Careers in the Fast Lane*, NOVA Private Industry Council, Sunnyvale

Wial H. 1991. Getting a Good Job – Mobility in a Segmented Labor Market. *Industrial Relations* 30:3, 396–416

Williams Frederick, ed. 1988. *Measuring the Information Society*. Newbury Park, CA: Sage Publications

Williams K., Cutler T., Williams J., Haslam C. 1988. The end of mass production? A review of Piore and Sabel's *The Second Industrial Divide*. *Economy and Society* 16

Williamson Oliver. 1975. *Markets and Hierarchies: Analysis and Antitrust Implications*. New York: Free Press

———. 1985. *The Economic Institutions of Capitalism: Firms, Markets, Relational Contracting*. New York: Free Press

Wilthagen Ton. 1998. *Flexicurity: A New Paradigm for Labour Market Policy Reform*. Rep. FS I 98–202, Social Science Research Center, Research Unit Labour Market Policy and Employment, Berlin

Wimmer Bradley, Townsend Anthony, Chezum Brian. 2000. Information Technologies and the Middleman: The Changing Role of Information Intermediaries in an Information-Rich Economy. *Journal of Labor Research* XXI: 3, 407–18

Winslow Ward, ed. 1995. *The Making of Silicon Valley: A One Hundred Year Renaissance*. Palo Alto: Santa Clara Valley Historical Association

Wolf-Powers Laura. 1999. Union-Sponsored Intermediaries in Regional Labor Markets: Mitigating the Negative Effects of Employment Flexibility. Presented at Association of Collegiate Schools of Planning Annual Conference, Chicago, IL. October, 1999

World Bank. 1998. *Knowledge for Development*. Oxford: Oxford University Press for the World Bank

Yellin Emily. 1999. American Medical Association to Form a Physician's Union: Some Doctors See Relief in Plan to AMA Union; Others Call Move an Inadequate Solution. In *New York Times*, May 25, 1999, pp. A18. New York

Yeung Henry Wai-chung. 2000. Organising "the firm" in Industrial Geography I: Networks, Institutions and Regional Development. *Progress in Human Geography* 24

Zabin Carol, Ringer Dan. 1997. *Flexible Manufacturing Networks and the Welfare of Workers*. Rep. No. 23, Lewis Center for Regional Policy Studies, UCLA, Los Angeles

Zabrowski Amy, Gordon Anne. 1994. *Evaluation of minority female single parent demonstration: Fifth year impacts at CET*, Mathematica Policy Research, contract for the Rockefeller Foundation, New York

Zimbalist Andrew S. 1979. *Case Studies on the Labor Process*. New York: Monthly Review Press

Zlolniski Christian. 1994. The Informal Economy in an Advanced Industrialized Society: Mexican Immigrant Labor in Silicon Valley. *Yale Law Journal* 103:8, 2305–36

Zuboff Shoshana. 1988. *In the Age of the Smart Machine: The Future of Work and Power*. New York: Basic Books

Index